War and Reconciliation

War and Reconciliation

Reason and Emotion in Conflict Resolution

William J. Long
and
Peter Brecke

The MIT Press
Cambridge, Massachusetts
London, England

This book was set in Sabon by Achorn Graphic Services, Inc., on the Miles 33
system, and was printed and bound in the United States of America.

Library of Congress Cataloging-in-Publication Data

Long, William J., 1956–
    War and reconciliation : reason and emotion in conflict resolution / William
J. Long and Peter Brecke.
        p.   cm.
    Includes bibliographical references and index.
    ISBN 0-262-12254-5 (hc. : alk. paper) — ISBN 0-262-62168-1 (pbk. : alk.
paper)
      1. Reconciliation.   2. Peace.   3. Civil war.   4. War (International law).
    I. Brecke, Peter.   II. Title.
    JZ5597 .L66 2003
    303.6'9—dc21

                                                                2002071834

10 9 8 7 6 5 4 3 2

For David and Nicholas

Contents

Preface

This project began during a conversation between the authors about a visit to the Yerkes Regional Primate Research Center. There, Peter had observed a presentation on primate conflict resolution by renowned animal behaviorist Frans de Waal. De Waal's team observed that a public, symbolic reconciliation between warring primates after a fight had a pronounced positive effect in restoring order within their groupings.

We remarked how public, symbolic reconciliation gestures by leaders of disputants in human societies became front page news, stayed firmly in our memories, and carried the strong presumption that these symbolic acts were associated with a reduction in future conflict between the groups the leaders represented. As political scientists we wondered, do reconciliation events—public, symbolic meetings between belligerents indicating a desire for improved relations—help restore lasting social order after wars, both civil and international? Is there empirical support for this presumption, and, if so, how and why do such events contribute to the long-run restoration of social order? Furthermore, we found these intriguing questions had gone largely uninvestigated by social scientists.

This book attempts to answer those questions. The answers we ultimately uncovered proved to be more interesting than we could have imagined. We discovered that reconciliation events were associated with reductions in international conflict because they operated as a form of costly and trustworthy signal that, under certain conditions, de-escalated violence and restored order. That such events served as successful signaling devices in international bargaining is consistent with a rational choice approach to conflict resolution. By making costly and reliable signals of a desire for improved relations, reconciliation events could serve as a dependable concession that changed the expected payoffs facing the parties so as to encourage them to choose peace.

More surprising, we found that these events also often correlated with the restoration of order after civil conflicts, but for very different reasons. There they helped reduce future conflict when they were part of a patterned, emotionally laden process of social forgiveness. That finding does not fit within existing models of rational decision making, however, and it opens the door to a radically different view of rationality and human problem solving. Unlike rational choice, which assumes that reason operates apart from emotion in applying universally logical principles to solving all types of problems, the forgiveness finding recommends a new approach to understanding rationality and choice. It argues for a model of human problem solving that integrates emotion and logic, and recognizes that we have numerous problem-solving processes to address different types of problems.

We believe this book will be of great interest to theoreticians and practitioners in the field of conflict resolution. Furthermore, constructive application of a new understanding of rationality carries broader implications for understanding psychological foundations for social theory generally. We suggest that is an equally important contribution.

We owe debts of gratitude to several others in making this book possible. We gratefully acknowledge Doug Bond, Phil Schrodt, and Rodney Tomlinson for making their events data available to us. We thank Louis Kreisberg, William Clark, Joshua Goldstein, and the editors and reviewers of The MIT Press for their constructive guidance. We have been helped by research assistance from Tracy Bius, Olivia Grimes, Ananya Lively, Kathleen Burke, and the 1998 master's degree class of the Sam Nunn School of International Affairs. We also thank Wanda Moore and Joy Daniell for deciphering editing squiggles as they typed changes and for assistance in preparing figures and tables. Any shortcomings in the book are exclusively our own.

Finally, we thank our wives, Mary and Julie, and our children for cheering us on in this extended endeavor. Both of us added members to our families while working on this project, and as we write this we realize that it is in large part for our children that we have done this work. We believe that this book improves our understanding of reconciliation as a process to restore and maintain society after conflict. We hope that this improved understanding will lead to a better world for them.

War and Reconciliation

1

Introduction

Through Ritual, Heaven and Earth join in harmony, sun and moon shine, the four seasons proceed in order, the stars and constellations march, the rivers flow and all things flourish; men's likes and dislikes are regulated and their joys and hates made appropriate.
—Hsün Tsu (ca. 313–238 B.C.E.)[1]

Reconciliation and Social Order

The most important and enduring puzzle for social scientists is explaining sociality and how it is maintained.[2] How do groups of individual actors maintain social order despite competition and conflict among themselves?[3] Johan Galtung succinctly captured the enigma: "The fact that we are around testifies to a lot of conflict resolution capacity. And reconstruction. And reconciliation. How come?"[4]

Formal and informal observations of many levels of social organization acknowledge the tension between aggressive pursuit of self-interest and societal harmony. Many of these observations also point to the importance of *reconciliation*—mutually conciliatory accommodation between former antagonists—as one process integral to mitigating future violence and maintaining societal relationships after violent conflict.[5] Consider four descriptions of reconciliation events in very different societies.

1. In primate society, Frans de Waal described a fight in the chimpanzee colony of the Arnhem Zoo:

It was the winter of 1975 and the colony was kept indoors. In the course of a charging display, the dominant male attacked a female, which caused screaming chaos as other chimpanzees came to her defense. When the group finally calmed down, an unusual silence followed, with nobody moving, as if the apes were waiting for something. Suddenly the entire colony burst out hooting, while one male worked the large metal drums in the corner of the hall. In the midst of the pandemonium I saw two chimpanzees kiss and embrace . . . the embracing individuals had been the same male and female of the initial fight.[6]

2. In subnational tribal relations, the letters of Samuel Sewall captured the following ceremony of Native Americans of the northeast colonies in 1680:

Meeting with the Sachem they came to an agreement and buried two axes in the ground . . . which ceremony to them is more significant and binding than all the Articles of Peace, the hatchet being a principle weapon.[7]

3. In the national society of contemporary South Africa, Archbishop Desmond Tutu's Truth and Reconciliation Commission collected testimony from victims and perpetrators of apartheid with the following goal:

The promotion of national unity and reconciliation . . . the healing of a traumatized, divided, wounded, polarized people.[8]

4. In the realm of international politics, contemporary historian Hendrick Smith described the signing of a peace treaty and public joining of hands among President Anwar Sadat of Egypt, Prime Minister Menachem Begin of Israel, and President Jimmy Carter of the United States:

The elusive, unprecedented peace treaty that Egypt and Israel signed today has enormous symbolic importance and the potential for fundamentally transforming the map and history of the entire region . . . the best diplomatic estimate here is that the treaty has markedly reduced the risk of a major war in the Middle East for a considerable time . . .[9]

Although the settings vary greatly, each anecdote contains, implicitly or explicitly, the same hypothesis: future violence is less likely to occur, and societal order more likely to be restored, if principals to a conflict engage in a formal, public reconciliation event indicating a desire for improved relations.

Is there systematic empirical support for the presumption that reconciliation events coincide with effective conflict resolution and, if so, why and how do these events contribute to restoring order and affinity in relations? As political scientists, we are particularly interested in the role and reach of reconciliation within and between states after conflict.

With these questions in mind, this book makes some important discoveries. It finds that reconciliation events do mark turning points in conflicts, leading to better relations in many cases, and substantially reducing rates of recidivist violence within and between nations. Intuitive observations of a relationship between reconciliation events and successful conflict resolution are supported by evidence from many civil and international wars.

This book explores reasons why these events might correlate with restoration of civil and international order in many instances. To guide that investigation, it develops two very different models of reconciliation, a signaling model and a forgiveness model; it derives testable hypotheses about expected behavior from the models; and it grounds each model in two different paradigmatic assumptions about human rationality, rational choice and evolutionary psychology.

Ultimately, both models prove useful in understanding the role of reconciliation events in conflict resolution, the forgiveness model in civil disputes and the signaling model in international disputes. Specifically, with regard to civil conflicts, this study finds that reconciliation events restore lasting social order when they are part of a forgiveness process characterized by truth telling, redefinition of the identity of the former belligerents, partial justice, and a call for a new relationship. The forgiveness model, however, does not explain why or how international reconciliation events contribute to successful conflict resolution between, as opposed to within, nations. International society lacks the will and the ways necessary to pursue a forgiveness process. Instead, the signaling model helps us understand why the events contribute to improvement in bilateral relations. It predicts correctly that when a reconciliation event was part of a costly, novel, voluntary, and irrevocable concession in a negotiated bargain, it contributed meaningfully to a reduction in future conflict. Reconciliation events that lacked these qualities generally failed to lead to a successful signal of a desire for improved future relations, and, in the end, relations were less likely to improve.

As noted, each model rests on a distinctive set of assumptions about human rationality. The signaling model is fully consistent with the paradigmatic assumptions of rational choice; that is, humans apply universal, general, reasoning rules to all problems in making choices in their current environment, including interpreting and acting on signals in reaching a negotiated settlement of conflicts. Rational processes include conscious reasoning only and are separated from emotions. The forgiveness process—an emotionally guided, specific pattern of problem solving—cannot be founded on psychological and physiological assumptions of general rationality, however. The search for paradigmatic assumptions about perception, strategy, choice, and behavior for the forgiveness model analogous to rational choice as the foundation for the signaling model, led to different assumptions about rationality consistent with aspects of evolutionary psychology and affective neuroscience. Those assumptions—that humans possess numerous, patterned, specific, problem-solving capabilities as a result of interaction with past environments, *and* that those capabilities work in synch with our emotional repertoire—are different from those underlying rational choice.

The utility of both models for understanding reconciliation in different settings opens the door to broadening what we mean by rationality in human problem solving and decision making. It illustrates certain limits to rational choice's general rationality assumption—that the mind applies the same dispassionate, logical principles to all types of problems—as *the* scientific foundation for social theory. The relevance of the forgiveness model to explaining reconciliation in civil conflicts forces us to reexamine and reinterpret fundamental assumptions about the microfoundations of rationality in the construction of social theories.

Findings in the natural sciences (particularly biology and neuroscience) and psychology support the notion that the mind possesses several different problem-solving mechanisms and suggest the need to reintegrate emotion into rationality and cognitive activities such as perception, preference formation, choice, and memory to capture how the mind addresses certain problems. Unfortunately, the social disciplines, political science in particular, have failed to use these conceptions about rationality to generate new social explanations. This book is the first to describe this alternative view of rationality and use it to generate a compelling new insight into a critically important social question: how do states restore civil order after war?

Efforts to generate new and useful social hypotheses based on an evolutionary, emotionally animated notion of rationality face many theoretical and practical problems and challenges. Some of these difficulties are the same as those faced by rational choice or any other broad, deductive method. Other problems apply only to this perspective, and some are the result of past failures at integrating the natural with the social sciences. We offer our thoughts on some of these challenges later in the book.

New approaches and new explanations for resolving social conflict also lead to novel possibilities for policy and practice and, in turn, generate opportunities for theory development. In our final chapter we offer some general insights for conflict resolution practice and policy, and identify future research paths suggested by our study.

But we are getting ahead of ourselves. The first step in this journey is canvassing civil and international conflicts to see if casual observations of a link between reconciliation events and order restoration are systematically supported by evidence.

Do Reconciliation Events Matter? What Is the Relationship between Them and Subsequent Relations between Belligerents?

The next chapter focuses on the role of reconciliation events in resolving intrastate conflict, which is the dominant form of warfare today. This form of conflict merits particular attention because, since the end of the Cold War, the number of civil conflicts compared with international conflicts has increased considerably. In the 1990s, the ratio of civil to international conflicts reached 5 to 1, historically very high (figure 1.1).

Moreover, today's civil conflicts have increasing international effects as they often destabilize their region through refugee flows, smuggling and organized crime, and opportunistic interventions by neighboring governments. Civil wars also engage the international community when they entail violations of international norms such as the prohibition against genocide and, more broadly, protection of human rights. If reconciliation events are linked to breaking the cycle of violence that has wracked so many countries, it is vital to understand how they operate to restore social order.

In chapter 3 we examine the role of reconciliation events after interstate wars. This investigation, like the one of civil conflicts in chapter 2, is warranted only, however, if prima facie evidence shows that such events

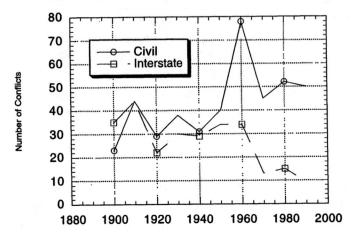

Figure 1.1
Number of conflicts per decade.
Source: Brecke (1999), available at www.inta.gatech.edu/peter/PSS99_
paper.html.

coincide with a reduction in subsequent civil or international violence.
We answer the question with the results of two broad studies that evalu-
ated the effect of reconciliation events in both national and interstate
arenas. These surveys allow us to accomplish three things: to assess, generally, the relationship between a reconciliation event and subsequent relations between belligerents; to select cases for further investigation; and
to generate explanatory models.

Reconciliation Events and Civil Conflict
We began with a broad survey that assessed reconciliation between participants of civil conflicts by examining the relationship between the presence or absence of a reconciliation event after the conflict and subsequent
relations between the participants. For the purposes of this study, we
define a reconciliation event as one that includes the following elements:
direct physical contact or proximity between opponents, usually senior
representatives of respective factions; a public ceremony accompanied by
substantial publicity or media attention that relays the event to the wider
national society; and ritualistic or symbolic behavior that indicates the
parties consider the dispute resolved and that more amicable relations
are expected to follow.

It is important to distinguish between reconciliation events and reconciliation. The former are a proxy indicator of reconciliation. We used them to identify potential reconciliations because they are *measurable* indicators of possible reconciliations. Reconciliation events can be identified in the historical record, whereas reconciliation (of this type) ultimately occurs within the minds of many, perhaps most, individuals in a society and is difficult to measure. A second justification is that it is difficult to envision reconciliation occurring among the general public if there has not been a reconciliation event.

To establish a set of countries for which the kind of reconciliation event we are interested in is an appropriate and meaningful concept, we assembled a list of all recorded within-country violent conflicts in the twentieth century. For the purpose of this study, the term "violent conflict" is used as shorthand for violent political conflict. Cioffi-Revilla's definition of war for his LORANOW project serves as the definition of violent conflict for this project:

A war (a "war event") is an occurrence of purposive and lethal violence among two or more social groups pursuing conflicting political goals that results in fatalities, with at least one belligerent group organized under the command of authoritative leadership.[10]

This definition provides sufficient generality such that it encompasses a wide variety of types of lethal conflicts that may occur within a country, such as civil wars, bloody coups, massacres, democides, or riots. At the same time, through the political goals criterion, the definition distinguishes violent conflict from other forms of lethal violence such as mob lynchings, gang turf battles, and organized crime vendettas. The line between violent conflict and other forms of lethal violence may be fuzzy in definition, but in practice they are seldom confused.

Furthermore, a conflict is deemed to be violent when at least thirty-two people were killed within a one-year period as a result of the point of contention that initiated the lethal violence. The thirty-two-person threshold results from a design criterion of the database we used, the Conflict Catalog, which is the only database that contains all recorded within-state conflicts in the twentieth century. That threshold enables all conflicts in the Conflict Catalog to satisfy the level two or higher classification level established by Richardson.[11]

Our search of the historical record identified 430 violent conflicts in 109 countries. We then explored the histories of each of those countries, using a wide variety of sources, to determine whether a reconciliation event had occurred and, if so, when. That effort unearthed eleven cases (ten countries) with reconciliation events satisfying the definition given above, all occurring in the latter half of the century.

We then determined which of those eleven cases had experienced a violent civil conflict subsequent to the reconciliation event. We found that seven (64%) of them did not experience a return to violent conflict. In contrast, only 9 percent of countries that experienced civil conflict without a reconciliation event avoided recurrence of that conflict in the time period demarcated by our reconciled cases (1957–present). Table 1.1 summarizes the results of our investigation and appendix A lists countries and classification of conflicts.

Reconciliation Events and Interstate War

What role, if any, do reconciliation events play at the level of international society?[12] To explore that question we first identified interstate wars during the past century. Second, we identified pairs of countries that opposed each other to determine specific dyads that might reconcile.

Table 1.1
Reconciliations after Civil Conflicts

Country	End of Conflict	Reconciliation Event	Outcome
Colombia		1957	War
North Yemen		1970	War
Chad		1971	War
		1992–1993	War
Argentina	1978	1984	Peace*
Uruguay	1980	1985	Peace
Chile	1978	1991	Peace
El Salvador	1992	1992	Peace
Mozambique	1992	1992	Peace
South Africa	1989	1992–1993	Peace
Honduras	1985	1993	Peace

*Peace refers only to the absence of civil violence exceeding the thirty-two-fatalities threshold.

Table 1.2
Set of International Conflicts with a Reconciliation Event

Dyad	End of Conflict	Reconciliation Event	Data Set Used*
1. USSR–West Germany	5/1945	8/1970	C, W
2. West Germany–Poland	5/1945	12/1970	C, W
3. USA–Japan	8/1945	4/1952	C
4. Japan–UK	9/1945	4/1952	C
5. China–Japan	8/1945	4/1952	C
6. India–Japan	8/1945	4/1952	C
7. France–Japan	8/1945	4/1952	C
8. Australia–Japan	9/1945	4/1952	C
9. Greece–Japan	8/1945	4/1952	C
10. New Zealand–Japan	8/1945	4/1952	C
11. South Africa–Japan	8/1945	4/1952	C
12. India–China	11/1962	12/1988	W, P
13. Honduras–El Salvador	7/1969	10/1980	W
14. USA–Vietnam	1/1973	7/1995	P
15. Israel–Jordan	10/1973	10/1994	L
16. Egypt–Israel	10/1973	8/1978	W
17. Ethiopia–Somalia	3/1978	4/1988	W
18. Cambodia–Vietnam	1/1979	10/1991	P
19. Uganda–Tanzania	4/1979	2/1981	W
20. Vietnam–China	3/1979	10/1991	P
21. U.K.–Argentina	6/1982	3/1990	P

*The authors used several data sets for the production of figures 2 through 9. C, Conflict and Peace Data Bank; W, World Event/Interaction Survey; P, Protocol for the Assessment of Nonviolent Direct Action; L, Schrodt and Gerner's (1997) data set for Middle Eastern events.

Next, we examined each relationship to determine if and when a reconciliation event had occurred between members of dyads (table 1.2). See appendix B for a detailed explanation of our methodology.

Then, using events data[13] drawn from four data sets we created plots showing the relationship for each dyad and demarcated the time of the reconciliation event at the appropriate spot on the plots. The result is a before-and-after picture of bilateral relations between former belligerents that experienced a reconciliation event.

Eight of twenty-one international conflicts with a reconciliation event offered clear visual evidence of the impact of that event: five dyads in

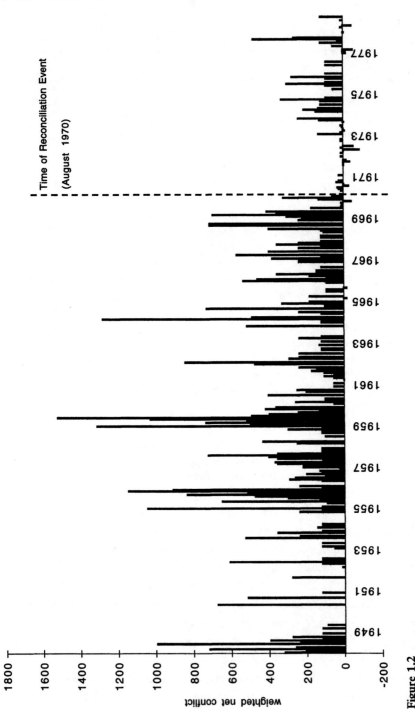

Figure 1.2
Relationship of USSR toward West Germany.

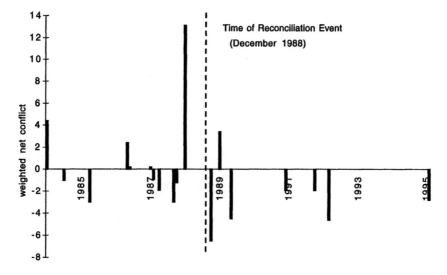

Figure 1.3
Relationship of India toward China.

which an event appeared to show improvement in bilateral relations and three that did not provide visual evidence of a reduction in conflict.[14] See figures 1.2 to 1.9 for individual plots and table 1.3 for a summary of visual findings.

In interpreting the figures, each dark vertical bar portrays a measure of the behavior of one dyad member toward the other for one month during the period of investigation. A tall bar indicates a month of high conflict and a short bar indicates a month with relatively less conflict. A bar that extends below zero indicates a month in which cooperative acts outweighed conflictual acts, and a horizontal gap between vertical bars indicates a month or months in which there were no recorded acts (or the quite unlikely possibility that conflictual acts were precisely counter-balanced by cooperative acts).[15] The long, dashed vertical bar indicates the time of a reconciliation event.

Time series plots such as these are useful because they enable us to visualize easily the basic dynamics of the behavior of one country toward another over a significant period of time and identify the impact, if any, of a reconciliation event in the relationship. An ideal example of a recon-ciliation event showing dramatically improved relations would be a figure

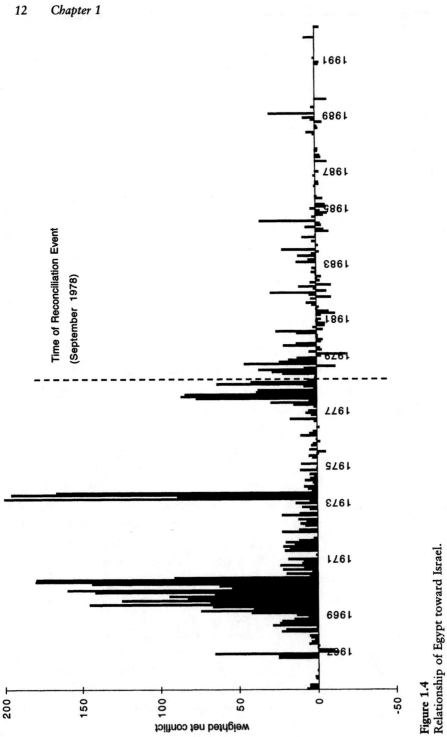

Figure 1.4
Relationship of Egypt toward Israel.

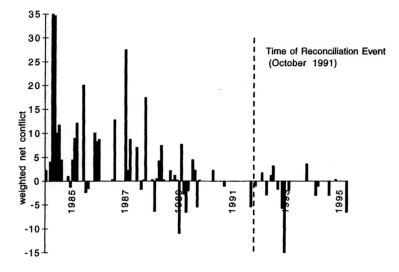

Figure 1.5
Relationship of China toward Vietnam.

in which many tall bars would be on the left of the event and, beginning at the time of the event, the bars being very short or even dropping below the zero line.

Summary of Survey Results

These results suggest that reconciliation events are often, but not uniformly, correlated with restoration of civil and international order. This finding merits further investigation. The eleven cases of civil conflicts and eight of interstate conflict provide a workable selection of cases for in-depth study with variation in the dependent variable—postreconciliation relations between former combatants.

Having found that a reconciliation event results in sustained peaceful relations between belligerents in some, but not all, cases, this study investigates the nineteen cases for answers to two questions: under what conditions does actual reconciliation occur and achieve reduction in future conflict? and what is the mechanism by which reconciliation has this effect? The answers will contribute significantly to the literature and practice of conflict resolution, and, in turn, illustrate the relative merits and limits of two approaches to social theorizing that guided our investigation.

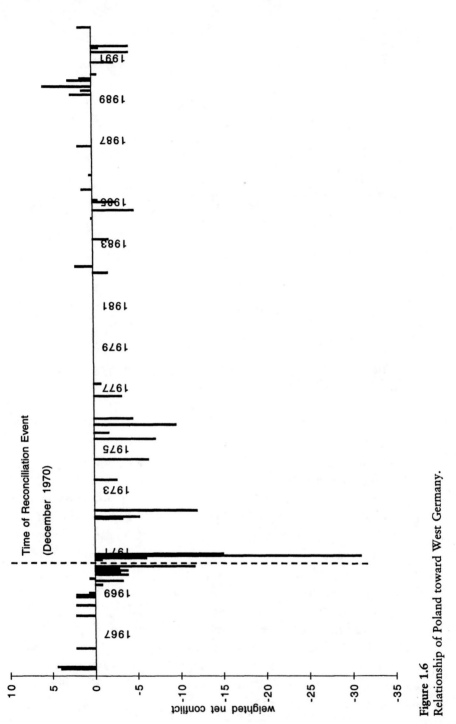

Figure 1.6
Relationship of Poland toward West Germany.

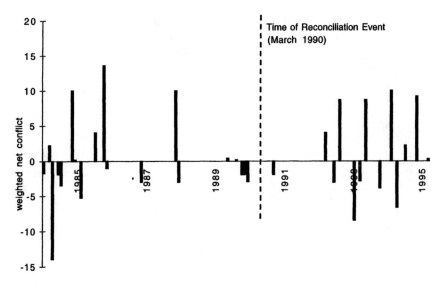

Figure 1.7
Relationship of the United Kingdom toward Argentina.

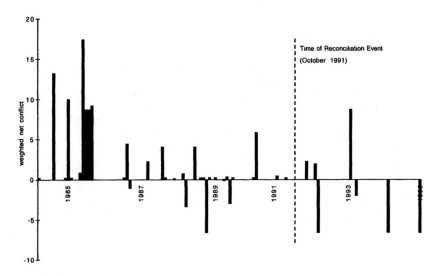

Figure 1.8
Relationship of Cambodia toward Vietnam.

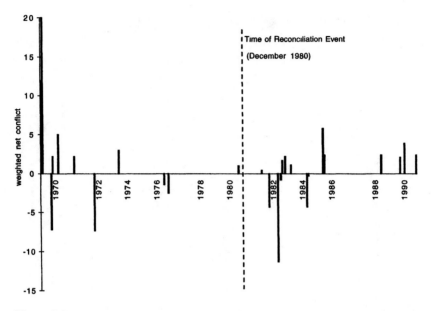

Figure 1.9
Relationship of Honduras toward El Salvador.

Table 1.3
Summary of Visual Analysis

Reconciliation Event with Visual Evidence of Improvement in Bilateral Relations	Reconciliation Event without Visual Evidence of Improvement in Bilateral Relations
USSR–West Germany	UK–Argentina
India–China	Cambodia–Vietnam
Egypt–Israel	Honduras–El Salvador
China–Vietnam	
Poland–West Germany	

Method of Investigation

Comparative Case Study
This study considered the questions *how* reconciliations are realized and, therefore, *why* they lead to restoration of peace after conflict through a detailed, theoretically informed, comparative case study analysis. An in-depth study of a small number of cases provides an opportunity to explore

those questions subtly yet systematically. This methodology also presents certain challenges. The major challenge, of course, is the problem of complex, multiple determinants of social phenomena and the risk of spurious or invalid inferences being drawn from a few cases in which many causal factors may be at play; in short, the problem of "over-determinancy."[16]

To control for this problem, the investigation will be defined by systematic use of theory and a within-case process tracing procedure. Two models, one drawn from rational choice and game theory and the second grounded in evolutionary psychology, will be used to establish relevant independent variables, and within-case process tracing will identify the intervening steps or cause-and-effect links between independent variables and outcomes.[17] To explore our research questions, this study used the nineteen cases that provide a substantial range of outcomes on the dependent variable (subsequent relations between former antagonists) and are relatively free of selection bias.

Theoretical Framework for Case Analyses: Model Development

Despite pervasive references to reconciliation in popular discussions of conflict resolution, the assumption that reconciliation events are an important determinant of subsequent relations within and between states is powerful, yet is not fully examined in the theoretical literature. Although impressionistic, narrative accounts of a single conflict abound, few examined postconflict reconciliation comparatively from a social scientific perspective.

In general, the conflict resolution literature identifies a surfeit of factors that can account for de-escalation of conflict. For example, Louis Kriesberg explained:

A combination of several changes is generally needed to bring about a transition into a de-escalation movement, particularly for protracted conflicts. The changes occur within one or more adversary, in their relations, and in their social context. Quite different combinations of changed conditions can bring about the shift toward de-escalation.[18]

This literature draws our attention to the complexity of conflict resolution in practice, a topic this book returns to in a discussion of explanatory reductionism in chapter 4. Nonetheless, most of this literature is descriptive, noting variable forms and the socially constructed nature of conflict and its resolution, and implicitly rationalistic in its assumptions.[19]

The approach here is explicitly social scientific in that it develops two models from general hypotheses about reconciliation processes, derives specific hypotheses about expected behavior, and connects each model to its underlying assumptions about human nature and human rationality, its "microfoundation." The study then examines evidence in our cases for patterns that support either model.

A Rational Choice Model

The first model of the reconciliation process emerges from rational choice and, more specifically, game theoretic approaches to explaining cooperative outcomes. Game theorists specify possible outcomes from the interaction of rational actors seeking to "win," that is, achieve desired strategies and satisfy their preferences.

This model describes a mechanism or process consistent with a general signaling hypothesis: the best strategy for breaking a pattern of hostile interactions is by sending signals that provide a measure of commitment to the pursuit of improved relations. Reconciliation events or gestures are particularly effective forms of this type of signal because they are almost always politically costly to leaders of opposing sides, and costly signals are more reliable determinants of a leader's true intentions for improved relations than low-cost or cost-free signals.[20] Reconciliation initiatives impose costs because of their "audience effect."[21] Leaders do not conduct policy in isolation, but before domestic and international audiences. Concern with adverse political reaction to a reconciliation gesture toward a former adversary, or with political humiliation should a leader decide to back down from an agreement if it fails to produce the intended effects or if it produces adverse reactions in key third-party actors, are important audience costs associated with reconciliation.

In short, a reconciliation event (and the reconciliation it symbolizes) is a costly (or potentially costly) signal that the other party is likely to interpret as a genuine offer to improve relations and thus may break a deadlocked conflictual situation. Because of associated costs of backing away from the event, it may also buttress initial attempts of the parties at cooperative interaction. Social science, since the work of J. David Singer, has maintained that for one actor to perceive another as a threat it must see the latter as having both the capability and the intent to block the attainment of one's desired strategies and goals.[22] Thus, by sending costly (and therefore trustworthy) signals indicating a less hostile intent, reconciliation events reduce the perception of threat between actors (other things being equal) and permit improvement in relations. Such initiatives may break through a conflictual relationship with its conditions of high ambiguity, high mistrust, and low credibility.

Specific behavioral hypotheses can be derived from this signaling model. Game theory and rational choice theory instruct us to investigate case studies for negotiated bargains associated with reconciliation events (offer and reciprocation) that increase or decrease costs to participating parties. Elements that increase costs should enhance chances for improvement in relations, whereas factors that reduce costs should reduce the likelihood of a positive impact on relations. For example, a reconciliation attempt made despite factional opposition would send a stronger signal to an adversary than one with little domestic consequence, and hence should be more likely to change the adversary's threat perception. Furthermore, factors that clarify or obfuscate the signal-sending effect of a reconciliation event should be important determinants of its success or failure. Clearer signals of a desire for improved relations should contribute to successful reconciliation.

Social psychology (the study of intergroup relations, including intergroup conflict and its de-escalation or resolution) identified several specific factors that improve recognition and increase the weight of a reconciliation signal and encourage reciprocation. For example, a conflict cycle or impasse in intergroup relations, what some political scientists label a "hurting stalemate,"[23] can be broken and relations enhanced by certain forms of contact and communication between parties, a so-called contact hypothesis.[24] Some place particular emphasis on contact between decision makers. Ronald Fisher's work maintains unequivocally that "movement toward resolution in the sense of searching toward creative, mutually acceptable, and self-sustaining solutions may only come about through direct dialogue between influential representatives of conflicting parties."[25] The relevance of reconciliation events to the broader process of reconciliation and thus our use of them arises from this set of findings.

According to social psychology, factors that facilitate the sending of successful (conflict-reducing) signals between individuals and groups include the following:

1. *Costliness.* The offer of a reconciliation must impose a cost on the initiator and its reciprocation a cost on the other party; the higher the cost, the better.[26]

2. *Vulnerability.* Reconciliation initiatives should involve risk and be vulnerable to exploitation.[27]

3. *Novelty.* Reconciliation attempts are most likely to break established conflict patterns when they are dramatic, positive (not merely refraining from a negative action), unexpected, and thought provoking.[28]

4. *Voluntariness.* Reconciliation signals are best when made unilaterally, rather than as the result of pressure or coercion. The offer of conciliation from the stronger party is prima facie evidence of voluntariness.[29]

5. *Irrevocability or noncontingency.* Making noncontingent and irrevocable offers that are likely to be understood as conciliatory, rather than quid-pro-quo, contribute to the success of a reconciliation attempt.[30] Carrying out conciliatory initiatives as announced[31] and making unambiguous offers that are open to verification[32] contribute to irrevocability and noncontingency.

From these findings we propose a signaling model of reconciliation as shown in figure 1.10. Actions in the reconciliation process involving novelty, voluntariness, and costliness contribute to successful reconciliation. Costliness, in turn, consists of actions entailing vulnerability and/or

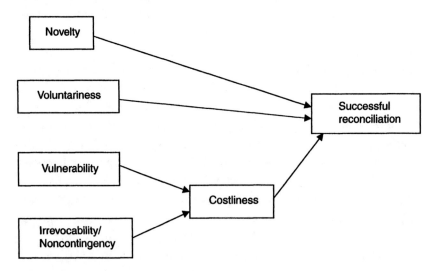

Figure 1.10
Signaling model of the reconciliation process.

irrevocability-noncontingency. These four factors have a relatively independent effect on the dependent variable, successful reconciliation.

With this model we further propose a specific hypothesis: a successful reconciliation emerges in cases manifesting these elements. Moreover, cases exhibiting a higher number of these elements will be the most successful. In chapters 2 and 3 the case studies are examined for each factor to determine whether this hypothesis is supported.

Cognitive-Behavioral Assumptions of the Signaling Model

Most works on signaling are consistent with a general rationality assumption about decision making: an individual (or individual acting on behalf of a collective) chooses an action from an array of potential actions that maximizes its interest or utility.[33] Assumptions of rational decision making are as follows:

1. Actors pursue goals.
2. These goals reflect the actor's perceived interests.
3. Behavior results from a process that involves, or functions as if it entails, conscious choice.
4. The individual is the basic agent in society.
5. Actors have preferences that are consistent and stable.
6. If given options, actors will choose the alternative with the highest expected utility.
7. Actors possess extensive information on both the available alternatives and likely consequences of their choices.[34]

These assumptions apply with equal force for all persons.

Deciding to go to war and, conversely, to resolve a conflict are both rational choices for decision makers under certain conditions. Bruce Bueno de Mesquita explained that for national leaders

the selection of war or peace is a choice that is initiated, conducted, and concluded by individual leaders who must accept responsibility for their decisions. . . . Their choices depend on their estimation of costs and benefits.[35]

Conflict resolution through conciliatory signals could also be an example of rationality.

These psychological assumptions confer certain important advantages to rational choice approaches: parsimony, the availability of equilibrium analysis,[36] deductive reasoning, and universality, or interchangeability of individuals.[37] Proponents contend that rationality assumptions allow for *scientific* investigation of politics and enhance our ability to explain and predict human behavior. Indeed, it is this specification about the micro-foundations of political behavior—deductive accounts of individual incentives, constraints, and calculations—that allegedly give rational choice theory its rigor.[38]

Many political and social scientists question and critique this model of decision making.[39] Some assert that the assumption about human behavior derived from economists—that people pursue self-interests subject to information and opportunity costs—does not apply to the realm of politics because most political acts concern public goods that are not explicable in market terms.[40] In a different vein, cognitive theorists criticize rational choice assumptions because of the limitations on decision making imposed by human cognition. The best-known examples of qualifications to strict rationality are models of "bounded" rationality and theories on the use of heuristics that recognize the limits on humans' rational processing capabilities.[41] A few theoreticians considered a possible role for emotion in decision making,[42] but most cognitive theorists either ignore emotion or see its role in decision making as secondary, marginal, or counterproductive. For most, assumptions of rational choice are accepted as an accurate depiction of decision making. Many others accept general rationality as a legitimate approximation of salient political interactions[43] or view rationality as a useful assumption that successfully establishes correspondence with observable phenomena.[44]

Rational choice assumptions, in turn, rest on a theory of human cognitive mechanisms that generate this expected behavior—a deeper, natural science microfoundation. The mind is assumed to be essentially content independent, taking its cues from the environment, and domain general; that is, its rational processes operate in the same manner in all domains of human activity. The paradigm sees the mind as a general-purpose computer that embodies rational, that is, universal, decision rules. The same reasoning mechanisms and principles operate regardless of content to address all challenges in one's environment: "how one acquires a language, how one learns to recognize emotional expressions, . . . how one acquires ideas and attitudes about friends and reciprocity—everything but perception."[45] With the exception of certain basic drives such as hunger and thirst, the human mind is content free, not designed to recognize, structure, or solve certain problems rather than others, but flexible, capable of applying rational rules equally well in any domain. Moreover, rationality refers only to conscious reasoning; it does not include subconscious mental processes and emotions.

Thus, general rationality from Gottfried Leibniz's calculus to Alfred Whitehead and Bertrand Russell's mathematics[46] maintains that rationality guarantees correctness independent of the material being reasoned about. The expected behavior of universal or general rationality—all individuals always act to maximize their well-being as they understand it, based on their preferences and strategic opportunities—and its assumptions about the human mind as a general-purpose, dispassionate calculator are stringent. The intellectual history of this view dates from the Enlightenment philosophy of progress and individual freedom through reason. This concept has deeper roots in the writings of the ancient Greeks, but it differs from the original Greek meaning of the word whose root *ratio* meant achieving balanced and proportional, not maximum individual, wants.[47]

The rational choice paradigm is silent on the question of why individuals behave in self-interested ways. It offers no explanation for the origins of a self-interested mind. It has great difficulty explaining behavior that is either manifestly not self-interested or emotive (a topic examined in chapter 4).[48]

An Alternative Model: Reconciliation as Forgiveness

An alternative approach asserts what we call the forgiveness hypothesis: reconciliation is part of a process of forgiveness, transforming certain emotions (moving from anger to affinity) and transcending certain beliefs about oneself and the other, that opens the possibility of new, beneficial relations. It begins by observing that reconciliation is a ubiquitous mechanism for solving the enduring problem of sociality. It then builds a model or explanation for this patterned behavior based on an evolutionary theory of the mind that assumes the mind has evolved to solve specific, recurring problems such as how to maintain social relations through integration of emotion and reason.

Specifically, the general forgiveness hypothesis suggests the following: an adaptive problem that humans and our ancestors[49] encountered for several million years (since they first lived in groups) is the problem of sociality, how to restore social order and the benefits of affiliation despite inevitable conflicts and injuries. In response, the often-witnessed and variously documented ability to forgive and the process of reconciliation are, hypothetically, modern manifestations of a functionally specialized, emotionally assisted, human problem-solving capability that we possess to explicate ourselves from this recurrent dilemma. Without such a mechanism, Hannah Arendt supposed, "Our capacity to act would, as it were, be confined to one single deed [conflict] from which we could never recover; we would remain the victims of its consequences forever, not unlike the sorcerer's apprentice who lacked the magic formula to break the spell."[50]

The universality of a problem such as sociality, or evidence of a ubiquitous problem-solving mechanism such as reconciliation, is not proof of an evolved human capability, but it does allow for generating hypotheses about behavior and designing observations and tests that are plausibly consistent with psychology and biology and otherwise would not have been thought of. Procedurally, the method of deriving and examining social science hypotheses from an evolutionary perspective begins by noting the existence of a complexly articulated and recurrent behavioral trait, in this case, reconciliation events. Second, one can ask, deductively, whether the trait could reasonably be the expression of an adaptation; that is, a response to a species-typical problem encountered over several million years of human evolution. If so, we might be witnessing a contemporary manifestation of an evolution-engineered, emotionally influenced problem-solving capability rather than simply the exercise of general reasoning. Human decision making has an emotive dimension that must be accounted for, not just our rational calculations. Third, armed with a plausible hypothesis, the posited behavioral characteristic must be linked with and understood in its cultural, social, or political system.

To appreciate this model it is necessary to elaborate the elements of this theory of the mind, the model's microfoundation; explain how it includes emotion with calculation; and link it to the forgiveness hypothesis. We turn now to the building blocks of this model.

Cognitive-Behavioral Assumptions of Evolutionary Psychology

Evolutionary psychology,[51] which is informed by evolutionary biology, offers an alternative framework for explaining the reconciliation process that connects social theory with the natural sciences and attempts to integrate human reasoning with human emotions. This approach begins by assuming that theories of human motivations and behavior must be consistent with the fact that the human mind is an evolved structure, a fact consistent with modern biology.[52]

Works in evolutionary psychology and neuroscience[53] begin by assuming that the human mind, like any other organ, can be understood as an evolved structure[54] that includes a large collection of functionally specialized, domain-specific mechanisms.[55] The mind's specific problem-solving capabilities, or circuits, to use the popular metaphor, are adaptations[56] constructed by natural selection[57] and other evolutionary processes over time[58] to cope with regularly occurring reproduction-threatening problems (so-called adaptive problems).[59] Form follows function. The function of a particular mental design refers to "how it contributed to its own propagation in ancestral environments"[60]; that is, how it addressed particular challenges over long periods of evolution. This is a very different understanding of the function of mental processes than that proposed by rational choice theorists, who posit a general problem-solving mind whose function is to maximize an individual's goals or well-being in response to its *existing* environment. From an evolutionary perspective, rationality of this kind exists as a side effect of a given evolved design, but it can play no role in explaining how such a design came into existence or why it has the organization it does. For example, the ability of mentally agile individuals to play chess derives in part from evolved spatial and navigational abilities. Similarly, our complex inner ear, designed to give us the ability to walk upright, permits the more agile among us to ride skateboards. But our balancing mechanism was not *designed* to enable us to ride skateboards, nor was our rationality designed to play games. The specific problems the mind was designed to solve date to the Pleistocene era, although those ancient problems do not exhaust the range of problems the mind is now capable of solving.

According to an evolutionary view, all normal human minds reliably develop a *collection* of functionally integrated reasoning abilities that interpret experience by providing frames for understanding events in our environment (such as the actions of others), that infer others' motivations and intentions, and that shape one's behavior. The mind possesses "privileged hypotheses" or crib sheets about how the world works, a phenomenon shared by humans ranging from infants as young as a few hours to adults at various ages and from various cultures.[61] This circuitry, which includes some rational methods, also has other inference procedures that are not universally logical, and both types of procedures or methods help us solve particular problems. These problems include, but are not limited to, acquiring language, recognizing faces and emotions, understanding physical principles, and diagnosing reciprocity and cheating. Moreover, these circuits enable problems to be solved faster and more reliably than a content-free rational computation device could, because a general-purpose computer can make no special assumptions about the problem to be solved and thus is constrained to apply the same methods to solving every problem. Having no privileged hypotheses, general rationality is quickly overtaken by combinatorial explosion. "*Combinatorial explosion* is the term for the fact that with each dimension of potential variation added, or with each new successive choice in a chain of decisions, the total number of alternative possibilities faced by a computational system grows with devastating rapidity."[62] Embedded knowledge about specific problems allows the mind to grasp problems much more readily because all possibilities need not be considered. A frame "carves the world into defined categories of entities and properties, defines how these categories are related to each other, suggests operations that might be performed, defines what goals might be achieved. . . ."[63] Of importance, a growing body of evidence supports the idea of these specialized,[64] but not indelibly fixed,[65] mental domains.

In sum, an evolutionary paradigm suggests that the human mind has developed reliable, specialized mechanisms that are preequipped to know many things about social interactions such as exchanges and threats, emotions, language, and expression, among others. The mind's flexibility and power result from the large number of specific problem-solving capabilities, not from absence of specific content and application of general rational principles. As David Buss maintained,

A carpenter's flexibility comes not from having a single, domain-general, "all-purpose tool" for cutting, poking, sawing, screwing, twisting, wrenching, planing, balancing, and hammering, but rather from having many, more specialized tools. It is the number and specificity of the tools in the entire toolkit that give the carpenter great flexibility not a single highly "plastic tool."[66]

So go human mental faculties as well.[67]

This approach clearly helps us reconcile the functions of the human mind with biological evolution. In addition to a large body of neuroscience that identified modularity in the human brain, this approach is consistent with the fact that evolutionary design generally favors specific organs and mechanisms designed to solve particular tasks.[68] It has not yet succeeded, however, in fully explaining humans' remarkable behavioral flexibility, including incredibly complex information processing.[69]

The evolutionary psychology account of general problem solving maintains that

Breadth is achieved not by abandoning domain-specific techniques but by adding more of them to the system . . . what is special about the human mind is not that it gave up "instinct" in order to become flexible, but that it proliferated "instincts" [i.e., adaptations] . . . which allowed an expanding role for psychological mechanisms that are (relatively) more function general.[70]

How specific reasoning is additive or compounding and how general rationality works with specific reasoning are not fully resolved. The road to explaining this process, however, cannot proceed without a new understanding of emotion's role in problem solving.

The Role of Emotion
Unlike rational choice theory, which treats emotions as exogenous to, or impediments of, reason, this understanding of the human mind incorporates emotion as well as reasoning in explaining human behavior because emotions are products of an evolutionary process: the results of functional adaptation.[71] Specifically, emotions, it is suggested, identify, establish priorities for, and help solve regulatory problems in, a mind filled with many functionally specialized mechanisms as well as general reasoning ability. Emotions "provide the 'go,' 'stop,' and 'turn' signals needed for much decision making and planning, even in regard to highly abstract topics."[72] In ways thus far only partially understood, they animate and help coordinate among problem-solving techniques and their appropriate application to situations.[73] Chapter 4 provides a fuller explanation of the role of emotion in rationality.

"Emotion" is subject to many definitions and connotations, but it is generally thought to include physiological arousal, sensations of pleasure and/or displeasure, and ideas or cognitive appraisals regarding the source of arousal.[74] The biological bases of emotions and their interaction with cognition are explored in chapter 4. Here, it is enough to note that emotion is incorporated into an evolutionary view of problem solving.

Recall that, in evolutionary psychologists' view of the mind, form follows function. Thus, it is presumed that the brain's systems are designed not for cool rationality, but for hot cognition, to respond to crucial events related to survival and reproduction. As such, these theorists assume natural interconnections between affect and cognition.[75] In general, emotions work hand in hand with cognition and behavior as interrelated parts of a functionally designed system.[76] Findings in neuroscience increasingly support this proposition.[77]

More specifically, reconciliation occurs when shame and anger that often lead to aggression or a desire for revenge are superceded by a different emotive and cognitive path—empathy and desire for affiliation. Although each of these terms is much debated in psychology and in other fields, for our purposes, anger can be understood as a strong emotion or experiential state ranging from irritation to fury that occurs in response to a real or imagined shame, frustration, threat, or injustice; aggression is an impulse to hurt as a possible response to anger[78]; and revenge is a more deliberate form of aggression.[79] Empathy implies a realistic understanding resulting from feeling with (not for) another,[80] and affiliation is a basic human motivation, a desire for belonging with another, even if only to enhance one's own chances for survival.[81]

The Forgiveness Model

These assumptions about the human mind and rationality generate a different set of predictions about human behavior and decision making than those of rational choice. Concerning reconciliation, they suggest a forgiveness model in distinction to the signaling model. As stated earlier, the forgiveness hypothesis proposes that reconciliation is a direct outgrowth or manifestation of patterned, emotively driven, problem-solving behavior, not merely rational calculations. Behind this hypothesis is the belief that a general rationality assumption may fail to account fully for conciliatory behavior. Below we describe a forgiveness model that explains how the reconciliation process can take place in a manner consistent with the forgiveness hypothesis.

Before going further, it must be acknowledged that discussing reconciliation this way might seem out of place in discourse about rough-and-tumble collective power conflicts. We ask the reader to suspend judgment on this score. Without engaging theological or normative approaches to forgiveness and reconciliation, we believe that this topic deserves serious examination by social scientists as a possible mechanism for resolving intergroup conflicts and for maintaining social order.

Furthermore, forgiveness takes time to consummate, and where collectivities are involved, it becomes much more complicated than in the one-on-one model of an injured person and a wrongdoer.[82] Louis Kriesberg, for example, noted that "After intense struggle between large-scale adversaries, it is not likely that reconciliation will be universal among all members of the opposing sides."[83] Nonetheless, forgiveness and reconciliation have a clear social function—restoring a neutral or more positive relationship after a transgression and reestablishing membership or affiliation in a larger society—that could occur between individuals, between an individual and a group, or between groups.

Behaviorally, the process of forgiveness and reconciliation as described across many different disciplines invariably includes four phases. First, parties to a conflict must recognize shame and anger from a perceived wrong, injustice, frustration, or injury. They must *acknowledge* the harm. "Official investigations, judicial proceedings, artistic productions, and mass media reporting are all ways to face openly what many experience covertly."[84] Potential mechanisms for coping with anger typically include conscious or unconscious denial, active or passive expression (aggression or revenge), or forgiveness.[85] The forgiveness option requires recognition first. As Joanna North explained, "Forgiveness does not remove the fact or event of wrongdoing but instead *relies* upon the recognition of wrong having been committed in order for the process of forgiveness to be made possible."[86] One does not forget to forgive, one remembers and forgives.

Second, forgiveness involves a changed understanding of oneself and of the other party to a conflict. Anger from an injury or wrong is closely associated not only with the desire for revenge, but with the "pain of injury," that is, emotions such as sadness or fear, and damage to one's self-esteem or identity.[87] Forgiving involves a self-transformation wherein the party sees itself as something other than a victim and achieves a more complete and balanced identity.[88]

Forgiveness is outwardly directed as well. Specifically, it requires constructing a new identity for the other, the enemy. Analysts describe this process in both cognitive and emotive language. Cognitively, it involves "reframing" the other, "separating the wrongdoer from the wrong which has been committed. . . . Reframing does not do away with the wrong itself, nor does it deny the wrongdoer's responsibility for it, but it allows us to regard the wrongdoer in a more complete, more detailed, more rounded way . . ."[89] The other party is recognized as separate from the injury he or she inflicted, and the humanity of that person is acknowledged by those who have suffered.[90] In Hannah Arendt's words, "*what was done is forgiven for the sake of who did it.*"[91] In addition, this phase is often described in emotive terms as an "empathic understanding" of the other,[92] a "willed change of heart,"[93] or "metanoia," a changed state of consciousness.[94]

Third, the parties must forego the option of revenge, however natural, desirable, or justifiable. This forbearance does not require abandonment of all versions of punishment, redress for wrongs or injuries, or abandonment of justice, only willingness to break the cycle of injury and counterinjury.[95] Retribution for a wrong must be less than total.[96]

Fourth, one or both parties make an offer that results in contact between them and a public expression of forgiveness, with the offer of a renewed but different relationship, what we call a reconciliation event. This reestablishes, at a minimum, mutual affiliation, coexistence,[97] mutual toleration, or respect.[98] As Murphy and Hampton described it, it is "at the very least the 'civil' relationship that prevails between strangers in a human community."[99] Although new, beneficial relations are possible, they are not certain: "Just as forgiveness accepts ambiguity in the past, so it does not seek to resolve all future conflicts ahead of time."[100] Rather, forgiveness and reconciliation enable members of a society to maintain stability and mutually beneficial affiliation with each other. This resolution may be in the context of high levels of integration or limited interaction.[101]

In sum, forgiveness requires recognition of harm—truth telling, development of a new understanding of oneself and the other, and willingness to forego prolonging hostility through acts of revenge. It also can include the offer of a renewed community in the future—a reconciliation event.[102] The fundamental argument of the forgiveness model is that although cognitive judgments and strategy are involved in the process of reconciliation, the process fundamentally represents an emotionally cued change to a *specific* problem-solving mechanism that helps us restore relations in our societal group rather than *general* rational calculation. Although the patterned behavior may vary in practice, one can visualize the stages of forgiveness by considering figure 1.11. Because these elements of forgiveness are themselves processes rather than discrete events, figure 1.12 illustrates the flow of the forgiveness sequence. In reality, all cases may not strictly adhere to such a sequence, but we would expect behavior to follow the general pattern.

Figure 1.11
Forgiveness model of the reconciliation process.

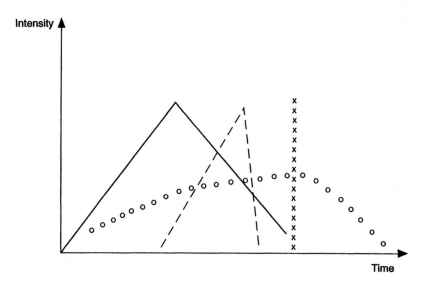

Figure 1.12
The forgiveness sequence.

Pulling together these insights and applying them to the question of reconciliation and conflict resolution gives us a very different model than that derived from a rational choice perspective. Compare these figures with the signaling model in figure 1.10.

Operationally, examining case studies in terms of the forgiveness model would involve a search for evidence of an acknowledgment of wrong and injury. We would expect to see a change of self-perception or identity from one who was wronged to one of autonomy and equivalence in the relationship. Furthermore, we would anticipate evidence of a change to a more holistic view of the other, expressed either rhetorically or in action, and a call for a new relationship coinciding with, or proximate to, the reconciliation event. Finally, we would expect efforts to find justice short of vengeance and full retribution. Evidence of this behavior would support the forgiveness model.[103] In practice, all these dimensions of reconciliation may not be fully realizable.[104] We must remember that this model is an ideal of reconciliation as forgiveness.

Organization

The next chapter presents eleven cases of reconciliation events after civil conflicts. The two fundamental models (or general hypotheses)—rational choice signaling and evolutionary psychology forgiveness—and the behavioral patterns they anticipate (our specific hypotheses) will guide the investigation. The chapter concludes by considering the fit between models and cases.

Chapter 3 considers the role of reconciliation in interstate, as opposed to intrastate, war. These eight cases allow a second opportunity to assess the contending models and explore the role and reach of reconciliation in the most diffuse of all societies—the society of states.

Chapter 4 considers in depth the relative merits, similarities, and differences to explaining human decision making between rational choice and evolutionary psychology as approaches to social theory. It reassesses the value and limits of social theory based on established rationality assumptions, and considers an alternative scientific approach to social theorizing based on reintegration of emotion and reasoning. Specifically, it explains how and why emotion should be reincorporated into rationality. Chapter 4 also considers common problems of rational choice and evolutionary psychology perspectives, the relationship between a constructivist and an evolutionary perspective, and the unfortunate history of attempts to integrate findings from the natural sciences into social theory.

Chapter 5 offers concise, general insights on the role of reconciliation as a tool for conflict resolution practitioners and policy makers. It identifies generic features, drawn from the case studies, of successful reconciliations and considers factors that often facilitate or complicate efforts to conclude social reconciliation. This chapter also identifies avenues for future research on reconciliation and conflict resolution, and suggests other political questions that might be amenable to an approach involving hypotheses derived from the integration of emotion into rationality.

2

Civil War and Reconciliation

To be social is to be forgiving.
—Robert Frost[1]

Before considering case studies, let us briefly restate the basic signaling and forgiveness models that attempt to explain the role of reconciliation events in reducing intrastate conflict. First, the signaling model holds that intrastate relations between belligerents can be understood as a bargain or game with a range of potential outcomes. Actors choose moves that maximize achieving their respective goals given environmental constraints and available information.

The offer of reconciliation or the event itself (offer and reciprocation) can be an important signal of an intention for improved, more cooperative relations because it is a costly signal that is likely to be interpreted as a reliable indication of a desire for improved relations by the other party. Reconciliation offers or attempts are costly because they are undertaken before domestic audiences and thus are potentially exploitable by the other party.

Because of attendant costs, reconciliation events potentially reduce threat perception between adversaries and permit improvement in future relations, because continuing the conflict in such an environment and with this new information may no longer maximize the utility of either party. Reconciliation initiatives may break through a conflictual relationship with its conditions of high ambiguity, high mistrust, and low credibility. We would expect signals to work when they are costly, exploitable, novel, voluntary, and irrevocable.

Works on signaling are consistent with a general rationality assumption about decision making. These assumptions, in turn, rest on a theory of human cognitive mechanisms that generate this expected behavior. The mind is assumed to be essentially content independent—it takes its cues from the environment—and domain general—its rational processes operate on all domains of human activity, including decisions of war or conflict resolution.

Alternatively, the forgiveness model maintains that reconciliation is part of an evolved, specialized, problem-solving mechanism. Specifically, it hypothesizes a four-phase behavioral process: recognition of the harm and public truth telling, a changed understanding of the self and other that transcends the narrow roles of victim and perpetrator, retribution short of revenge, and the offer of a new but different relationship that establishes, at a minimum, mutual affiliation and coexistence. Although cognitive strategies are part of this process, it fundamentally represents an emotionally animated process entailing a specific problem-solving technique that exists to restore relations in one's societal group. This hypothesis instructs us to look for this four-phase process in the case studies.

Next, we provide concise narratives of the history of the ten countries that experienced civil conflict and a reconciliation event. These case studies are not meant to be the definitive history of the conflicts and are limited in scope and depth to capture the essence of conflict, reconciliation event, and postreconciliation relations. The brief narratives allow the reader to discern empirical referents of the two models without getting lost in the complexity of each case. Notably, the first three countries—Colombia, Yemen, and Chad—are cases in which reconciliation events failed to restore lasting social order. The next seven cases—Argentina, Uruguay, Chile, El Salvador, Mozambique, South Africa, and Honduras—are cases of successful, order-restoring reconciliations. After the narratives, we offer a set of findings that assess the utility of the two models in explaining the outcomes, and our conclusion comments preliminarily on the broader implications of these findings.

Case Studies

Colombia

An independent republic by 1819, Colombian politics have been dominated by Conservative and Liberal parties since the 1850s. Aside from two brief military takeovers, civilian rule has been the norm. Despite this democratic tradition, Colombian history has also been characterized by violence, including two civil wars resulting from rivalry, the War of a Thousand Days (1899–1902) and *La Violencia* (the Violence) of the late 1940s and early 1950s.

In 1948, competition between political parties turned violent after the assassination of Liberal leader Jorge Gaitán. An estimated 100,000 to 200,000 people died in the violence, and several armed insurgent groups were spawned.

In 1953, a military coup supported by the parties brought General Gustavo Rojas Pinilla to power. Although he was successful initially in reducing the level of internal violence, eventually the military and the two political parties became frustrated over his failure to restore civilian rule and overthrew him in favor of a provisional government. Colombia's reconciliation event occurred in 1957 when Conservative and Liberal leaders met and publicly issued the Declaration of Sitges. The declaration led to creation of a National Front whereby the two parties would govern jointly. Under this arrangement, the presidency would alternate between parties every four years, and the parties would share appointed and elective offices. The goal was to reduce the level of violence and give the country twenty years to recover from *La Violencia*. This arrangement remained formally in effect until 1974, and de facto, it continued into the 1990s. The accommodation, designed to permit return to democracy, effectively closed political participation to groups outside the two dominant, oligarchic parties. As a result, political claims from many parts of Colombian society had no legal institutional channel, and they soon overflowed legal bounds into continuing armed insurrections by those effectively disenfranchised.[2]

Although the compromise ended interparty violence, it did not restore order. Colombia remains the "most troubled country in the hemisphere," engulfed by a civil war without end, besieged by a "permanent armed insurgency."[3] In the four decades since creation of the National Front, internal armed conflict has claimed over 35,000 lives. An average of ten citizens is killed every day in political violence. Government control is tenuous and geographically limited, and leftist guerrillas and rightist paramilitary forces have expanded and, with the advent of the drug trade, become increasingly well financed.

The major challenge to the government came from several leftist guerrilla organizations: the Revolutionary Armed Forces of Colombia, National Liberation Army, Popular Liberation Army, and the ideologically heterogeneous M-19 group.[4] Colombia's internal violence worsened in the mid-1980s with the rise of right-wing paramilitaries and the influx of illicit money. The guerrillas, for example, are thought to derive close to one billion U.S. dollars annually in revenue from taxing cocoa producers, extorting money from oil producers, and kidnapping. The paramilitaries, believed to number over 5,000, are supported primarily by payments from drug traffickers and from landholders who fear guerrilla interference in their operations or a peasant uprising. Drug money has also corrupted and weakened many of the country's traditional political institutions, particularly the judiciary. In short, the rise of the drug economy worsened Colombia's woes by strengthening the guerrilla movements, weakening the government through corruption, and prompting the rise of extreme paramilitary forces on the right.[5] Several military crackdowns and peace initiatives have not stemmed the violence.

Paradoxically, Colombia continued to hold election after election throughout its internal crisis, and during much of this period maintained respectable levels of economic growth. Yet, more than forty years since creation of the National Front, the political system is not inclusive, the society remains distrustful and unreconciled, and the state has not consolidated its authority.

Yemen

For centuries Yemen was under the rule of Imams usually of the Zaidi Muslim sect. This traditional theocracy survived into modern times. In 1918, North Yemen threw off the yoke of Ottoman domination. Great Britain kept South Yemen, known as the Aden Protectorates, under its colonial rule.

In 1962, North Yemen leader Badr Yahya was deposed by revolutionary republican forces composed of urban populations, army officers, Shafai (a different Muslim sect from the Zaidi) merchants, intellectuals, industrial laborers, and expatriated dissidents. These republican forces took control of the capital, Sanaa, and created the Yemen Arab Republic (YAR, or North Yemen). Despite creation of a new republic, the dominant feature of Yemeni politics remained intact: a struggle between the central government and tribal leaders whose base of support lay outside the cities in the northern and eastern sections of the country.[6]

A costly and divisive civil war between republicans and royalists followed the revolution. Republicans received support from Egypt and royalists from Saudi Arabia, adding regional and east–west dimensions to the conflict. Fighting continued periodically until 1967, when Egyptian forces were withdrawn after Eygpt's defeat in the Six-Day War, and the Saudis agreed to end support for the royalists. Although the republicans would survive, the civil war tipped the balance of power in favor of the tribal periphery at the expense of the centralized state, and limited the scope of national building and modernization.

By 1968, after failure of a royalist siege of Sanaa, the civil war entered a period of stalemate. Extremists in both republican and royalist camps lost influence. Negotiations for the war's end ensued under Saudi auspices, and most of the opposing forces participated in a reconciliation event in 1970.[7]

That year a modern constitution was adopted and the republic began again the slow process of state building under the neutral leadership of President Abdal-Rahman al-Iryani. The reconciliation event brought some tribal shaykhs into high government offices for the first time in exchange for their allegiance to the republic. The tribal chieftains' influence in the government, in their homelands, and among the army enabled them to limit the overall influence of the central state. Furthermore, "reconciliation" meant expulsion of the modernist left from politics, thus weakening the state, slowing modernization, and antagonizing relations with the newly independent People's Democratic Republic of Yemen (PDRY, or South Yemen). The result of the reconciliation event was creation of a narrowly based, right-of-center regime, not a restructuring of society. This compromise, despite frequent changes of governments, assasinations, and a military coup, persisted into the 1980s.[8]

Relations between YAR and PDRY deteriorated rapidly, however, as one drifted right and the other lurched to the left. A border war between them erupted in September 1972 and flared again the next spring. After mediation by other Arab states, presidents of YAR and PDRY agreed to take steps toward unification.[9]

Despite these pledges, war again broke out between the Yemens in 1979. The Arab League mediated a temporary peace, and the two countries reaffirmed the goal of unity. But skirmishes and full-scale conflicts continued until 1988, when a negotiated settlement brought the war to a close and set the countries back on the path of reunification.

In November 1989, YAR and PDRY agreed on a draft unity constitution, drawn up originally in 1981. The unified Republic of Yemen was declared on May 22, 1990. The fragile unity was not to hold, however, and civil war broke out in 1994. The war lasted only a few months before rebels, largely in the southern part of the country, were defeated militarily.

In sum, the impact of the Yemeni reconciliation event of the early 1970s was equivocal. On the one hand, it restored tenuous order to North Yemen. On the other hand, conflict was exported to its border with PDRY in the 1970s and then emerged again as a civil war in the 1990s after reunification in 1989.

Chad

During its history this "improbable country" has been beset by entrenched ethnic animosities and divergent patterns of social organization.[10] The government has never possessed full administrative control over some groups within its territory, nor has it fully controlled its borders. Over its forty-year history Chad has known virtually continuous civil war or insurgency punctuated by two concerted efforts at national reconciliation.

Chad emerged as an independent country under the presidency of François Tombalbaye in 1960. In 1965, a tax revolt sparked a long civil war that set the Muslim north and east against the government in the south. Although supported by French troops, Tombalbaye never fully quelled the insurgency.

Urged by his French backers, Tombalbaye began a national reconciliation plan after his "election" as president in 1969 (he was the sole candidate). Elements of the reconciliation event included release of several hundred political prisoners and a reshuffling of his cabinet and the political bureau in May 1971. A few weeks later at the party congress, Tombalbaye admitted errors and mistakes of his administration that had given rise to injustices and caused discontent and subversion.[11] The congress approved the new political bureau, which included participation of former political prisoners.

This attempt at incorporation of dissident elements into the regime was short lived. Two attempted coups against the Tombalbaye government implicated some of those individuals recently granted amnesty. These intrigues occurred against a backdrop of civil unrest, a financial crisis, worsening drought, and cabinet infighting, and prompted Tombalbaye to purge dissident elements and order the incarceration of up to 1,000 real or suspected enemies of the state. *Le Monde* described the reaction as evidence of complete failure of reconciliation. The massive arrests also further eroded support for the regime and alienated Tombalbaye from reformists in his own bureaucracy.[12]

Increasingly, Tombalbaye's rule became violent and self-destructive, leading to a military coup in 1975 that installed General Felix Malloum, a southerner, as head of state. Although Malloum's government would reach out to include some northerners, internal dissent within the government led northern Prime Minister Hissein Habré to send his forces against the national army at Ndjaména in February 1979. Civil war broke out and the state splintered into eleven factions.

Civil war continued for the next ten years. It was interrupted by two failed mediation efforts by the Organization of African Unity and was complicated by interventions by Libya. By November 1988, Habré reestablished himself and his alliance, the *Forces Armees Nationales Chadiennes*, in Ndjaména, but his hold on power was short lived. One of his leading generals, Idriss Déby, defected and fled to Darfur in Sudan, from which he mounted a series of attacks on eastern Chad. In November 1990, Déby widened the attack and by December 2, 1990, his forces entered Ndjaména without a battle, Habré and his forces having fled the city. During the final phase of Habré's rule, he too attacked his perceived enemies, killing, by one estimate, more than 20,000 people.[13]

After three months of provisional government, a national charter was approved by Déby's Patriotic Salvation Movement (MPS) on February 28, 1991, with Déby as interim president. Déby's tenure also was one of civil unrest, attempted coups, reprisals, and a reconciliation event, this one beginning at year-end 1992. Déby convened a Truth Commission in 1992 designed primarily to villify his predecessor, Habré. Even as the commission gathered testimony and evidence of past killings and torture, identifying Habré's henchmen in the security forces, Déby began rehabilitating and reincorporating many of the same individuals into his renamed security police. By the time the report was completed, the struggle for accountability was lost; Déby was already relying on the same tactics and torturers to fight new battles.[14]

Urged on by Western pressure for democratization, Déby called for a national conference that was convened on January 15, 1993. It called for a transition to democratic government through elections, but did little to come to terms with Chad's many ethnic, religious, or economic divides. Even during the conference, ethnic violence raged in various parts of the country, reflecting both old divisions and the more recent growth of Islamic fundamentalism among northern populations.[15] Déby's government engaged in military battles with the *Front de Libération National Tchadien* insurgency in the north and the Armed Forces for a Federal Republic (FARF) in the south.[16]

Unable to convince armed opposition groups and legalized parties and associations to join him in a comprehensive settlement, Déby moved forward with a national constitutional referendum that provided for a presidential-style system of government with a popular legislature. The measure passed with 65 percent of the vote, allegedly helped along by some ballot fixing. Of significance, the constitution was opposed by 95 percent of southern voters.[17] In June 1996, Déby was elected president with 69 percent of the votes. Legislative elections held in January and February 1997 saw the MPS party control Parliament also.

Turnout for the elections was low, and insurgencies in the south and north continued after the election. Déby continued to face trouble in the south from FARF and other groups, and there were accusations of government reprisals against civilian populations there in 1997–1998. A more determined insurrection in the desert north also dogged the regime.[18]

In short, despite two negotiated reconciliation events, one in 1971 and the other in 1992–1993, Chad has remained in turmoil for most of its history: a state "suspended between creation and destruction."[19]

Argentina

With the country independent by 1816, Argentine politics was dominated by conservative forces during its first century. In 1916, the Radical Party won control of the government and began a fourteen-year period of democratic opening to a larger proportion of the Argentine people, especially the growing middle class. A military coup in 1930 ended this era and began a decade of Conservative Party rule.

The military again deposed the constitutional government in 1943, and in 1946 elected one of the coup's leaders, Juan Peron, as president. Peron, reelected in 1952, broadened the base of political participation to include Argentina's growing urban working class and, urged by his wife, Evita, extended the franchise to women. Alarmed by Peron's economic nationalization and political populism, the military deposed him in 1955. Throughout the 1950s and 1960s, military and civilian administrations traded power, neither coping with Argentina's growing social unrest and deteriorating economic conditions.

Worsening economic and social conditions facilitated return to power of Peronists in the 1973 elections, and Juan Peron himself assumed the presidency in a second election that year. Peron's third wife, Maria Estrela Isabel Martinez de Peron, became vice president. Peron's return was beset with the rise of political extremism on the left and right, and growing, violent, social disorder. The government resorted to a number of emergency decrees in response, including unlimited imprisonment without charges of those suspected of disturbing the public order. Peron died after a year in office and was succeeded by his wife. Her administration was overtaken by economic problems, intraparty struggles, and terrorism from the left and right. On March 24, 1976, a military coup removed her from office and began a period lasting until December 10, 1983, during which commanders of the three branches of the armed forces exercised power through a junta.[20]

The armed forces dissolved Congress and dismissed federal judges in what it called the Process for National Reorganization. It claimed these actions were necessary to combat leftist guerrillas responsible for hundreds of political assassinations during the Peron years and to attempt to solve the nation's economic crisis. The junta assumed all executive, legislative, and judicial power, but avoided formally declaring war on the guerrillas to avoid giving them legitimate status as belligerents in a civil war.

But it was war nonetheless, what became known later as the Dirty War against suspected internal subversives. During that period, thousands of suspected dissidents were secretly kidnapped and tortured in more than 240 detention centers established throughout the country. More than

10,000 people were murdered (some human rights groups estimate three times that many), and strict censorship allowed the military to hide some of these facts from civil society and the international community while feeding the society's desire for order and an end to guerrilla violence. A frightened and ill-informed society did not oppose what was happening.

Repression reached its peak within a year or two of the military takeover, and by 1980 the military had closed most of the detention centers. But by 1981 the economy was imploding, with the peso plummeting in value and foreign debt tripling in the period 1980–1982. The unions rose in protest against the government's economic policies in large public rallies. Against this background of public unrest, the military made its ill-fated decision to invade the Falklands/Malvinas Islands to recapture political support and to rebuild the civic–military alliance.

The economic crisis, victory for Great Britain in the Falklands/ Malvinas war, public revulsion at the level of internal violence and human rights abuses, and mounting allegations of corruption combined to discredit the military regime and led it to return the country to democratic rule. Argentina's reconciliation events were precipitated by fatigue and failure.

Truth emerged as the first step. The military lost its control over public information, and reports of the regime's atrocities began to appear in the print media and on television. Acting under public pressure, the junta removed the ban on political parties and restored some political liberties. Elections for national, provincial, and local administrations were scheduled for October 1983.

Raul Alfonsin, candidate of the Radical Civic Union, won election to a six-year term as president. Elected with 52 percent of the vote, he responded to human rights groups and others in society pushing to see crimes against civilians investigated and those responsible punished. As promised, the first law enacted by the new Congress nullified amnesty granted by the military to itself.

Alfonsin's government then proceeded with two remarkable reconciliation initiatives: creation of an independent commission to investigate the truth, and a search for justice through prosecution of former members of the military junta. The investigatory commission, the National Commission on Disappeared People, collected about 50,000 public testimonies from victims of the repression and their relatives, and documented close to 9,000 "disappearances" that occurred under military rule. From its investigation, a television report was aired, and its final report took the form of a record-selling book, *Nunca Mas (Never More)*, that laid bare the events of the Dirty War.

Information contained in the report served as the basis for judicial investigations. Public trials were held in 1985 and 1986 focusing on the masterminds and architects of military repression. In all, 481 military and police officers were indicted; 16 were tried and 11 convicted, including top junta officials. Although Alfonsin was satisfied that sufficient justice had been achieved without risking a military uprising and was ready to turn a page in Argentine history, the courts continued their investigation into the activities of others, primarily lower-ranking officers. After squelching a military uprising among younger officers, Alfonsin's administration passed the Due Obedience Law, ending prosecutions for all officers whose rank was below colonel.[21] Although Alfonsin's actions had shattered the notion of the military's impunity and fundamentally changed their role in Argentine society, amnesty left human rights activists and the families of victims understandably distraught.[22]

Alfonsin also solidified civilian control over the military. He retired more than half of Argentina's generals, slashed the military budget, eliminated compulsory military service, and reduced the military's role in the economy. Congress also assented to legislation limiting future jurisdiction of the military courts.[23] The military's role was reoriented away from internal and toward external threats, and later its role included participation in international peacekeeping operations. One observer called this the "institutional debilitation" of the military, a complement to its political debilitation.[24]

In 1989, Carlos Menem of the Peronist Party was elected to succeed Alfonsin. He assumed office amidst a deteriorating economic situation and unrest among the military. Among his first actions was to grant pardons to convicted officers in the name of national reconciliation while simultaneously crushing further military dissent. In all, Menem pardoned 277 people, including 40 generals awaiting trial for human rights abuses, lower-ranking officers, and members of guerrilla groups. Menem, like Alfonsin, expressed concern for stability. His amnesty was unpopular with the public at the time. Also, despite his Peronist affiliation, he set Argentina on a path of neoliberal economic reform designed to rein in inflation and privatize the economy. Menem served two terms as president of a democratic, stable, and, for a time, economically improving Argentina.

Uruguay

Uruguay achieved national independence in 1825. At the beginning of the twentieth century it was a model of democratic stability to many countries in the region.

The country enjoyed sustained economic growth until the 1960s, which saw the onset of economic crisis. But that dimension was only one aspect of a crisis that was also political, social, cultural, and ethical. Growing discontent within large sectors of the population gave rise to an armed minority movement (National Liberation Movement, the Tupamaros), which emerged together with other revolutionary groups in the mid-1960s. Despite relatively small membership of such groups, the government became increasingly authoritarian and declared a state of internal war, unleashing a campaign of persecution against those groups and individuals considered seditious, including all opponents of the government, whether they were engaged in guerrilla activity or not. Thus began the dismantling of trade unions, student organizations, and other major social organizations.

In 1973, the constitutionally elected president, Juan Maria Bordaberry, unable to control urban terrorism, dissolved Parliament and installed a military regime that lasted until 1984. During military rule thousands of Uruguayans were imprisoned and routinely tortured for political crimes. Uruguay became the country with the world's highest per capita rate of political incarceration, with one in every fifty citizens detained at one point, and many of them systematically tortured.[25] Some 100 persons disappeared (some estimates run as high as 300) and several thousand fled into exile abroad.

In 1980, a new constitution drawn up by the military regime was rejected by a popular referendum. That signaled the start of a process of restoration of democracy through mobilization of social forces, international pressure, and discrediting of the armed forces.

Strengthened by the public's frustration with twelve years of military rule, Uruguay's dominant political parties engaged the military in largely secret negotiations resulting in several pacts leading the country toward reconciliation. The imprisoned Tupamaros and others would be freed and granted unconditional amnesty, and elections would be held, but the military would also receive amnesty for any responsibility for the "excesses" of the military regime during a time of "internal war."

In 1985, Julio Maria Sanguinetta of the traditionalist Colorado Party was elected president. Soon thereafter, the ruling Colorados, with the military's urging, presented Parliament with the Law on the Expiration of the State's Right to Prosecute, which was approved on December 2, 1986. The law expressly renounced investigation and trial of individuals involved in excesses that may have been committed by the army. After its enactment, a group of relatives of victims of the dictatorship—politicians, artists, and intellectuals—formed the Pro-Referendum Committee for the purpose of calling a referendum to repeal the law. A massive campaign was launched to collect signatures for holding the referendum, and 25 percent of eligible voters signed. The referendum was held on April 16, 1989, and failed by a 12 percent margin (35% to 47%). Sanguinetta's administration had maintained that democratic peace and stability must be paid for by forgiveness of the repressors. That appeal and the public's desire for a return to normalcy prevailed.

Since 1986, social identities have been rewritten in Uruguay. The military's role in civilian politics was substantially decreased. The armed forces tried unsuccessfully to resist the government's decision to cut their budget and reduce their numbers. The once-feared Tupamaro guerrillas became a legal political party. Democratic practices were restored, if not renewed.

On the other hand, there was little immediate "moral cleansing" of society through truth telling, recognition of suffering, and punishment of the guilty, as in Argentina. In part, this is attributable to the military's ability to fragment internal opposition to human rights abuses, Uruguay's insulation from international pressures for reform, failure of political parties to unify around the theme of human rights, and an executive who had already struck a bargain with the military. No external or internal force pressured the parties to adopt immediately a truth and justice program.[26] Most human rights criticism came initially from exiled opposition groups, and the undefeated military remained a threat. Instead, freeing all political prisoners, blanket amnesty, and a return to democratic practices would be the initial steps along the route to national reconciliation.

During the subsequent period of democratic consolidation, however, a truth-telling process was originated from below by civil society. An initiative known as the "Never Again" project became the focus of church-related and newly emergent human rights groups. These groups worked for three years to produce a report, also called *Nunca Mas,* in 1989. The report lacked the force of a public document and produced no formal response from the government or military. It did become the focus of media attention and public debate, however.

Chile

For most of the twentieth century Chile enjoyed democratic government and political parties broadly representative of the ideological spectrum that peacefully vied for power. Events of the 1970s led to a September 1973 military coup that brought General Pinochet and the military to power. The short rule of Socialist President Salvador Allende precipitated the coup. Allende, elected by a slim majority in 1970, embarked on wide-ranging reforms of industrial nationalization and land redistribution. These policies challenged conservative interests and led the armed forces to depose the government by force.

The junta named Pinochet head of state. He pledged to rid Chile of Marxism and to reconstruct the national economy. The country's economic elite and much of the middle class supported his economic plan. Pinochet dissolved the legislature, banned all political activity, and censured the press, and his internal war violated the human rights of thousands of citizens. In 1978, the government decreed statutory amnesty for itself for crimes committed during the first five years of the military regime (1973–1978), when most of the worst abuses occurred.

In October 1980, a national plebiscite ratified a new constitution developed by the military government. The document established a blueprint for transition to a "protected democracy," one that guaranteed the military a prominent role. The plebiscite ratified the presidency of General Pinochet but called for another plebiscite on continued military rule to be held eight years later.

Resistance to continued military rule increased during the 1980s from several sectors: the Roman Catholic Church, guerrilla organizations, human rights groups, and political moderates from the right and left. Chile also encountered international censure for its human rights violations.

In anticipation of the October 1988 plebiscite on continued military rule, sixteen opposition parties joined forces to create *El Comando por el No* as a unified opposition. On October 5, the No forces carried the plebiscite with 54.7 percent of the vote compared with the government's 43.1 percent. Apparently Pinochet had misread the mood of the public and was shocked by the results.[27] Nonetheless, the plebiscite set in motion a transition to civilian government as the electoral results triggered constitutionally mandated elections for a national president and congress, scheduled for December 14, 1989.[28]

Patricio Aylwin, a moderate former senator and candidate of the *Concertacion de los Partidos por la Democracia,* a coalition of seventeen center and center-left opposition parties, won the election. His party, the Social Democrats, won the largest bloc of seats in the lower house of the legislature and held a majority together with his coalition partners. The upper house, the forty-six-member Senate, remained in conservative hands, however, buttressed by eight members appointed directly by Pinochet according to the 1980 constitution.

Despite election of a civilian president, Pinochet remained head of the army (until 1998), and military and judicial structures remained unchanged. In these circumstances, the new president confronted the problem of human rights violations committed by the military during the civil war, including summary executions, forced disappearances, widespread torture, arbitrary detention, and forced exile.[29]

The new government's first and most important reconciliation initiative was creation of the Commission on Truth and Reconciliation appointed by President Aylwin in April 1990 to investigate those violations. The Commission's mandate was to "clarify in a comprehensive manner the truth about the most serious violations committed in recent years" and "to gather evidence that may make it possible to identify the victims by name and determine their fate or whereabouts." The mandate did not extend to all violations of human rights, such as torture not resulting in death, and did not call for prosecution of individuals responsible. The commission was also to propose measures for reparations and reinstatement, and to recommend legal and administrative measures to prevent recurrence of these acts through institutional redefinition.

The commission presented its final, unanimous report in February 1991. President Aylwin accepted the report and a month later announced its main findings on national television. At this highly public event he offered a formal apology on behalf of the government for the acts of its agents and begged for forgiveness from families of victims, promising reparations and special benefits for them. The report was printed and circulated widely in the press.

The report included an explanation of the origins of the violations, their nature, and institutions responsible. It provided individual information on a large number of victims. The commission did not provide information on those individuals who carried out the killings and disappearances, limiting its discussion to naming branches of armed forces, security forces, or opposition groups believed to be responsible. The report did not individually address cases of exile, internal exile, censorship, or detentions that affected the lives of thousands. In short, this approach to truth and justice was a relatively comprehensive inquiry that named and exonerated those who were victims or disappeared in an effort to restore the identity and dignity of many of the victims. It placed blame on relevant groups, but it left specific cases to individuals to pursue through the courts for punishment of specific wrongdoers.

Securing justice in Chile was complicated by a number of legal and political realities. Under the 1980 constitution, Aylwin did not have authority over the armed forces; Pinochet, as Commander in Chief, did. Furthermore, it denied civilian jurisdiction over many cases and prohibited overhaul of the Supreme Court. As a result, the 1978 amnesty law decreed by Pinochet and upheld by the Supreme Court complicated the lower courts' role, although Aylwin claimed it did not bar judicial investigations. That law, recall, barred prosecutions for crimes committed during the period from the commencement of the coup until 1978 when the military had largely consolidated its power. Furthermore, Pinochet himself publicly threatened that the state of law would end if any of his men were touched by the new government.[30] Given these constraints, extensive truth telling, general attribution of blame, and government acceptance of the findings may have been the least unsatisfactory way of pursuing truth, a partial redefinition of social identities, and justice in the Chilean context.

Eventually, the courts convicted a score of soldiers and police for crimes committed after 1978 and investigated several hundred others

with the possibility of more investigation as judges found new loop-
holes in the 1978 amnesty law. Pinochet himself was extradited from
Britain to Spain and later to Chile to face charges on human rights
violations.[31]

The commission devoted a large portion of the report to the effects of
these crimes on the victims, their families, and the larger social fabric. It
recommended reparations to the victims for past violations, including
both moral and material compensation. A direct outgrowth of the commission was the February 1992 law that called for a National Corporation for Reparation and Reconciliation. The corporation established a
monthly pension for families of those named in the report, medical benefits (including psychological counseling) for families, and a subsidy for
high school and college education of victims' children.

The report also called for human rights education for both the military
and civilians, especially lawyers and judges, greater judicial independence, and changes in laws on states of emergency, military jurisdiction
over civilians, and criminal procedures generally. It recommended greater
adherence to international human rights treaties and standards, including
specific changes in domestic law. It also called for creation of a human
rights ombudsman's office. Finally, it called on the government to com-
memorate victims through monuments and support for cultural and artistic works.[32]

The air force and police acknowledged some responsibility, although
the army and navy, the most powerful branches of the Chilean military,
rejected the commission's findings. The army and navy did not challenge
any of the facts presented, but claimed their actions were necessary to
protect the nation from internal attacks. The report was endorsed by
Chile's Congress, political parties, the Catholic Church, and human rights
groups.[33]

President Aylwin was succeeded in March 1994 by Eduardo Frei, who
was elected for a six-year term. Frei, a Christian Democrat, headed a
coalition of the center-left known as the *Concertation,* roughly the same
group that had backed Aylwin. He received 58 percent of the popular
vote, the largest victory for a presidential candidate in sixty years. The
election marked a consolidation of democracy in Chile and legitimation
of civilian rule.

El Salvador

Violence and authoritarian repression dominated Salvadoran politics during the twentieth century. By 1979, leftist guerrilla warfare, headed by the Farabundo Marti Front for National Liberation (FMLN), broke out in cities and the countryside and was fueled by external support for both sides.

Amid the chaos and violence, however, elements of democracy were emerging. In 1983 the National Assembly drafted a new constitution that called for greater protection of individual and workers' rights and that strengthened the legislature and judiciary. The year 1984 saw the first freely elected president of El Salvador in fifty years when Jose Napolean Duarte, leader of the Christian Democrats, defeated Roberto D'Aubuisson of the nationalist Republican Alliance (ARENA). In 1989, ARENA's Alfredo Cristiani won the presidential election, marking the first time in the country's history that power passed peacefully from one elected official to another.

At his inauguration in June 1989, Cristiani called for direct dialogue between the government and the FMLN. For two months, the sides met for unmediated talks that broke down in November 1989, when the FMLN launched a nationwide military offensive.

In early 1990, prodded by a request from Central American presidents, the United Nations offered to mediate a new round of talks and the sides returned to negotiations. Three factors figured prominently among many as precipitates to this second, and ultimately successful, round of negotiations. First, the FMLN's military offensive had demonstrated that the war was stalemated. Second, the killing of six Jesuit priests at the Central American University in November 1989, for which four officers of the Salvadorian military and five enlisted men were charged, unleashed a torrent of domestic and international revulsion. Finally, external pressure on the Salvadoran right by the United States and a cutoff of Cuban money to the rebels reinforced attempts to solve the conflict through negotiation.

The two sides staged a reconciliation event at the signing of a final agreement, the Accords of Chapultepec, in Mexico City on January 16, 1992. The United Nations monitored implementation of the Accords until June 1997.

The Accords established a Truth Commission under U.N. auspices to investigate the most serious cases of human rights violations and report its findings by 1993. The parties recognized the need to make the complete truth known and to "put an end to any indication of impunity on the part of officers of the armed forces particularly in cases where respect for human rights is jeopardized."[34] It was also to recommend legal, political, or administrative measures to prevent repetition of the kinds of social unrest that occurred in the past and to promote national reconciliation.

With a six-month mandate to carry out its enormous task, the commission could only selectively investigate some of the tens of thousands of cases of alleged human rights violations that occurred during the war. It received more than 22,000 testimonies about such violations involving more than 7,000 victims. Approximately 85 percent of these violations were attributed to the armed and security forces, paramilitary groups linked to the state, or death squads. Five percent of denunciations were made against the FMLN.

Having assigned general responsibility for human rights violations to institutions, the commission focused on a smaller universe of particularly important or representative cases for in-depth examination, and, where there was sufficient proof, named the individuals involved. The commission published the results of its investigation in thirty-two cases, naming some forty former or current military officers and six guerrilla leaders.

The commission's report officially confirmed what many in El Salvador already knew about the war, although many military leaders vehemently denied its findings.[35] Still, the report had a cathartic effect on both antagonists. It breached the wall of impunity around the military and began a process that substantially reduced their role in Salvadoran society.[36]

Nonetheless, on March 20, 1993, just five days after publication of the Truth Commission's report, the Legislative Assembly adopted an amnesty law for people implicated in atrocities during the civil war. There appeared to be some acceptance, both nationally and internationally, that amnesty would be necessary for El Salvador to move toward democratization and to implement the report's wider recommendations. Even before the report was issued, President Christiani urged amnesty given the country's precarious political stability, its nascent democracy, and its still powerful military.[37]

In addition to the Truth Commission, the Accords created several other institutions to implement the agreement and reforms urged by the commission itself. These included a commission to purge the military of human rights violators (the Ad Hoc Commission), a new human rights ombudsman, replacement of military security forces with a new civilian police force, and constitutional reforms to increase the independence of the judiciary.

These reforms restructured Salvadoran society. The Ad Hoc Commission recommended transfer, retirement, or discharge of more than 100 officers implicated in human rights abuses. Citizens can now file complaints about such abuses with the National Council for Human Rights, a government agency. Consistent with the Accords, three discredited public security forces were abolished, and a new civilian police force was created to replace them. The National Civilian Police grew to a force of over 10,000 officers (including former rebels) deployed throughout the country by the mid-1990s. Finally, the commission recommended that all members of the Supreme Court immediately resign to hasten the appointment of new justices under a new constitutional formula. This recommendation was fulfilled in 1994 when an entirely new court was elected. The government also moved to remove incompetent judges from the lower courts and to strengthen attorneys general and public defenders' offices, although that process has been slow.

In accordance with the peace agreement, the constitution was amended to prohibit the military from playing an internal security role except under extraordinary circumstances. The military demobilization aspect of the Accords was achieved ahead of schedule.

The political left was reintegrated into the country with legalization of the FMLN as a political party, and the country has had two highly successful elections since 1992. In 1993, the U.N. confirmed that the FMLN had demobilized its military structures and destroyed its arms. Perhaps most remarkable was reconciliation of the warring groups. There have been virtually no incidents of violence between former adversaries.[38]

In sum, in resolving a vicious and protracted civil war and restoring order and democracy, the case of El Salvador has been to date, a remarkable, but not unqualified, success. Changes include a substantial reduction in the armed forces, purging of the officer corps, redefinition of military doctrine, abolition of internal security forces and creation of a civilian police, establishment of an office for human rights complaints, improved judiciary, and incorporation of the political left into the electoral process. El Salvador faces considerable challenges—law and order, economic growth and equity, and stable leadership—but it has restored political order and made fundamental changes in its society.

Mozambique

After 470 years of Portuguese colonial rule, Mozambique became independent on June 25, 1975. The first president, Samora Moises Machel, had been head of the National Front for the Liberation of Mozambique (FRELIMO) for much of its ten-year guerrilla war for independence. The Front established a one-party Marxist state and quickly moved to nationalize the economy. The new state faced enormous challenges, with over 90 percent of the population illiterate and much of the country's weak infrastructure destroyed by embittered ex-colonists.

Beginning in 1976, antigovernment guerrillas organized as the Mozambique National Resistance (RENAMO), and their backers in Rhodesia and South Africa began a destabilization campaign that would lead to a sixteen-year civil war with FRELIMO. With external support, RENAMO grew from 500 to 8,000 fighters by 1982 and posed a serious threat to the government.[39]

By 1984, the Machel administration was locked in a paralyzing and cruel war with RENAMO. In 1986, Joaquim Chissano became president after Machel's untimely death. By 1988, with external support for the conflict declining for all sides, the war was stalemated. Chissano began a policy review of FRELIMO's economic, foreign, and civil rights policies. As part of that review, he gave permission to senior church leaders to open talks with RENAMO as a step toward direct peace negotiations between the belligerents. These intermediaries returned from talks in Kenya, stating that RENAMO was also spent from the war and was open to negotiations. A few months later Chissano renounced Marxism as Mozambique's guiding ideology at FRELIMO's congress in 1989, and sought direct negotiations with RENAMO, which eventually began in 1990 in Rome.

The two-year negotiation was drawn out by absence of a formula that would recognize the current government yet grant equal standing as a political party to FRELIMO. Under urgency created by widespread drought and food insecurity, a cease-fire agreement and reconciliation event in the form of a general peace agreement was finally signed by

Chissano and RENAMO leader Afonso Dhlakama on October 4, 1992. The war had caused an estimated loss of life ranging from 600,000 to 900,000 soldiers and civilians.[40]

One week after the signing, the U.N. Security Council approved the establishment of operations in Mozambique to monitor and verify implementation of the peace accord. The U.N. sent 6,800 troops to supervise withdrawal of foreign troops from the country and to oversee the cantonment, demobilization, and disarmament of approximately 100,000 soldiers from both sides.

The peace accord also called for a new national army, resettlement of 5 to 6 million refugees and displaced persons, and organization of elections. Mozambique earned high marks for reducing the size of the armed forces and reintegrating soldiers into civilian life.[41] Peaceful and fair elections were held in October 1994. With a voter turnout of 85 percent, Chissano was reelected president, and FRELIMO captured 129 to RENAMO's 112 seats in the new 250-seat parliament. The government was installed in December.

Although the government has not officially recognized a truth commission, the churches have been actively pursuing peace and reconciliation through recognition of human rights abuses and encouraging forgiveness since the early 1980s. The Mozambican Christian Council (CCM), in consultation with other churches not in the council, began discussions with President Machel on peaceful ways to end the devastating war. In July 1984, in a confidential memo to Machel, the CCM called for dialogue among all Mozambicans caught up in the war, which the president received negatively. In November, the CCM launched a Peace and Reconciliation Commission to use as a vehicle for peace. The next May it repeated the request for dialogue between the government and RENAMO, but again the response was negative. With ascension of Chissano to the presidency in 1986, the CCM stepped up its calls for dialogue and circulated a pastoral letter calling for talks and reconciliation between the government and RENAMO.

After recognizing the CCM initiative, Chissano gave his permission for a CCM delegation to pursue contact with RENAMO. After several visits by the delegation to Kenya, RENAMO agreed to meet the churchmen in Nairobi. The churchmen emphasized their neutrality, stressing that reconciliation was a basic vocation of the church. After this breakthrough meeting, the church acted as a messenger between FRELIMO and RENAMO until direct negotiations in Rome in 1990. Members of Mozambic churches became officials of the negotiating team. The CCM is credited with playing a key role in speeding up the peace process by emphasizing to the two parties the civilian consequences of continuing the war during a period of severe drought. The peace initiative would not have borne fruit without the persistence of the churches.

During the peace process, the churches' role was not limited to bringing together leaders of the two opposing groups, but included reconciling the citizens who supported them. In 1989, the bishop in Nampula began "to announce the names of people killed in the war during the Sunday mass. Increasingly, combatants and residents from both sides would pass the church information, and the list became more extensive, making the reading of the lists a powerful call for peace."[42] The CCM, together with several other parochial organizations, also began a program in which people could trade in their guns for household necessities.

After the Rome accords, the church continued its work by explaining to the people what peace meant. Father Pier Mazzola stated that they "preached reconciliation and used their pastoral newsletters, consisting of pictures and local language texts, to spread the message of peace. Because we had a good reputation, the newsletters were taken seriously. Some 15,000 copies were printed and could be seen everywhere in Nampula after the signing of the peace accords."[43] Local healers, using traditional methods of purification and appeasement for past transgressions, facilitated the process of reconciliation in rural communities.

The consolidation of peace in Mozambique has gone well despite social divisions, political alienation, and poverty left by the war. At a national level, the parliament has become the primary arena of competition between FRELIMO and RENAMO, although intermittent violence persists in some rural areas. In general, the United Nations High Commissioner for Refugee Office commended the process of reconciliation in Mozambique as a source of future stability, noting, "We have not come across widespread violations of human rights, there is no private revenge."[44] The disquieting aspect of cessation of human rights violations is that virtually no attempts have been made to hold anyone accountable for the many heinous crimes committed during the war through official war crimes trials or tribunals.[45]

In December 1999, voters concluded three days of peaceful balloting for the second democratic elections since the civil war. The electoral commission reported that Mr. Chissano had won 52 percent of the vote and Mr. Dhlakama 48 percent. The governing FRELIMO won 133 seats in Parliament, with 117 for RENAMO. Remembering its political inheritance of colonialism, revolutionary Marxism, and civil war, these free and fair elections were impressive, and even more important, few believe that resumption of war is even a possibility.

South Africa

South Africa has seen several forms of civil conflict over its history. In the latter half of the twentieth century, internal conflict arose out of the policy of white domination and racial separation—apartheid. In 1948, the Nationalist Party came to power and codified apartheid's discrimination with the goal of racial separation. It denied the franchise to vote to the majority black population and severely limited their access to education and economic opportunities through a comprehensive system of laws that "turned the African majority into nonpersons, beyond the pale of political life."[46]

All this led black opposition groups to launch a defiance campaign in 1952 and support a Freedom Charter in 1956 that called for negotiations, peaceful change, and universal suffrage. The Sharpeville massacre of 1960 marked a turning point. There, 69 protesters were killed and 180 injured when police opened fire on peaceful demonstrators. In response, leading South African black political movements—the African National Congress (ANC) and the Pan-African Congress (PAC)—adopted the option of armed insurrection against the regime and were banned by the ruling Nationalist Party. The ANC leader, Nelson Mandela, and many others were charged with treason and imprisoned. The ANC, PAC, and other groups were forced underground and began a program of guerrilla warfare and sabotage against apartheid, in addition to nonviolent resistance.

Growing domestic violence followed popular uprisings in black and colored townships in 1976 and 1985. Radicalization of young blacks in segregated black townships increased levels of both domestic violence and government repression.

Spiraling internal violence and increasing international ostracism led ruling Nationalist leaders to begin secret negotiations with Mandela and the ANC in the mid-1980s. After the election of new Nationalist President F. W. de Klerk in 1989, the Nationalists announced the unbanning of the ANC, PAC, and other antiapartheid groups, and within days of the announcement, Mandela was freed from prison. De Klerk's reforms were apparently motivated by the belief that apartheid simply failed to work, rather than by any meaningful change of heart.[47]

Negotiations continued based on a formula of legality for opposition groups in exchange for a pledge of nonviolence. Each side had come to recognize the need to accommodate the other to reach their desired ends. Eventually, nineteen political players, originally called the Congress for a Democratic South Africa, began a dialogue on political transition. Of importance, the two key players, ANC and Nationalists, agreed on the need to facilitate a peaceful transition from apartheid to a nonracial democratic state.

In 1991, the legal pillars of apartheid were abolished and lengthy negotiations for creation of a new system ensued. In 1993, the government and ANC agreed on a new constitution including creation of a National Assembly that would be elected by party based on proportional representation. The National Assembly, in turn, would elect a president and form a permanent constitution. In the spring of 1994, the country held its first nonracial elections on the principle of one person, one vote, resulting in the election of Mandela as president.

From the start, the new government was determined to confront the past. Among its first reconciliation acts was creation of the Truth and Reconciliation Commission (TRC) in 1995. The TRC was headed by Nobel peace prize laureate Archbishop Desmond Tutu and charged with investigating human rights abuses committed during the years 1960–1994. It was given power to grant amnesty selectively to those who voluntarily confessed their crimes to the commission and to recommend compensation to victims of abuse. A final report was to be delivered to the state president on July 31, 1998, and made available to all South Africans.

The TRC sought a middle course between demands for truth and justice in a new society where apartheid (and its adherents) had been politically deposed, not militarily defeated. Truth was essential if violations of apartheid were to be avoided in the future, and to give voice, dignity, acknowledgment, and a measure of compensation to apartheid's victims and their families. "Truth" was not intended to provide all South Africans with one uncontestable history. Rather, as Tutu argued, revealed truth was designed to provide "frameworks" through which "the past can be explored, the present viewed, and the future approached, in a spirit of understanding, tolerance, unity, and reconciliation; they share perceptions, attitudes and experiences with others, with the objective of forging new perceptions and attitudes."[48] Justice could not be ignored nor could it be fully pursued. Instead, the goal was somewhere between "amnesia and justice." Vengeance was not possible, given apartheid's negotiated demise and the fact that the scope of discrimination would overwhelm the judicial system. Nor was total justice desirable, given the goals of reaching the truth and peacefully reuniting all South Africans. South Africa sought what is called restorative rather than retributive justice. Restorative justice, as described by Tutu, derives from the Xhosa concept of *Ubuntu:*

Ubuntu says I am human only because you are human. If I undermine your humanity I dehumanize myself. You must do what you can to maintain this great harmony, which is perpetually undermined by resentment, anger, desire for vengeance. That is why African jurisprudence is restorative rather than retributive.[49]

The instrument of this middle ground was limited amnesty that would be granted to those whose crimes were politically motivated and who disclosed all they knew. Those who failed to come forward could be prosecuted.[50]

Partial amnesty was acceptable to members of the former government because they would not necessarily be prosecuted after the transfer of power. For ANC and the new regime, partial amnesty was satisfactory because it was granted by a new legitimate government rather than imposed by apartheid, and it set out objective conditions and' procedures for the prosecution of some offenses, thus enshrining due process and equality before the law and providing some measure of retribution.[51] In practice, amnesty has been addressed on a case-by-case basis, with only a small percentage of those requesting it receiving approval by the TRC. By year-end 1998, for example, only 125 of 7,060 applicants had been approved and 4,570 had been refused; the rest were pending.[52]

But public reporting of the truth and granting limited amnesty were only part of the TRC's mandate. Equally important goals were to establish the basis for reparations, to recover and restore the identity of victims, and to recommend institutional and legislative changes that would establish a new society based on principles of fairness and equality. Toward these ends, the TRC held more than 120 hearings throughout the country, gathered over 22,000 statements from victims of human rights abuses, investigated the role of professions and institutions in upholding apartheid, recommended reparation payments to victims, and suggested reforms in the political system designed to avoid repetition of past wrongs. Much of this process was conducted publicly and broadcast on radio and television as well as covered in the print media. Despite denunciations by the Nationalist Party and last-minute efforts to scuttle the report by ANC, the TRC delivered its 3,500-page document for public review.

The TRC's efforts are part of a larger process of reconciling the often-conflicting political, economic, and cultural interests held by South Africa's diverse people. Political stability and greater racial peace were established with decidedly few racial recriminations despite the country's past. South Africa has not rid itself of a culture of violence, intolerance, distrust, or racial hatreds, but these characteristics are no longer its governing principles or predominant practices. Peaceful coexistence is the norm, and thus far the nation has been spared the cycle of violence seen in places such as Yugoslavia and Rwanda. The TRC, although criticized by many and subjected to intense media scrutiny, must be credited with fortifying political stability by reorienting the country's moral climate and establishing new respect for the rule of law and human rights.

South Africa substantially redefined its past. Its constitution and bill of rights provide extensive guarantees for equality before the law and outlawing of discrimination. The bill of rights also extends protection of individual civil and economic liberties, including life, privacy, individual security, speech, assembly, fair trial, safe environment, housing, education, and health care. An independent judiciary was created to enforce these provisions, and its authority has been respected.

Since the abolition of apartheid, political violence has decreased dramatically, but not disappeared. Certain regions of the country, such as Kwa-Zulu Natal Province, continue to experience high levels of political tension, and nonpolitical criminal activity remains a national concern. South Africa also faces daunting economic challenges given levels of poverty, illiteracy, and income inequality that are legacies of apartheid.

Honduras

Since becoming independent in 1821, Honduras has seen nearly 300 internal rebellions, civil wars, and changes of government, half of the conflicts occurring in the 1900s. Until the midtwentieth century, Honduran politics was authoritarian and dominated by the interests of foreign capital and large domestic landholders.

In the 1950s, the military emerged as an important political actor in Honduran politics. By the 1980s, although ruled by nominally civilian governments, the armed forces had become the country's most powerful political actor.

In that decade, the armed forces, particularly the counterterrorism unit known as Battalion 3-16, the National Investigation Directorate (DNI), and the Public Security Force, led a campaign of clandestine detention, torture, and murder against suspected internal subversion. These domestic security forces also infiltrated and disrupted labor, student, and peasant groups they suspected of threatening national security. Fearful of revolutions in neighboring countries, the private sector backed the military, and civil society was too weak to provide meaningful resistance. During this time, although not a civil war in name, several hundred people disappeared, and others, especially peasant and union organizers, were killed in an attempt to head off creation of antigovernment insurgencies then flourishing in neighboring countries. In addition, Honduras soon became the main base for the U.S.-backed Contra war against Nicaragua and counterinsurgency efforts in El Salvador, further increasing the power of the armed forces.

By 1990, international, regional, and domestic forces were compelling changes in Honduran society. The end of both the Cold War and regional revolutions led the United States to slash military aid to Honduras from a high of $81.1 million in 1986 to $2.7 million in 1993. The U.S. embassy, a former proponent of the Honduran armed forces, became a severe critic and urged greater civilian control of the military. The electoral defeat of the Sandinistas in Nicaragua in 1990 and the end of the Salvadoran civil war hastened the army's decline in power and spurred institutional reforms under President Rafael Callejas. Responding to the changed external environment and the turnaround in U.S. policy, domestic society (human rights groups, students, the Roman Catholic Church, the press, and business) joined in a strong antimilitary movement.

Pressures from these groups and from the United States compelled a reluctant President Callejas to initiate a series of reconciliation measures by appointing a respected jurist, Leo Valladares, to the new post of human rights commissioner and by creating an Ad Hoc Commission for Institutional Reform. To guarantee its independence, the human rights commissioner was to be selected by the president from a list provided by a National Reconciliation Commission and could be removed only by a two-thirds vote of that commission. All civil and military authorities were to cooperate with, and could not suspend, Commissioner Valladares's investigations.

Shortly after his selection, Valladares began investigating a pattern of disappearances that had taken place in Honduras from 1980 to 1993, most during the early 1980s. He justified his efforts on two grounds. First, it was necessary to know the truth and to do justice to achieve reconciliation of all Hondurans because it was impossible to forgive without knowing what happened or who was responsible.[53] Second, investigation was necessary to restore public confidence in state institutions, especially the judiciary.

Valladares found 179 cases of disappearances masterminded by the armed forces. He named several members of the army high command and specific units, such as Intelligence Battalion 3-16, as responsible for them, and criticized the court system for its inaction in the matter. His report recommended that those apparently involved be tried by appropriate courts, and provided a list of those who occupied military posts during the years involved. In addition, the report recommended investigations of all judges and magistrates who denied *habeus corpus* petitions filed by family members of the disappeared, changes in laws governing detentions, periodic visits of human rights groups to detention centers, and establishment of a special commission to find clandestine cemeteries. It further recommended extradition of foreign military advisors or Contras involved in disappearances, separation of military and police functions, civilian control over military intelligence, institution of human rights education, and adhesion of Honduras to several human rights treaties. Finally, it recommended an official apology, compensation, and an official monument to the disappeared. The report was published in January 1994, and excerpts appeared in the local press.

As Valladares's investigation proceeded and in response to private sector complaints about the nation's flawed judicial system, President Callejas appointed a high level Ad Hoc Commission chaired by Archbishop Andres Rodriguez. In 1993, the Ad Hoc Commission recommended that an independent public ministry be established under the jurisdiction of a prosecutor general that would include a new civilian Director of Criminal Investigation (DIC) to replace the notorious, military-controlled DNI. The commission further recommended reforms of the entire Public Security Force with the aim of its eventual demilitarization. Congress passed enabling legislation for creation of the Public Ministry and DIC by December 1993, about the same time that Valladeres issued his report and President Roberto Reina took office.

The Reina administration sped up political reforms, solidified civil order, and increased civilian control over the armed forces. Important achievements of this administration included abolition of military draft and legislation transferring the national police from military to civilian authority. Reina drastically reduced the size of the armed forces from 26,000 in the 1980s to less than 12,000 by 1996. He exercised the prerogative of appointing his own Defense Minister in 1996, breaking the precedent of accepting the nominee of the armed forces leadership.[54]

Reina's administration also implemented many institutional reforms recommended by the Ad Hoc Commission. In June 1994, the military's DNI was disbanded and replaced by the civilian-controlled DIC. The Public Ministry began its operations and appointed a prosecutor general. The administration also created an important precedent by paying financial compensation to families of two victims who disappeared in the 1980s in fulfillment of a finding by the Inter-American Court of Justice. Reina prudently reduced the military budget while avoiding unnecessary confrontation with the military.

Limits to civilian control over the military remain, however, as the armed forces retain certain specific roles under the constitution. They remain guarantors of the electoral process and executive succession, and the president must share commander-in-chief powers with the chief of the armed forces. Perhaps the strongest evidence of limits to reform has been the difficulty of the judiciary in bringing active-duty or retired military officers to trial for alleged human rights violations. In July 1995, for example, nine officers and enlisted men were called to testify in a case involving illegal detention and torture of six students in 1982. All nine refused to cooperate, and when arrest warrants were issued for three of the officers that fall, they went into hiding.

In 1997, Honduras held democratic elections for a new president, unicameral congress, and mayors. Although its history is one of poverty and praetorian governments, Honduras made progress in restoring order after a period of increased internal conflict. Several democratic reforms were consolidated in the 1990s, and a return to the political violence of the 1980s does not appear likely. Supported by the media and several national and international groups, human rights and civil liberties are reasonably well protected. The role of the military as a political actor has been substantially reduced, and the range of political participants has broadened.

Findings

Although each case study is different, these brief summaries of national conflicts, reconciliation event or events, and postreconciliation relations reveal certain distinct patterns. Most important, those countries that reconciled successfully, that is, restored lasting social order, did so through a protracted process of recognition of harm and public truth telling, redefinition of identities and social roles of antagonists, and partial justice short of revenge, not merely through signal sending in a negotiated bargain. An untidy, seemingly idiosyncratic, but undeniably patterned process of national forgiveness was the foundation of successful national reconciliations. The three instances of reconciliations confined to a negotiated bargain—Colombia, Yemen, and Chad—did not lead to long-term restoration of peace (table 2.1).

Negotiation and signal sending were initial steps in many of these cases. The impetus for negotiation was not always the product of precisely reasoned signal sending designed to maximize interest, although some cases fit this description (e.g., South Africa). In other cases, negotiation was

Table 2.1
Presence of Forgiveness Factors and Outcome

Country	Public Truth Telling	Partial Justice	Redefinition of Social Identities	Call for a New Relationship	Outcome
Colombia	No	No	No	Yes	Conflict
North Yemen	No	No	Partial	Yes	Conflict
Chad	Partial	No	No	Yes	Conflict
Argentina	Yes	Yes	Yes	Yes	Peace
Uruguay	Partial	Yes	Yes	Yes	Peace
Chile	Yes	Yes	Yes	Yes	Peace
El Salvador	Yes	Yes	Yes	Yes	Peace
Mozambique	Yes	No	Yes	Yes	Peace
South Africa	Yes	Yes	Yes	Yes	Peace
Honduras	Yes	Yes	Yes	Yes	Peace

the last resort of belligerents driven by fear, revulsion, loss of control, or simple exhaustion with violence.

Although negotiation was part of all the cases, the rational choice signaling model provides little guidance as to how and when it leads to restoration of civil order. Negotiation and signaling may be a necessary part of a reconciliation, but they clearly are not sufficient, as the examples of Colombia, Chad, and Yemen illustrate. Furthermore, reconciliation signals can meet virtually all conditions for signaling success noted in chapter 1—costliness, novelty, irrevocability, and noncontingency—yet fail to restore lasting order, as the case of Chad reveals. Conversely, secret, low-cost, and highly contingent negotiations, as was the case in Uruguay, can be part of successful national reconciliation. In short, the mere existence of, or conditions surrounding, negotiations is not a good predictor of possibilities for long-run restoration of social order (table 2.2).

Instead, the cases strongly suggest that much more than launching, or even concluding, negotiations is required for reconciliation to restore order to state and society. Below, we consider how the pattern of recognition of the harm through truth telling, redefinition of self and other, and limited justice were reflected in the cases and how this pattern established successful national reconciliation.

Table 2.2
Presence of Signaling Factors and Outcome

Country	Costliness Vulnerability	Novelty	Voluntary	Irrevocable/ Noncontingent	Outcome
Colombia	Yes	Yes	No	Yes	Conflict
North Yemen	Yes	Yes	Yes	No	Conflict
Chad	Yes	Yes	Partial	Yes	Conflict
Argentina	Yes	Yes	No	No	Peace
Uruguay	No	No	No	No	Peace
Chile	Yes	Yes	Yes	No	Peace
El Salvador	Yes	No	Partial	No	Peace
Mozambique	No	Yes	Yes	No	Peace
South Africa	Yes	Yes	Yes	Yes	Peace
Honduras	Yes	Yes	Partial	No	Peace

Recognition of Harm and Truth Telling

Extensive truth telling was a part of each successful reconciliation and absent from the three unsuccessful ones. Moreover, with the exceptions of Uruguay and Mozambique, it was one of the first acts of interim or new governments.

In many instances the victimized population was clear about what abuses had occurred and who had carried them out. In small, densely populated societies such as Uruguay and El Salvador, few were untouched by violence and few did not know their victimizer. Thus the importance of a truth commission was not only in uncovering the truth, as was the case in Argentina or Chile, but in acknowledging it. Aryeh Neier wrote, "Knowledge that is officially sanctioned" becomes "part of the public cognitive scene that is not there when it is merely the 'truth.' "[55] Official acknowledgment of what has long been denied can psychologically begin to heal societal wounds because it unmasks an official lie and strips away impunity. Acknowledgment can be especially important when justice, in the form of punishment of the guilty or reparations for the victims, is difficult to extract. In such cases, truth may act as a substitute for, rather than a complement to, justice.[56]

The degree of official acknowledgment of truth varied considerably from case to case. In Chile, President Aylwin formally received the report and in a televised speech accepted responsibility as head of state for the actions of the state's agents. In Honduras and South Africa, reports were prepared in existing state institutions, carrying the message of official acknowledgment. In contrast, in El Salvador the truth was accepted grudgingly and partially, and in Uruguay the government did not formally accept or reject the truth report.[57] In Mozambique, truth was unearthed by civil society.

In every case, results of investigations into truth were widely publicized and disseminated in the forms of best-selling books, television shows, movie documentaries, sermons, and newspaper exposes. The truth was not buried in an inaccessible government report, but deliberately packaged and promulgated so as to be accessible to a large swath of the public. Jon Sobrino, commenting on the Salvadoran report, noted the power of public truth: "It is a known anthropological fact that we human beings develop knowledge when we express it in words. . . . We cannot avoid facts which are aired publicly."[58]

Truth telling is not always in a society's immediate self-interest, however, as it entails substantial risks to social order. It runs the risk of creating greater resentment among participants to civil conflict and of opening old wounds and inflicting new ones on an already fragmented society. Those implicated in truth telling—the military, judiciary, and guerrillas—often have a strong interest is seeing that certain facts are not uncovered and publicly acknowledged. These groups could, if unduly threatened, resort to violence to stop the process. Even those not culpable have warned of the danger of investigation and promulgation of truth in a politically fragile environment.[59] Nonetheless, many countries chose to pursue this path despite the paradoxical fact that such inquiry risks intensifying animosity and conflict and rekindling violence. Guillermo O'Donnell and Philippe Schmitter suggested a deeper logic to the process of pursuing truth: "By refusing to confront and purge itself of its worst fears and resentments, such a society would be burying not just its past but the very ethical values it needs to make its future livable."[60]

Truth telling was directly linked to the pursuit of justice and redefinition of the identities and roles of parties to the conflict. In many cases, findings of truth commissions provided the evidentiary foundation and a pool of witnesses for the pursuit of justice against those named in reports. For example, Argentina's *Nunca Mas* was turned over directly to

federal prosecutors and led to numerous inquiries and prosecutions. This ·
was the case in Honduras and South Africa as well.

The process is also linked to a different notion of justice: reparations
for, and restoration of, the identity and good name of victims of violence.
Truth telling acknowledges victims and restores their identity, as well as
identifying the perpetrators. Or, as a Chilean commentator said, without
memory "we do not know who we are . . . we wander aimlessly, not
knowing where to go. Without memory there is no identity."[61]

Social and political roles also are reshaped. Armed with the authority
of official truth, truth commissions and fact-finding bodies are often empowered to make detailed policy and institutional recommendations and
push fundamental reforms and a redefinition of societal relations. El Salvador and South Africa are perhaps the most graphic examples of the
connection between official truth and redefinition of social actors, but
this feature of redefinition was present in most cases.

Truth telling does not complete the process of reconciliation. Instead
it opens up a public space for reconciliation by allowing a formerly taboo
subject to become amenable to the action of political bodies and future
policies. Truth telling is "one part of a broader process . . . [to] help spark
a longer term process of national healing and reconciliation."[62] It plays
a critical, perhaps indispensable, role in the process of national reconciliation and contributes directly and indirectly to the redefinition of identity
and limited justice essential to complete the process.

Redefinition of Self and Other

Evidence of redefinition of parties to a conflict whereby the narrow identities of victim and perpetrator or repressor and insurgent are replaced
with a new sense of self and other that makes a new relationship possible
appears throughout cases of successful reconciliation. The process can
begin with recognition and dialogue, as was the case in El Salvador. Combatants may first recognize each other as both part of the problem and
part of the solution in a negotiation.

Recognition and redefinition can also occur during truth telling and
remembrance of those who disappeared, the ultimate loss of identity because "they are deprived of the last link they had with society . . . the
right of being at a particular place at a particular time."[63] For survivors
and their families, truth telling can provide a means for redefinition of

self. Truth commissions often provide the first sympathetic hearing for these victims. Listening to their stories offers a sense of redress and wholeness for participants. Recording and publishing these reports is an opportunity for those affected to transcend their role as victim and assume again the role of citizen. South Africa's truth and reconciliation reports provide numerous examples of this.

Successful reconciliations also redefined the role and relationships of important social groups and institutions. Former belligerents from the left were often brought into the political process. The military was often depoliticized or its role in the political process subjected to new constraints. Although its impunity was removed, its role as protector of the nation was never completely disavowed. That is, its power was circumscribed, but its legitimate institutional prerogative, or identity, was reoriented, not destroyed. What often changes is the armed forces' "messianic self-image as *the* institution ultimately interpreting and insuring the highest interests of the nation."[64] The military's identity shifts from that of ultimate guardian of the national interest with a preoccupation with internal security to "some more credible and orthodox role as defender of the country's (or the region's) external security."[65] This change is seen most clearly in Argentina and El Salvador. In addition to a new role for the military, in many cases judiciaries were strengthened, civil society was restored or encouraged, and political parties were empowered.

The cases vary in their forms of institutional redefinition. In Chile the emphasis was on reparations to victims, reduction of the military's role, and restoration of identities of the disappeared. In El Salvador and South Africa the emphasis was on judicial and political reform and restoration of victims, in Uruguay and Mozambique on restoring or rebuilding democratic institutions and the role of political parties, in Argentina on victims' rights and restricting the military's influence in the political process, and in Honduras on instituting civilian control over the government security apparatus. In every case, countries that successfully reconciled established a set of new identities for key social actors.

Justice Short of Revenge
In every instance of successful reconciliation save Mozambique justice was meted out, but never in full measure. This fact may be lamentable, even tragic, from certain legal or moral perspectives, yet it is consistent

with the requisites of restoring social order postulated in the forgiveness hypothesis. In all cases of successful reconciliation, retributive justice could neither be ignored nor fully achieved.[66]

Full judicial accountability was inhibited by the possibility of a backlash from a still-powerful military or other group involved in civil violence that could endanger the larger process of restoration of peace. Furthermore, in some cases the judiciary was implicated in abuses and was incapable of applying justice impartially. Instead, the decision was often made to draw a line under past human rights violations in the name of national reconciliation. Balance was struck between the needs of moral and legal responsibility against the actual balance of power in fragile societies and the compromised ability of local judiciaries.

Therefore, we see the granting of full (Uruguay), near total (Chile), or partial (Argentina and South Africa) amnesty to those potentially responsible for wrongdoing. Amnesty, a word whose root is from "amnesia," is often a palliative for the powerful prescription of truth telling and redefinition of social identities. The timing of amnesty is important to the level of justice achieved. Blanket amnesty given early in reconciliation, as was attempted in Chile and implemented in Uruguay, severely limited the realization of justice. Granted later in the process, as was the case in El Salvador, Argentina, and South Africa, it allowed for prosecution of some of the guilty, helped push out of office abusive political or military figures, and speeded the process of institutional reform.

Disturbing as it may be, people appear able to tolerate a substantial amount of injustice wrought by amnesty in the name of social peace. One commentator acknowledged that in choosing between them, "people will take a high degree of peace and some imperfect realization of justice."[67]

Reasons for the limitations on justice are several. As noted, there is the danger of provoking still-powerful security forces or other elements of society to take recourse by destabilizing society and the rule of law.

Second, some elements of the society, not just perpetrators, viewed violence as occurring during a state of war. This context for interpreting events makes it difficult to determine which actions were excessive or criminal and which were legitimate in warfare. As one white South African lamented, "How can I apologize for an act of war? War is war."[68] This justification, or rationalization, depending on one's point of view, was offered in virtually all of the countries as a reason to limit the scope of judicial inquiry.

Third is the problem that guilt and responsibility for the evils and crimes of the previous order were widely shared. Some maintained that where state repression and terror received political support from most of the population, and where a large part of the population was recruited into active or passive collaboration, national reconciliation is best served not by settling past scores but by accepting a measure of truth telling and acknowledgment that violation of rights occurred, while making a fresh start with all sides eligible to participate in the work ahead.[69]

Finally, it is possible that amnesty is not merely the distasteful price of compromise. At least in instances when it is endorsed by most of the population (Uruguay) or their legitimate representatives (South Africa), it represents an expression of mercy and is a gift of those who have suffered.[70] Whereas it may abridge the rights of the suffering to grant amnesty of expediency, so too would it abridge the rights of those who suffered to deny them the right to be merciful.

Whether for reasons of *force majeure* or other considerations, imperfect justice is often tolerated in the name of societal order.[71] What justice is secured is usually achieved through extensive truth telling, material reparations for some victims, and limited prosecutions of individuals, with punishment being loss of impunity, reputation, moral standing, office, or privileges, more often than incarceration.

Commitment to a Renewed but Different Relationship

Finally, each case of order-restoring reconciliation was accompanied by a national commitment to a new social relationship that transcended the antagonism of the war years. Legislatures passed solemn resolutions, peace accords were signed and embraces exchanged by heads of formerly rival groups, statues and monuments to the tragedy were erected, textbooks were rewritten, and a thousand other actions, large and small, were undertaken to underscore the notion that the past was different and the future more hopeful.

Conclusion

These findings are significant from theoretical and practical perspectives, points we will return to in chapters 4 and 5. For now, our study illustrates that a key political challenge at the start of this century—resolving civil conflict and obtaining or restoring social stability and peace through reconciliation—cannot be understood, and patterns of human behavior that explain sociality cannot be fully perceived, using a rational choice signaling model. Negotiation among self-interested players was a part, but only a part, of a much deeper, more protracted, more emotive pattern of behavior that can be recognized and understood only through a different model based on different assumptions about human nature. Assumptions of evolutionary psychology, a theory of the mind and human behavior that looks for evolved, emotionally directed, mental processes and patterns of behavior, allows us to generate a forgiveness hypothesis that carries more insight as to why and how national reconciliation serves as a mechanism for restoring social order after civil war. This approach integrates human rationality and human emotion in a hypothesis of social behavior that is more efficacious with regard to understanding the important political problem of national reconciliation.

This finding, which neither proves nor disproves either model or their paradigmatic assumptions, is a challenge to rational choice as the only foundational approach to the study of politics. It also questions its role as *the* scientific approach to politics. Rational choice is scientific in the sense of making its assumptions explicit and following the scientific method of generating and testing hypotheses. On the other hand, it may be unscientific in that it is not wholly consistent with the most widely accepted scientific finding of the past two centuries: humans, like all species, are the product of an evolutionary process that shaped our physical features and characteristics, including the structure and, in some measure, function of our minds. We must ask if a theory can be scientific if it rests on assumptions about the human mind and human behavior that are not well supported by the majority of evidence generated by other fields of human inquiry; in this case by modern biology and neuroscience. We consider this question in chapter 4.

Many, ourselves included, can accept this limitation when rational choice models provide useful insights into explaining political behavior, and in many instances they do. But even as a heuristic device, rational choice may not always be appropriate. As illustrated in this analysis of civil war and reconciliation, excessive reliance on its assumptions can be limiting for those seeking explanations of important political phenomena.

An evolutionary biological foundation for generating political hypotheses has its own strengths and weaknesses, some theoretical, some methodological, and some historical, although some critiques are misguided. But it is equally as or more scientific in the explicitness and accuracy of its assumptions and its amenability to the scientific method. Moreover, it is consistent with established facts and predominant theories in the natural sciences—a basic problem for most social science. Evolutionary psychology integrates emotion and specific rational processes, currently our best understanding of the human mind, rather than leaving those findings outside the model and substituting an assumption of general rationality in generating hypotheses (we discuss these and other broad questions in chapter 4). Furthermore, as a heuristic it provides a foundation for a model that illuminates and helps explain a critical question not explicable by a rational choice approach: why and how does reconciliation often work to restore civil order?

3

International War and Reconciliation

As man advances in civilization, and small tribes are united into larger communities, the simplest reason would tell each individual that he ought to extend his social instincts and sympathies to all the members of the same nation, though personally unknown to him. This point being once reached, there is only an artificial barrier to prevent his sympathies extending to men of all nations and races.
—Charles Darwin[1]

What role, if any, do reconciliation events play in international relations? For a variety of reasons, that question is rarely considered in the literature of international relations.[2] We saw in chapter 1, however, that belligerents involved in international conflicts also engage in reconciliation events and that, in some cases, those events appear to coincide with a reduction in future bilateral conflict. Could the signaling or forgiveness models also explain in some way postreconciliation conflict reduction between states?

That question presupposes the possibility of an international society, that states exist in a social system that possesses many features of individual nations or small-scale societies.[3] The presumption is a fundamental point of contention in international relations theory.

The realist tradition in international relations generally denies the existence of an international society. Rather, states exist in an international *system*[4] that is fundamentally anarchic. At the other extreme, the communitarian tradition sees the fundamental unit, or goal, of international relations as the community of humankind. Both approaches have deep roots: for realists, Hobbes, Machiavelli, and Thucydides; for communitarians, Kant and Rousseau.

Between these extremes lies what writers since Grotius have described as a middle way, an international society of states.[5] This view holds that the anarchy of international relations and the actions of states, the most important agents of the system, are tempered by a society that regulates state behavior and to which states are committed to maintain. Hedley Bull provides a succinct and widely cited definition:

A society of states (or international society) exists when a group of states, conscious of certain common interests and common values, form a society in the sense that they conceive themselves to be bound by a common set of rules in their relations with one another, and share in the workings of common institutions.[6]

International society reveals itself in institutions such as diplomacy, international law, the balance of power, the concert of powers, and accepted norms of behavior[7] for a particular historical and sociological context.[8] The chief function of these institutions and principles is to maintain societal order.[9] They are essential to the survival of the international system.

It is not our goal to resolve this long-standing theoretical dispute here, only to note that its existence means that a plausible case can be made that, despite differences in size, complexity, or decentralization of authority, international society may be a society nonetheless. It is, Evan Luard proposed, "at least an association of nations, groups, and individuals, in regular communication with each other, engaging in formal and official relationships as well as unofficial contacts, having economic, cultural, and social, as well as military interrelationships, with its own traditions of intercourse, expected norms of behavior, and its own institutions for mutual discussion of common problems."[10] As such, it is appropriate to consider the applicability of the models of reconciliation developed and applied earlier to nations to the international arena. In so doing, we will test the scope and utility of the models and perhaps shed additional light on this debate.

We briefly examine the eight cases of international reconciliation cited in chapter 1. Each one has been the subject of earlier study and some, such as the Egyptian–Israeli case, have received extensive examination. As in our discussion of civil conflicts, our goal is only to summarize succinctly the cases to assess the overall applicability of the contending models. In the findings section, we consider the relevance of the models to an explanation of the cases. In our conclusion to this chapter we return to the implications of these findings for this broad theoretical debate and to the question of the reach and relevance of reconciliation in international conflict resolution.

Case Studies

USSR–West Germany

Russian–German relations have a long history of mistrust based on political and ideological differences tempered by mutual admiration for elements of each other's culture. Neither state has natural boundaries, so it is perhaps inevitable that Russian desires for westward expansion and inclusion in Europe and German desires for eastward expansion and unification of the Germanic people have resulted in conflict between the nations.

Hitler's fascist ideology was based largely on the concept of pan-Germanism, that the German people had a special historical destiny. In the 1930s, Hitler came to regard the Soviet's Bolshevist government as "Semitic" and an obstacle to the goal of pan-Germanism.[11] Both he and Stalin suspected that war between them was inevitable, but Hitler's more immediate concerns focused on full German rearmament and avoiding a two-front war.

With little alternative in light of the weakened state of the Russian military after the purges, Stalin concluded a nonaggression pact with Hitler in 1939 to avoid military engagement, and, subsequently, a secret treaty dividing Polish lands between them. Having bought peace, as he believed, Stalin was unprepared for Hitler's 1941 decision to attack Russia, resulting in the German army reaching Stalingrad and almost entering Moscow. The Soviet counterattack drove Hitler back, and Soviet forces eventually defeated the German army, resulting in the liberation of eastern Europe from the Third Reich. However, the cost was catastrophic. Russian cities lay in rubble, and the final count of Russians dead from combat or concentration and labor camps was over 27 million.

After giving part of its lands to Poland, Germany was divided in two, with East Germany under Soviet occupation and West Germany under the Western sphere of influence. Communism soon replaced Nazism as the enemy in the eyes of the West. Western Europe threw its lot in with the United States as the North Atlantic Treaty Organization (NATO) was founded with the purpose of keeping the Communist threat confined. From the Russian perspective, they had paid a terrible price to German expansionist ambitions, and they were determined to keep Germany from ever uniting again to prevent future attempts at pan-Germanism. Thus, its post-World War II goals placed the Soviet Union in an inherently troubling position: keeping the Germans apart while trying to achieve normal relations with West Germany and keep it from participating wholeheartedly in the American agenda. This goal was complicated further by two factors: economic stagnation inside the USSR and Russian economic reliance on West German trade.

The Soviet Union did not recognize the West German government for several years, considering it an American puppet. West German Chancellor Konrad Adenauer was struggling to effect rapprochement with the West and to rebuild the state, so he had little interest in the East except as it involved East Germany.[12]

It was not until 1967 that a crucial link to reconciliation was forged. Social Democrat candidate for chancellor Willy Brandt had been West German ambassador to the Soviet Union. He advocated improved ties between West Germany and the USSR and eastern Europe to improve, in turn, relations with East Germany. His *Ostpolitik* won him recognition in the Kremlin.[13]

With Brandt's accession as chancellor, relations between West Germany and the USSR improved, although they were constrained by the context of the Cold War and the East–West alliance structure. Nonetheless, Brandt and Foreign Affairs Minister Walter Scheel pursued negotiations with the Soviets. Their efforts bore fruit in a reconciliation event when the Soviet Union signed a treaty with West Germany, whereby, in exchange for trade agreements and credits, the Soviets recognized the existing borders of eastern European states. The USSR–West German Renunciation of Force Treaty of 1970 rejected the use of force in their bilateral relationship and called for respect for the territorial integrity of the present European states. An amended letter to the treaty stated, however, that this renunciation did not conflict with German political obligations to seek reunification.[14] Of importance, this agreement allowed Brandt to pursue his *Ostpolitik* with other eastern European countries.

In the 1980s, the domestic economic situation in the USSR was declining rapidly, and Moscow relied increasingly on its intra-German economic relationship for technology and finished products. By decade's end, East Germans, realizing Moscow's weakened economic state and disinclination to use military force, took advantage of a window of opportunity afforded by a new travel law to take a stand at the Berlin Wall and demand to be let through. As people on both sides of the wall became caught up in the surge of emotion, they began to disassemble the barrier that had been erected during the height of the Cold War. Faced with the realities of the situation, Moscow conceded to the wishes of the German people to be reunified, but demanded that the USSR have an integral part in the negotiations for reunification and substantial reparations.

Soviet President Mikhail Gorbachev initially believed that unification should not be forced but should take place gradually.[15] He and Soviet Foreign Minister Eduard Sheverdnadze initially rejected a united Germany in NATO, stressing that the idea of Germany allied with the Western camp was unacceptable to the Soviets after they had sustained such enormous losses during the Second World War.[16] After the Berlin Wall fell, however, the Soviet leadership had no clear concept of a unified Germany or the rights of the former allied powers. After much debate during the "Two Plus Four" talks, which included the two German states and the four former allied powers, the Soviet government conceded to all terms of unification desired by the Germans, including the right to choose which alliance system they would join.[17] In exchange, the Germans promised to honor all trade and debt obligations between the Soviets and the German Democratic Republic, increase future trade, extend more than eight billion in Deutsche marks (DM) loans, and provide more than DM 15 billion in compensation for troop withdrawal. The Germans also agreed to the concept of reparations for Soviet victims of Nazi Germany.[18]

The German desire for rapid troop withdrawal and the willingness of the Soviets to bring their troops home in exchange for additional compensation helped the nations cooperate. In September 1990, the two nations signed a twenty-year friendship treaty that agreed "to finally be done with the past, and to use understanding and reconciliation to achieve an important contribution toward the overcoming of Europe's division."[19] This reconciliation event is the first of its kind since the one negotiated by Brandt in 1970, and maintains that neither side will use force against the other and that both will honor the territorial integrity of the current borders of all European states. It also calls for greater technological exchange and trade as well as protecting Soviet war memorials and banning the National Socialist (Nazi) movement.

The war and reconciliation between these countries was profoundly influenced by domestic factors—the civil conflict and partition of the

German people—and international systemic factors—the Cold War and the bipolar East–West alliance structure. Nonetheless, it is possible to focus on the applicability of the two models to the relationship. We find a strong fit between the expectations of the signaling hypothesis and improvement in bilateral relations. The reconciliation events were characterized by costly concessions on both sides (for example, Soviet concessions left leaders vulnerable to charges of ideological weakness and threatened to undermine the internal alliance relations of the Communist bloc), novel breaks with the past (particularly Brandt's *Ostpolitik*), and largely voluntary and irrevocable commitments, all leading to lasting improvement in the relationship. In contrast, factors associated with forgiveness—truth telling, partial justice, redefinition of identity, and the call for a new relationship—were not pronounced. Neither country has fully explored the truths of the wartime years, especially in the East, as archives are only recently available. Russia has not secured formal reparations for the war. A fundamental redefinition of identities was not possible within the alliance structure of the Cold War and is only recently a possibility as Germany is reunified, the Soviet Union dissolved, and Russia democratized. The 1990 Friendship Treaty does represent a call for a new relationship, however.

India–China

Sino–Indian relations during the twentieth century were characterized by regional competition for power, distrust, and political miscalculation. The cause of the brief border war in 1962 was a territorial dispute, underlying which were their respective regional and international roles. China's desire to be a world power and regional leader clashed with Indian aspirations for regional leadership and economic development.

Colonialism sowed the seeds of the dispute. In 1914, at the Simla Convention, British and Tibetans established a Himalayan border that gave a strategically advantaged position to British India; this became known as the MacMahon Line. China, the dominant power in Tibet, never ratified the agreement, however, and refused to recognize the new border. Historically, eastern countries had seldom concerned themselves with designating precise borders, many of which were imposed by western nations as they raced to define the extent of their imperial holdings.[20] However, with the departure of the British from India in 1949, and despite mutual desires for neighborly relations, China and India found themselves in the midst of a boundary dispute fueled by nationalism and conflicting strategic interests.[21]

The initial British boundary agreements served the purpose of placing a buffer state, Tibet, between China and India. The Chinese held suzerainty, but not sovereignty, over this region. India and China in the post-imperialist era agreed that the concept of a buffer state was a remnant of imperial politics and therefore undesirable. Nevertheless, neither country was willing to give up its claim to these disputed border lands. To China, Tibet rightfully belonged to it, and negotiations made with the British under imperial domination were seen as void, especially since the Simla Convention agreement neglected to obtain Chinese consent to the MacMahon Line.[22]

In 1950, China's People's Liberation Army (PLA) invaded Tibet, occupying the land and exercising direct control over the Tibetan government in contravention of Indian interests in limited Chinese control. The Indian government, recognizing it could do nothing to dislodge the PLA, worked to improve relations with China bilaterally while courting other Himalayan nations such as Sikkim, Nepal, and Bhutan.[23] These efforts culminated in China and India signing the Panch Sheel (Five Principles) Treaty in 1954. These principles were nonencroachment of territory, noninterference in each other's internal affairs, nonaggression, peaceful coexistence, and equality of status for mutual benefit. By design, the treaty was bound to fail because the two nations had not agreed on their borders and, hence, what was considered an internal affair. Indian Prime Minister Jawaharlal Nehru hoped the treaty and his country's acquiescence on the Tibet issue would lead China to reciprocate by granting India's border claim to the MacMahon Line.

Such efforts to placate China were undermined by Indian public opinion, which was far more outspoken than the government regarding China's occupation of Tibet. India was home to more than 100,000 Tibetan refugees, including Tibet's head of state and spiritual leader, the Dalai Lama. These refugees worked to raise awareness of their plight and opposition toward China's policies in their country.[24] Inflammatory comments by the media and the public about China's Tibet policy heightened tensions with the Chinese government, who considered the rhetoric as meddling in its internal affairs. Despite the Panch Sheel Treaty, relations continued to worsen due to failure to resolve key territorial disputes. Five years later Chinese and Indian troops exchanged fire on the border south of Migytun, heralding the border war of 1962.

The war resulted in India suffering a quick and humiliating defeat and China occupying 14,500 square miles of Indian territory and laying claim to another 30,000 square miles. The conflict did nothing to settle the dispute about the MacMahon Line, and it heightened hostility between the countries to such an extent that negotiation was out of the question.

Postwar relations continued to be stormy as India supported Tibetan autonomy and China supported insurgencies in the northeast of India and West Bengal. In part because India felt threatened by China's power and influence in the region, it signed a treaty of friendship, cooperation, and peace with the Soviet Union in August 1971. The Sino–Soviet split made this treaty a source of Chinese concern.

The Indian government's position on Tibet began to change after Bangladesh (East Pakistan) liberated itself from Pakistan in 1971. The Indian government, fearing Chinese support for independence movements in India, especially after India absorbed Sikkim in 1974, adopted the position that Tibet was part of China.[25] Although China did not recognize India's absorption of Sikkim, New Delhi's change in posture diffused some of the tension between the Asian giants.

Indian Prime Minister Indira Gandhi made a tentative first step toward reconciliation in 1976 by restoring ambassador-level relations between the countries. The deaths of Mao Zedong and Zhou Enlai, main architects of the 1962 war, facilitated this move. Relations suffered a setback in 1979, however, when Indian Foreign Minister Atal Behari Vajpayee toured Beijing to discuss normalization and the border dispute. His visit became a source of political embarrassment for the Chinese and shock for the Indians when China attacked Vietnam during his visit. Deng Xiaoping, in a public address, compared the attack on Vietnam to China's punitive war with India, stating that China would "teach the Vietnamese a lesson" just as it had India. This insensitivity was mirrored eighteen months later by the Indians when Indira Gandhi recognized the Vietnamese-imposed, Soviet-supported regime in Cambodia.[26]

Despite these political miscues, the two governments agreed to a series of annual talks from 1981 until 1988 to discuss the border issue. The talks accomplished little and were marred by an exchange of fire in 1987 at the Sumdurong Chu border, which almost led to a second war. Nevertheless, the dialogue helped to pave the way for a major breakthrough in diplomacy when Prime Minister Rajiv Gandhi visited China in December 1988. This visit was the first to China by an Indian prime minister since Jawarhalal Nehru visited Mao thirty-four years earlier. Deng Xiaoping met with Ghandi as part of the reconciliation event and called for setting aside differences between the countries and expanding cooperative relations.[27]

Motives for the reconciliation event on both sides were varied, but in 1988, with the weakened state of the Soviet Union and the possibility of Sino–Soviet rapprochement, reconciliation with China was a strategic move for India. Moreover, a foreign policy success in the form of Sino–Indian reconciliation could help quell domestic dissatisfaction and reverse the tide of public opinion that was increasingly critical of Rajiv Gandhi's leadership. In addition, India was eager to tap into the enormous Chinese market and expand its trade relationship. For China, reconciliation with India would strengthen its influence in Asia at the expense of a declining Soviet Union.[28] China also saw India as a gateway through which it could gain influence in the nonaligned movement and access to global forums such as the G-77 and the G-15.[29]

The summit culminated in the establishment of a Joint Working Group to deal exclusively with the border question, and it was partially successful at bringing about a rapprochement. The visit, however, furnished new fuel for the Indian public's fire of disapproval for Rajiv Gandhi when he stated that Tibet was an internal matter for the Chinese. India's longstanding sympathy for Tibet had increased over the years, so Gandhi's statement did not reflect the opinion of most Indians. The Chinese made no reciprocal statement concerning Kashmir or Sikkim that might have redeemed Gandhi's concession.

China and India achieved partial reconciliation: the territorial dispute remains unresolved, as does the underlying geopolitical rivalry, but diplomatic relations and trade between the countries have resumed, and a regular, high-level dialogue continues. Rajiv Gandhi's visit to China and acts immediately before and after it fit the rational actor signaling model rather than the forgiveness model of reconciliation. The visit was not the culmination of a process of forgiveness; it was a costly, novel, and voluntary signal of a desire for improved relations during a time when India sought to take advantage of strategic opportunities in a changing political environment. Gandhi's interests included domestic political motives for securing a foreign policy victory and strategic reasons to avoid alienating China in the wake of normal Sino–Soviet relations and a weakening Soviet economy. China's economic reform and liberalization increasingly led the United States and other Western powers to treat China as a world power, and with the regional balance of power in danger, India chose to take a gamble on reconciliation rather than face a hostile China with full global power status. An additional motive for the Indian government was the hope that by diffusing hostilities between itself and China, its relations with Pakistan would improve. Thus, although Rajiv Gandhi's statement that Tibet was an internal matter for China was criticized by the Indian public and by his political opponents, it reassured China and symbolized India's dedication to maintain peaceful relations. Ghandi's efforts were novel, irrevocable, and costly, and even though the Indian government hoped for a reciprocal act in the form of China's recognizing Kashmir or Sikkim as Indian territory, there was no assurance of that. As events proved, China did *not* reciprocate the recognition, and the majority of the Indian public does not support its government's official attitude toward Tibet.

Egypt–Israel

The uneasy peace that has existed for more than thirty years between Egypt and Israel was the result of protracted negotiation after five wars.

War came almost immediately after the creation of Israel. Faced with bankruptcy after World War II, Britain negotiated with Egypt to withdraw its colonial presence provided the Suez Canal remained under its protection. Britain also gave up its mandate over Palestine and, pursuant to the Balfour Declaration, advised the U.N. General Assembly to partition Palestine into an Arab state (Transjordan) and a Jewish state. Arab riots broke out in Palestine in response to the declaration, but thousands of Jews continued to filter into Palestine from Europe. British withdrawal from Palestine began in 1947, and Israel declared itself an independent, sovereign Jewish state on May 14, 1948.

Egypt viewed the British-supported state of Transjordan and the Israeli declaration of independence as challenges to the concept of pan-Arabism and to its role as leader of the Arab world. Concerned that Britain and

Transjordan would resolve matters in Palestine themselves, Egypt led the Arab League in a preemptive strike to "liberate" Palestine and return the land to the "local Arab populace." Israeli forces faced Syrian, Iraqi, and Egyptian armies on three fronts. The assault was costly to both Egypt and Israel, and accomplished little except to wrest the Old City of Jerusalem away from Israeli control. After a brief truce, fighting broke out again until the United Nations could impose a second cease-fire.[30]

The outcome of the first war gave Israel 22 percent more land than originally allotted in the U.N. Partition Resolution. The city of Jerusalem was partitioned, and Egypt was able to retain the Gaza coastal strip and the town of al-Auja and its vicinity, but negotiations stalled with failure of the parties to come to an agreement over Palestinian refugees.

The second Egyptian–Israeli war, led by President Gamal Abd al-Nasser of Egypt and Prime Minister David Ben-Gurion of Israel, widened the conflict into an East–West struggle when Nasser concluded an arms deal with the Soviet Union to procure modern weapons. International pressure limited Israel's full prosecution of the war, and the United Nations demanded Israeli withdrawal from Gaza and Sinai after Britain's failed attempt to nationalize the Suez Canal in 1956. Israel, however, had achieved its main objective by regaining access to the Strait of Tiran and having the United Nations guarantee international access to the waterway. Furthermore, the U.N. agreed to station its expeditionary force in the Gaza Strip until an understanding could be reached for a permanent settlement. Israel was careful to add that it reserved the right to take defensive action in the event of renewal of threats against Israeli shipping.[31]

The third war was initiated by hostilities between Israel and Syria. Israel, feeling threatened by increasingly provocative attacks at the Syrian border, threatened to take decisive action to protect itself. When its counterattacks became more aggressive, the Soviets urged Nasser to become involved. Because of Egypt's increasing reliance on Soviet arms and other supplies, Nasser felt obliged to heed this request. He launched an attack into the Sinai and ordered U.N. troops out of Egyptian territory and the Gaza Strip. Diplomatic efforts by France, the Soviet Union, the United States, and Great Britain failed, and the Arab countries rallied around Egypt. Israeli troops responded by launching a tactical air strike that wiped out Egypt's air force and then targeted ground troops in the Sinai. Within six days Israel had taken the Sinai Peninsula, the West Bank, and the Golan Heights, in all, 28,000 square miles of territory inhabited by at least a million Arabs. For the first time, Israel was in a position to dictate terms for peace.

The United Nations, after much deliberation, adopted Security Council Resolution 242, which required Israel to withdraw its armed forces "from territories occupied in the recent conflict" and for all parties to terminate all hostilities and recognize the rights of sovereignty and peace for every state in the region.[32] The language of the document was so vague that the Arabs understood it to mean complete Israeli withdrawal, whereas the Israelis believed partial withdrawal would be sufficient. Nasser ignored the cease-fire and, together with the other Arab nations, pledged "no peace with Israel, no negotiations with Israel, no recognition of Israel, and maintenance of the rights of the Palestinian people in their nation."[33] The Egyptians mounted several offensives to breach the canal, sunk Israeli destroyers, and engaged in sporadic outbursts of warfare that were met with Israeli counterstrikes. The hostilities became known as the War of Attrition. United States intervention and Moscow's refusal to provide more weapons forced Nasser to accept a cease-fire agreement. New Israeli Prime Minister Golda Meir and her cabinet also acquiesced to the plan after American pressure and offers of financial support.

After the death of Nasser, Vice President Anwar al-Sadat assumed the presidency. At first his policies seemed to be a continuation of Nasser's, so Egypt–Israeli relations changed little. Later, Sadat began contacting the United States, expressing a desire to "reduce tensions in the Middle East."[34] He cautiously made an offer to the Israelis to open the canal in return for withdrawal, but it was rejected. By signaling cooperation to Washington, Sadat put Israel on the defensive and won a diplomatic and propaganda victory. Because diplomacy had not brought about Israeli withdrawal, Sadat turned to the military option and prepared a carefully organized attack aimed at recapturing the Sinai during a decline in Israeli preparedness.

At 2:00 P.M. on October 6, 1973, the Jewish Yom Kippur holiday, Egyptian forces began shelling and bombing the eastern bank of the Suez Canal, and Syrian forces did the same along the cease-fire line at the Golan Heights. Egypt's planes took out air bases and radar stations behind enemy lines while its infantry moved across the canal in boats. Although the Israelis tried to stop the amphibious assault with jets, antiaircraft weapons shot their planes down. Egyptian forces breached the Bar-Lev defensive line and, when the Israeli counteroffensives failed, the Israeli government stated it would be willing to consider a cease-fire. This time, however, Egypt was unwilling to offer one.[35]

United States Secretary of State Henry Kissinger convinced the Nixon administration to supply the struggling Israelis with weapons and equipment, enabling them to launch a concerted attack to regain the Sinai.[36] The Israeli counteroffensive brought the United States and the Soviet Union to the bargaining table to fashion two proposals under U.N. Security Council Resolutions 338 and 339. The latter called for an immediate end to hostilities and the dispatch of U.N. monitors to the region.

After a failed negotiation effort and a protracted round of Kissinger's so-called shuttle diplomacy, the two countries signed a new, binding cease-fire at Geneva. Further negotiations failed to bring results until Sadat, driven by economic necessity, decided to reopen the Suez Canal and rebuild the canal cities.[37] Matching his "gesture of goodwill," the Israelis withdrew their tanks and troops eighteen to twenty-five miles from the waterway. These acts defused tension between the Middle Eastern countries and between the United States and Israel, and led Israel to agree to withdraw its forces past the Mital and Gidi passes and the southwestern Sinai area of oil fields. As a result, Egypt acknowledged Israeli rights to use the canal and promised to relax its boycott of foreign companies doing business with Israel.

After a series of scandals in Israel, Prime Minister Itzakh Rabin resigned and was succeeded by Menachem Begin, a rightist from the Likud party. Begin sent out feelers to Egypt that he was willing to strike a deal. He delivered drafts of peace treaties to the United States that Sadat at first disregarded as a ploy. Shortly thereafter, however, Israeli intelligence intercepted a Libyan and Palestinian plot to assassinate Sadat, and Begin not only ordered the information relayed to Egypt, but also indicated that Israel would do nothing to disturb Egypt in the Sinai during its punitive border war against Libya. These gestures won Sadat's appreciation, and he began to take Begin's offers seriously.

Through intermediaries, the two governments discussed their main issues for settlement. Sadat wanted the Sinai returned, all Israeli troops withdrawn from Egyptian territory, and a settlement for the Palestinian people that would link the West Bank and Gaza with Jordan. In return,

Egypt would adhere to security guarantees and an agreement of nonbelligerence. Israel was willing to restore Sinai to Egypt, but would not abandon its settlements in the northeast or the air base at the Gulf of Aqaba, or withdraw troops and settlements from the West Bank and Gaza. Despite these disagreements, Americans continued to pressure the two nations to sign a comprehensive peace agreement. At this point, Sadat made the unanticipated announcement to the Egyptian People's Assembly that he himself would "go to the ends of the earth," that is, to the Israeli parliament (the Knesset), to discuss a settlement for withdrawal and for Palestinian rights.[38] Other Arab leaders reacted bitterly to what they considered betrayal of Arab brotherhood and the Palestinians. Sadat's visit to Israel was afforded full ceremonial honors as a visiting head of state. His address to the Knesset was eloquent and poignant, proclaiming the importance of peace as an objective for both Egypt and Israel.[39]

Although the speech was hailed as a breakthrough by the media, the meeting between Begin and Sadat produced agreement on only three issues: rejection of war between their countries, restoration of Egyptian sovereignty over the Sinai, and demilitarization of the largest part of the Sinai. Begin refused to compromise over Jewish possession of a unified Jerusalem or his opposition to Palestinian self-determination on the West Bank. Nevertheless, the two men agreed to continue talks. Growing tension over these issues and Israeli authorization of new settlements in Judea and Samaria prompted American involvement.[40] President Jimmy Carter did not wish to see the momentum of peace falter and invited both Begin and Sadat to Camp David, the presidential retreat in the Maryland mountains, to discuss proposals for a peace agreement.

After seven days of intense negotiations, a compromise was reached among Carter, Sadat, and Begin. The three agreed to separate the settlement with Egypt from a broader settlement in the Middle East.[41] Begin agreed to evacuate the Sinai fully and return it to Egypt, after Carter persuaded Begin to give up the Sinai air base in exchange for two air bases built in the Negev by the United States before full evacuation. Sadat agreed to restore full diplomatic and commercial relations with Israel only nine months after signing a peace treaty, and he made no preconditions for Palestinian autonomy or the West Bank. Sadat also agreed to use the Sinai airfields for civilian purposes only, and he guaranteed the right of free passage for Israeli ships through the Gulf of Aqaba, Strait of Tiran, Suez Canal, and Gulf of Suez. A third agreement, subject to approval from Jordan, concerned construction of a highway between Sinai and Jordan near Eilat, with freedom of passage for Egyptians and Jordanians. Details for a phased withdrawal of Israeli troops from the Sinai were worked out, together with other specifics governing the presence of Egyptian forces and U.N. troops.

On the Palestine problem, a three-step framework was established involving participation from Israel, Egypt, Jordan, and representatives from the Palestinian people. Its purpose was to determine guidelines for establishing an elected, self-governing authority in the West Bank and Gaza, for withdrawal of Israeli troops during a five-year transition period, and finally, for determining the final status of the administered areas.[42] The timetable was purposely vague, allowing the Israelis to postpone dealing with the issue.

Efforts to forge a final peace treaty were endangered by renewal of Israeli settlement-building in the West Bank and Gaza Strip and refusal of the other Arab states to support the framework set up for Palestinian self-determination. In fact, Sadat was thoroughly demoralized when the Arab states decided to impose an embargo on Egyptian businesses and withdraw financial support. Not wishing to see his diplomatic efforts go to waste, President Carter pledged to go to Egypt and Israel himself to oversee the negotiation and signing of a peace treaty. After wringing further promises from Sadat and Begin to work on the Palestine issue and other technical issues, the peace treaty was completed. Sadat and Begin signed it at the White House on March 26, 1979, and it was ratified by the parliaments of both countries.[43]

The peace treaty was the culmination of a step-by-step process of hard bargaining consistent with a rational actor theory of cost-benefit analysis and benefit maximization, and shows few signs of fitting the forgiveness model. Sadat's trip to the Knesset was a grand gesture of reconciliation that imparted momentum to the process. This gesture was motivated by both strategic and economic goals as well as a genuine desire that suffering from warfare should end. Strategically, Egypt wanted the United States to fill the void created when the Soviets vacated their position as Egypt's great power sponsor. Sadat knew he would lose the support of his Arab neighbors if he unilaterally pursued peace, but he thought that with United States support and with domestic support from his own people, Egypt could survive this isolation. Regaining the Sinai Peninsula and progressing a step toward a greater Middle East settlement, even if the step was ambiguous, seemed worth the cost. For Sadat, friendship with the United States could bring financial support, investment, and trade to his country, which was suffering from the economic and psychological burdens of the continuous war with Israel. In his calculation, the welfare of Egypt took precedence over pan-Arabism.[44] Moreover, he realized that to cut through the fog of mistrust that characterized their relationship, he would have to convince not only the Israeli leadership and public, but also the rest of the world, including Egypt, that he was sincere in his desire for peace.[45] Sadat wrote, "I had reckoned that my Jerusalem trip would break the vicious circle within which we had been caught up for years."[46]

The act was one of voluntary public acknowledgment, for it involved Sadat making a special trip to speak before the Israeli parliament that would likely be broadcast around the world. It was novel; no Arab leader had ever visited Israel or even acknowledged Israel's right to exist. The dramatic import of Sadat's visit and his words to the Knesset played on this concept of novelty and of just how far he was willing to go for peace. It was a costly and vulnerable act because Sadat knew he could lose the economic support of the Arab countries and risk his own political career back home if it did not yield tangible results. He might even have risked his own life, as Arab leaders who had shown flexibility toward Israel before had faced assassination attempts from Palestinian extremists and the Arab League. The visit was irrevocable because once Sadat proclaimed his serious intentions toward reconciliation, he put too much at stake to back away from the attempt.

Begin also risked his own political standing and the security of his country by taking Sadat's intentions seriously and by pursuing a peace settlement in which he agreed to return the Sinai Peninsula to Egypt and withdraw all troops. He did so because he decided the benefit of being able to guarantee that at least one of Israel's neighbors would no longer pose a security threat and would recognize the Israeli state as legitimate far outweighed the costs of abandoning the Sinai, where Israel had developed numerous settlements, airfields, and oil wells totaling several million dollars worth of investment.

The rational actor-signaling process resulted in a settlement that was successful in bringing about improvement in postreconciliation relations because the parties abstained from warfare to solve their problems. The outcome—improved relations—is therefore consistent with the reconciliation process.

The forgiveness hypothesis fits poorly with the facts of the case. Neither Egypt nor Israel engaged in truth telling to paint a clear picture of what went on during the course of their five wars. On the contrary, each side, up until the signing of the peace treaty, vilified the other and played down its own role in provoking hostility. To a small extent, after the treaty was signed, an exchange of civilian and military accounts provided some idea of the injury they had inflicted on each other. Since the signing of the treaty, bilateral relations suggest that Egypt's identity has not significantly changed, as the country still allies itself with the other Arab states and considers itself obligated to stand up for Palestinian rights; and Israel still fights against the notion of a Palestinian homeland within territory it considers its own.[47] The relationship thus continues to be thorny.

Vietnam–China

Historically, these neighbors have struggled for territory along their 796-mile common border and in the waters of the South China Sea (the Oriental Sea, to the Vietnamese) along the Tonkin Gulf and the Paracel and Spratly Islands.[48] In addition, Chinese support of the Western powers' plan in the 1950s to divide Vietnam and create independent nation status for Cambodia and Laos was a major obstacle in Sino–Vietnamese relations.

Cambodia was the crux of the conflict between Vietnam and China. Vietnam had good relations with Laos and signed a Treaty of Friendship and Cooperation with them in 1977, but its relationship with Cambodia was more distant. The Cambodian people resented Vietnam for interfering in their internal affairs and for past attempts to subjugate their nation. Vietnam considered both states vital to its security and therefore, wanted to keep anti-Vietnamese elements out of power in Cambodia. In 1974, the Soviet Union recognized the Lon Nol government as the legitimate government of Cambodia, whereas China recognized the Khmer Rouge, an extreme militant arm of the Cambodian Communist Party (KCP). Neither the Soviet Union nor China had a special relationship with either faction, except that the Lon Nol faction was vehemently anti-Chinese, and the Khmer Rouge was anti-Vietnamese and anti-Soviet. A power struggle in Cambodia ensued as the two sides fought for control, with Vietnam shipping supplies and aid to Lon Nol and China doing the same for the Khmer Rouge.

The Vietnamese government could not afford to let the Khmer Rouge gain control of Cambodia, so it invaded Cambodia on December 25, 1978. It launched a concerted attempt to influence Cambodian politics by attempting to oust the Khmer Rouge militarily, capture Phnom Penh, and install a puppet government under Heng Samrin.[49] The Association of Southeast Asian Nations (ASEAN) called for immediate withdrawal of Vietnamese forces, as did the United Nations. The Khmer Rouge retreated to the northwest highlands and regrouped to battle the Vietnamese army. China denounced the attack by Vietnam and called for international support in condemning it. Privately, China's leadership discussed the need to teach Vietnam a lesson. In response to these denouncements, Vietnam stated that it was willing to talk with China about ceasing hostilities, settling boundary and territorial issues, and addressing the issue of thousands of ethnic Chinese living in Vietnam. It made no mention of the Cambodian crisis, however.

China's antipathy toward Vietnam and its Cambodian policies had been building for more than two years before Vietnam's invasion. In April 1976, reports of fighting along the Sino–Vietnamese border began to circulate. Despite a widening rift, the governments continued cautiously to project an image of fraternity and goodwill. In April 1977, however, Vietnam's Premier Pham Van Dong went to Beijing to request aid from Chinese leaders. Memoranda of the meeting indicate that the talks were "tense and heated," as the Chinese expressed their concern over closer links between Hanoi and Moscow and claimed the Vietnamese government was inciting anti-China sentiment among the Vietnamese people.[50] As relations deteriorated between these nations, the Cambodian power struggle took on new dimensions. China's support for Pol Pot, secretary of the KCP and the real power behind the Khmer Rouge, angered the Vietnamese. Hanoi strongly opposed the Khmer Rouge, although they were not necessarily anti-KCP. China began making statements laying the blame for the Cambodian conflict on Hanoi. Foreign press services reported that Beijing was sending arms to Cambodia to resist Vietnamese forces at the border and stave off an invasion. By 1978, the Khmer Rouge had shifted its strategy to take the offensive by launching raids into Vietnamese territories.[51] As fighting between Cambodia and Vietnam became fiercer, relations between China and Vietnam approached a crisis.

As rumors of a China–Vietnam war began spreading, Hanoi implemented policies directed against the ethnic Chinese living in Vietnam. The postreunification Vietnamese government policy of collectivization was particularly burdensome to the ethnic Chinese population. These changes, in turn, triggered a refugee crisis,[52] which spurred a series of largely unproductive talks between the countries. By early 1979, an estimated 1.4 million ethnic Chinese and Vietnamese had fled Vietnam (approximately 50,000 of these perished at sea), 725,000 of whom settled in the United States.

Another source of Sino–Vietnamese friction was Vietnam's close relationship with the Soviet Union. As financial aid from China decreased, and it became clear that the United States had opted for normal relations with China rather than Vietnam (closing off another possible source for assistance), the Vietnamese government was forced to turn to the USSR for help. To Moscow, a strong Vietnam allied with the Soviets and dominating Laos and Cambodia was desirable because it gave the Soviets a sphere of influence in an area of the world where it had little experience and a strategic edge against the Chinese. In 1978, Vietnam joined the Moscow-based economic organization, the Council for Mutual Economic Assistance, giving Hanoi greater access to aid and technical assistance, but also requiring the Vietnamese government to reciprocate by giving greater consideration to Moscow's aims. That same year Vietnam signed a Treaty of Friendship and Cooperation with the Soviets. It stated that in the event that either country was attacked or threatened with attack, the other would be consulted and would be obligated to lend appropriate assistance. China saw this treaty as a direct military threat to itself and a sign of Soviet and Vietnamese ambitions in Indochina.

On February 14, 1979, China invaded Vietnam, justifying the attack by claiming Vietnamese troops had repeatedly crossed into Chinese territory and provoked those living along border areas. Although increased tensions along the border may have contributed to the overall conflict, this was probably just a legal justification for the invasion. Chinese forces moved twenty-five miles into Vietnamese territory within nine days, but the costliness of the invasion in terms of lives, and the unexpected strength of Vietnamese resistance prompted China to suggest a truce.

Vietnam agreed on condition that China withdraw all its troops from its territory. The war continued, with China announcing on March 4 that it had captured the town of Long Son and claimed that its campaign had been a success. Vietnam also claimed victory. The next day China announced a formal troop withdrawal. Vietnam followed with an announcement that if troops were actually withdrawn, Hanoi would be ready to commence negotiations.[53] The cost to both sides in lives had been dear, and in areas where the Chinese invaded, almost 80 percent of the infrastructure was destroyed.

Cambodian–Vietnamese negotiations began in 1979 but accomplished very little because the Vietnamese invasion of Cambodia was central to the conflict between China and Vietnam, and both countries were actively seeking to blame the other for that conflict. Vietnam continued its Cambodian campaign despite mounting pressure to desist, but eventually, domestic economic concerns and international isolation and sanctions prompted Hanoi to compromise its position vis-à-vis Cambodia. Chinese leaders also began sending signals indicating willingness to compromise.

In 1984, the People's Republic of China announced that, although it would not conduct direct talks with Hanoi as long as Vietnamese troops remained in Cambodia, they would not object to other countries pursuing direct talks with Vietnam. Thailand, in particular, began a process of negotiation with Vietnam on settling the Indochina issue. In late 1986, a younger, more liberal and reformist faction headed by Nguyen Van Linh replaced the anti-China Vietnamese Communist Party (VCP) leadership. Shortly after entering office they announced policies of economic liberalization. This change in leadership was crucial to normalization because it allowed Vietnam to emphasize the importance of economic interests, and it presented China with negotiators who were not hard-line Soviet supporters. In 1989, China and the Soviet Union developed normal relations, and this encouraged several high-level meetings between Vietnamese and Chinese deputy and vice foreign ministers that year. Vietnam announced toward the end of the year that it would withdraw all of its troops from Cambodia.

Beginning in 1990, several reconciliation events occurred that were decisive to normalization. First, VCP Chief Nguyen Van Linh, Premier Do Muoi, and former Premier Pham Van Dong met in China at a secret meeting with Chinese Premier Li Peng and Communist Party General Secretary Jiang Zemin. The absence of Foreign Minister Nguyen Co Thach from the meeting may have been a conciliatory signal toward China from the Vietnamese leadership, who were aware of China's dislike of the man. Thach was later replaced, as was Interior Minister Mai Chi Tho, whom the Chinese accused of being responsible for the expulsion of thousands of ethnic Chinese from Vietnam.[54] Scholars believe the secret meeting resulted in some sort of understanding between the countries regarding the Cambodian situation, for shortly thereafter, Vietnam signed the terms of the Paris peace proposal on Cambodia, allowing for a provisional power-sharing government made up of the Vietnam-backed Heng Samrin government and representatives from all rival factions, which would be replaced by an elected government.[55] Vietnam had to forego its opposition to representatives from the Khmer Rouge in the provisional Cambodian government and, consequently, its special relationship with Cambodia.

Relations also were helped by several other factors. The Chinese, after harsh international criticism for the Tiananmen Square massacre, were facing diplomatic ostracism of their own and were seeking broader international engagement. Furthermore, the Soviet Union was showing alarming signs of economic weakness after Gorbachev's *Glasnost* and *Perestroika* partially opened the Soviet economy.[56] Vietnam relied on the USSR for subsidized oil, fertilizer, and loans in excess of two billion dollars a year. With these sources of aid diminishing, Vietnam had to find a replacement financial supporter, and China and the United States were the obvious choices. The *Economist* noted that the Chinese had been hinting at offers to replace the oil, fertilizer, and other goods supplied by the Soviets in return for a satisfactory conclusion to the Cambodian situation.[57] To gain the support of both nations, Vietnam was compelled to withdraw troops from Cambodia.

The situation between Vietnam and China remained at a standstill until 1991, when the Paris Agreements on Cambodia were signed. Immediately thereafter, Jiang Zemin and Li Peng invited Do Muoi and chairman of the Council of Ministers, Vo Van Kiet, to a high-level talk in China for five days in November. After the talks, a joint communique was issued stating that the result was normal relations between the countries. The communique spelled out principles for good neighborliness that would guide the two countries; agreements to cooperate in scientific, economic, technological, cultural, trade, and other endeavors; agreements to continue work on the border and territory issues; acceptance of the Paris Agreements; and promises on the part of both nations not to seek hegemony in the region. Although this reconciliation event led to normal relations, it did not end outstanding teritorial disputes concerning the Paracels, Spratlys, and Gulf of Tonkin. Vietnam was forced to accede to Chinese terms because of its weakened economic state. Its strategic security interests in Laos and Cambodia had not changed, but the government put these issues on the back burner until the economy could recover from the devastation wrought by the flight of ethnic Chinese, the Sino–Vietnam war, international sanctions and isolation after the Cambodian invasion, and the fall of the Soviet Union.

It appears that Vietnamese leaders conceded to China's demands at the negotiating table in Paris and Beijing in attempts to arrive at a rational bargain. There were no truth telling, attempts at justice, or fundamental redefinition of identities between parties. It is not apparent that all conditions necessary for a successful, lasting restoration of order through negotiation exist, yet relations have improved since 1991. The signaling factors of costliness, vulnerability, novelty, and irrevocability do not pertain in this case despite what appears, thus far, to be a successful reconciliation. Underlying issues of regional roles and disputes over territory and resources remain beneath the surface.

West Germany–Poland

Poland's geopolitical position, sandwiched between the two major powers of Germany and Russia, contributed to a conflictual and often tragic history. During the past 400 years, German and Russian states partitioned the lands of Poland four times. Although nominally maintaining its Polish origins, the government was often run from either Germany or Russia.

The devastating effect of World War I resulted in the rise of an independent Polish Republic. By 1939, Poland had signed similar treaties of nonaggression with Hitler's Germany and with the Soviets.[58] The September 1939 invasion proved that Germany had not changed its historical goal of expansion and domination of Poland. Stalin and Hitler had made a secret pact to partition Poland between them as part of their nonaggression treaty. The Soviets would take the eastern half of the territory consisting of Byelorussia and the West Ukraine, and the Germans would absorb Pomerania, Posnania, and Silesia. The rest of the country was designated as the General–Government, a colony whose capital, Krakow, would be run by Hitler's cohort Hans Frank.

The historical animosity between Poles and Germans was further complicated by atrocities committed by the Nazis during the war. The Soviet government had also massacred thousands of Polish prisoners and sent more than a million others to forced labor camps. More than six million Poles died as a result of atrocities and serving in the Resistance.

In 1944, Polish Resistance forces staged the Warsaw uprising as Soviet troops approached the Vistula to overthrow German forces, but they received no help from Russian troops, who refused to let Allied planes land on Russian airfields after supply drops. The uprising led to complete destruction of the city as Germans bombed Warsaw for almost 70 days. The political and military institutions of the Polish underground were decimated, opening the way for a Soviet takeover[59] and exacerbating Polish antipathy for its eastern neighbor.

In return for Stalin's cooperation, Britain and the United States agreed to let the Russians profit from their invasion of Poland by keeping the absorbed lands, about one-third of Polish territory. Germany was partitioned and the eastern half came under Soviet control. The Polish people were "awarded" all the German territory east of the Oder and Neisse rivers, although the Poles themselves wanted to annex East Prussia, the free city of Danzig (Gdansk), and Upper Silesia. The Western powers, however, wanted a substantial buffer zone between themselves and the Soviet Union. Poland was chosen as the sacrificial victim, and the Oder–Neisse line was ostensibly selected as the western border of Poland.[60]

The postwar settlement left the Polish people feeling their interests had again been sacrificed. They received little in the way of reparations or aid from the Federal Republic of Germany or the West. Their economy was in ruins; their historical, cultural, and artistic centers were either looted or destroyed; and their population was devastated. Some of their animosity was turned on Germans living in the country, many of whom were expelled or subjected to repressive policies. These actions sowed the seeds of continued discord with the Federal Republic of Germany (FRG).

In 1970, German Chancellor Willy Brandt made the first overture for reconciliation with Poland. Having placed diplomats in Prague and Warsaw, Brandt took the opportunity to meet with the Polish people. His visit to Warsaw culminated in an agreement in which West Germany recognized the Oder–Neisse line as the western border of the Polish state and renounced all future German claims to Polish territory. Brandt went further, demonstrating West German atonement for Nazi crimes by walking to the memorial for the Jewish victims of the Warsaw Ghetto Uprising and falling to his knees in a gesture of repentance and reconciliation. As Brandt remarked, "No people can escape from their history."[61]

Brandt's actions were not met with universal approval at home, especially by some conservative West Germans who believed he had betrayed his country. Nevertheless, he did not lose sight of his concrete political goals. The Treaty of Warsaw, in which Germany gave the same assurances to Poland as it had given to the USSR in return for agreement that ethnic Germans could emigrate to the FRG, was the culmination of ten months of negotiation. Brandt also tied ratification of all the renunciation of force treaties with eastern Europe to guarantees that West Germans would have access to West Berlin by land. Although Brandt's actions did not lay to rest all issues of territory, reparations, aid, and the treatment of the German minority in Poland, they did allow the governments of the two countries to commence a dialogue on reconciliation.[62]

In the late 1980s, German Chancellor Helmut Kohl made overtures toward reconciliation with Polish Prime Minister Mieczyslav Rakowski. The German government claimed it would be willing to accept normal relations if the Polish government addressed certain issues. Particularly, the German minority in Poland had to be granted dual citizenship and greater rights to practice their culture and language.[63]

Poland's elected Solidarity government was willing to meet all of these demands in exchange for more lenient terms for debt repayment and various political and financial assistance measures to help the fledgling democracy improve its dismal economic conditions and standard of living. To guarantee the security of its borders, the Polish government also wanted a proclamation from the West German government giving up all claims, present and future, to lands awarded to Poland after World War II. It sought war reparations for victims of Nazi concentration camps and the return of valuable works of art. Despite the desire of political leaders of both nations for normal relations, public opinion was mixed. Kohl initially failed to meet his commitment to pursue an official declaration to relinquish the Oder–Neisse territories, and the West German government was unwilling to meet the expense of reparations.[64]

Reflecting the split in public opinion, in 1989 Polish President Richard von Weisacker, who had marched with German troops during the invasion of Warsaw in World War II, planned to make a historic visit of atonement on the fiftieth anniversary of the beginning of the war. His plans were cancelled when West German finance minister, Theo Waigel, made inflammatory comments about one-third of Poland still technically belonging to Germany. The embarrassing situation stalled financial aid to Warsaw and, for a time, further efforts at reconciliation.

During German reunification after the fall of the Berlin Wall in 1989, Kohl worked to reassure the Polish government as to the territorial integrity of their country. He delivered on his assurances when the nations signed two treaties, one that officially revoked German claims to the territory east of the Oder–Neisse known as The Boundary Treaty, and The Friendship Treaty that officially implemented channels of communication, cooperation, and cultural exchange between the countries.[65] Scholars generally recognize these two treaties as the second major reconciliation event between Germany and Poland.[66]

This case is something of a hybrid: it contains traces of the forgiveness model—notably, a public acknowledgment by Brandt—but lacks many other elements of forgiveness. Viewed over the longer period encompassing both *Ostpolitik* and the Boundary and Friendship Treaties of 1990–1991, the case fits solidly within a rational choice-signaling explanation, with the emotive dimension of reconciliation lagging behind bargaining over interests.

Brandt's initial reconciliation overture was a powerful symbolic gesture that served as a form of acceptance by the West German government for the part it played in World War II. It was not followed with policies that addressed many of the issues in conflict, however. Most important, although Brandt declared that the West German government would not seek to reclaim its lost territories, the declaration was not accepted by many in positions of power in West Germany, and, because of lack of whole-hearted German acceptance, Poland did not regard Brandt's declaration as an official and final acknowledgment of its territorial rights. Furthermore, the West German government refused the costly reparations Poland had demanded. As a result, events of the 1970s did little to change the Polish people's views of themselves as victims, and for many, the war was too recent to be able to forego the desire for revenge.

The second major reconciliation event between these nations does, however, meet most requirements for successful signaling. Concessions made by Germany to give up its rights to territory without contingencies and to offer aid to Poland by rescheduling and canceling several loan obligations, as well as other forms of political and financial support, were costly, voluntary, and irrevocable commitments. These concrete concessions, after openings created by Brandt and others, led to improvement in bilateral relations and gradual transformation of Polish identity into a member of Western economic and security institutions, in this sense, becoming a partner with its former adversary.

United Kingdom–Argentina

The 1982 conflict between the United Kingdom and Argentina over the Falkland/Malvinas Islands had its roots in a centuries-old disagreement about sovereignty. Control over the islands, which are located 300 miles east of the Argentine coast, has resided with France, Spain, Argentina, and the United Kingdom over the past 400 years. The United Kingdom maintained control since 1833, when Argentine settlers were forced off the eastern islands after the United States military destroyed their settlement in retaliation for the arrest of three American ships by the Argentine government. This episode ended Spain's, and later Argentina's, sixty-year colonial presence on the islands.[67]

In 1982, a military dictatorship controlled Argentina's government and faced severe economic problems and internal discontent. The junta decided to make a play for the islands as a way to draw attention away from internal problems and to encourage the populace to solidify around an issue of strong national sentiment.[68]

The conflict began with an attack by the Argentine Navy on the islands and the small British battalion stationed there.[69] After the attack, thousands of Argentine troops were sent to occupy the islands. The British responded by declaring a 200-mile war exclusion zone around the islands and dispatching additional forces to the south Atlantic.[70] International and American attempts at mediation failed,[71] and after several months the violence ended when British troops defeated the Argentines at the capital of Port Stanley on West Falkland Island. The conflict lasted from early April to June 1982, and resulted in nearly 1000 deaths.[72]

Initially, Argentina's citizens supported the government's attempt to gain control of the islands. They were ill informed of the conduct of the war, however, and surprised by the defeat. Thus, the conflict ultimately undermined the military government and led to the ousting of General Galtieri from the presidency and eventual restoration of civilian control.[73]

Immediately after the conflict, the relationship between Argentina and the United Kingdom was highly antagonistic. Conflicting claims to the islands were as intractable as ever, and the island inhabitants remained fully committed to their British citizenship. The British removed a 200-mile exclusion zone, but kept a 150-mile Falklands protection zone in place. Diplomatic relations were severed, and the states imposed trade bans on each other.[74] They attempted to negotiate over sovereignty in Berne in 1984, but failed.[75] In 1985 and 1986, the United Kingdom built a military airbase on the islands, which the Argentines viewed negatively.[76]

By the mid-1980s, the two nations took some initial steps toward improving relations, but the question of sovereignty remained contentious. In 1985, Britain lifted its ban on trade, hoping that this would spark a similar action by the Argentine government.[77] The two nations managed to participate in a relatively peaceful quarter-final World Cup soccer match in June 1986.[78] In March 1988, Argentina filed a complaint with the United Nations Security Council about British military maneuvers being conducted on the islands, claiming that such actions undermined and "disregarded negotiations as a basis for the settlement of disputes."[79] The Council took no action, but in a March 1988 resolution the U.N. General Assembly urged the two parties to resolve problems about the future of the islands.[80]

On March 11, 1989, Argentina's new president, Carlos Menem, made an opening for further discussion by announcing that, although Argentina would continue to pursue its sovereignty over the islands as called for in its constitution, it would renounce the use of force in achieving that goal.[81] That fall, negotiations began under an arrangement that placed the issue of sovereignty under an umbrella and placing it to one side, so other issues important to both parties, such as fishing rights and economic cooperation, could be resolved.[82]

Negotiations in Madrid between October 1989 and February 1990 reestablished consular relations as a step toward resuming diplomatic relations, and direct air and sea links between Great Britain and Argentina resumed. As a result of these high-level negotiations, Argentina lifted financial and bureaucratic restrictions on British companies, and the United Kingdom opened the 150-mile protection zone around the islands to Argentine fishing vessels and permitted military ships and planes to enter the area with advance notification.[83] Both sides also agreed to provide advance notice of military maneuvers in the area surrounding the islands and off the coast of Argentina.[84] After this agreement, the two nations publicly restored full diplomatic relations in March 1990.[85]

Following this reconciliation event the relationship was characterized by a mix of positive and negative interactions. Decisions to allow visitation by families of Argentine soldiers buried on the islands received a mixed response from islanders,[86] as did a later decision to allow Argentine tourists to visit.[87] The Argentine constitution of 1994 proclaimed that the islands belonged to Argentina, a concept taught to the country's schoolchildren. Immediately after the reconciliation event, trade between the countries grew rapidly, although in 1991 it was only one-tenth of the level before the conflict.[88] Military-to-military courtesy calls began again in 1994, and in 1995, Great Britain and Argentina set up a joint commission to handle issues regarding oil exploration in the waters surrounding the islands.[89]

Hopes for an improved relationship increased when Menem announced that he would visit England in 1998. During his visit, Menem laid a wreath of flowers at a monument to fallen soldiers of the war, expressed "regret" over the war, and held high-level and generally positive discussions with British Prime Minister Tony Blair and the Queen. The visit was marred, however, by an argument over whether or not an article released by Menem was an apology for the war.[90] Both sides noted that they would continue to agree to disagree about the islands' sovereignty.

Menem's visit concluded with plans for growing British investment in Argentina's recovering economy and expanding bilateral trade. In 1998, the U.K. and Argentine defense ministers signed a memorandum of understanding and, in 1999, Great Britain relaxed its arms embargo against Argentina, permitting sales on a case-by-case basis. That year, the two countries negotiated an agreement to allow Argentine tourists to visit the islands, although the requirement that they travel with passports continues to upset the Argentines.

The reconciliation event is missing most features of the signaling or forgiveness models necessary for a substantial improvement in long-term relations. Regarding the signaling model, by leaving the sovereignty issue outside the negotiations, the event was not particularly costly to either side. Similarly, the movement to reestablish relations was not novel, as months of negotiations preceded the final act, and restoration of diplomatic relations had been expected for nearly a year.[91] Negotiations were largely voluntary, but were not irrevocable, proceeding instead in a highly contingent manner.[92] In sum, the reconciliation event lacked many factors that make signaling successful.

Similarly, it lacked most features required under the forgiveness model. Initially, there was no public truth telling or recognition of harm. Neither side admitted to having made a mistake, nor did either press for a public reading of the events of the war.[93] Limited justice was abandoned as both sides decided in October 1989 that "neither would pursue claims for loss or damage against the other."[94] Regarding a change in identity, the two countries have moved away from wartime enmity toward normal trade and diplomacy that existed before the war. The transformation of the Argentine government from the wartime junta of the Falklands/Malvinas war to a civilian democracy contributed to changed relations for the better. With regard to islanders and the Argentines, little has changed in their identities. The islanders view the Argentines as invaders and with suspicion. Argentines maintain that the islands are a legitimate part of their territory, although their leaders have attempted to reduce the islanders' antipathy.[95]

The figure representing the relationship between the nations before and after the reconciliation event shows no visual evidence of improvement. The countries became closer economic partners after the reconciliation, and stronger connections resulted when they lifted exclusions and bans. However, their relationship is still hindered by their contradictory stances on the issue of sovereignty. The issue is still debated in committees of the U.K., and Argentina expresses its claim to sovereignty regularly.[96]

Cambodia–Vietnam

Cambodia's history is dominated by the desire of its people to maintain independence against foreign intervention and the inability of its government to secure it. Cambodia's historical relationship with Vietnam can be summarized as one of shared antagonism over issues of territory and identity.

For example, when Cambodia was a protectorate of France, the French encouraged Vietnamese immigration into the country the better to exploit its commercial and agricultural potential.[97] As Vietnamese and Chinese minorities gained superior positions in Cambodia, the largely agrarian Khmer majority developed an anti-West, anti-Vietnamese bias and an extreme self-reliant attitude, reflected in the rise of several proindependence factions within the government.[98]

With the defeat of Japan at the end of the Second World War, British-led Allied land forces arrived in Phnom Penh to take control of Japanese forces and impose external authority over the country. A brief taste of independence the Cambodians experienced in 1945 further strengthened the resolve of various internal factions to fight against a return to colonialism.

Vietnamese-led forces spearheaded an Indo–Chinese resistance movement against the French force struggling to regain their lost territories. They also operated in Cambodia and Laos. France and North Vietnam fought in the east of Cambodia, and a Thai-sponsored Free Khmer guerrilla movement set up a government in exile in the west. The two nationalist factions eventually combined forces to try to oust both King Sihanouk and the French.

In 1954, the Vietnamese Communists advanced from Laos to invade parts of Cambodia. Cambodia then became embroiled in a military conflict that engulfed the whole region as North Vietnamese Communist forces used Cambodia and Laos as staging areas for their war against South Vietnam. To protect Cambodian sovereignty, Sihanouk made an arrangement with North Vietnam to support the Viet Cong but projected an overall nonaligned role for his country. Despite these measures, Cambodian civil unrest increased, and a young dissident named Saloth Sar (later Pol Pot) gained control of the radical wing of the Kampuchean or Khmer Communist party and went underground with attacks against the Cambodian government in the early 1960s.

In 1970, a new Khmer Republic government under Lon Nol proceeded to fan anti-Vietnamese sentiment among the rural Khmer population and called for the ouster of the Viet Cong from Cambodia. Paradoxically, a United States and South Vietnamese offensive against the Viet Cong shortly thereafter drove the Viet Cong units farther inland instead of forcing them off Cambodian territory. There they encountered ineffectual Cambodian forces and swept them away.

North Vietnam undertook training of the Khmer Rouge guerrillas and temporarily assumed the burden of keeping Khmer Republic forces at bay. By 1973, the Khmer Rouge (an extreme arm of the Khmer Communist party) was able to conduct military strikes against Phnom Penh by itself.

By 1975, Sar, now Pol Pot, led the Khmer Rouge into a full-scale offensive against the Phnom Penh government. On wresting control over the government, he pursued Cambodian self-sufficiency through accelerated agricultural production and forced labor. The purges, atrocities, malnourishment, and overwork of the rural Cambodian populace under the Khmer Rouge led to the deaths of between 1 and 3 million people. The regime's xenophobia also led to further animosity toward the Vietnamese, a relationship already inflamed by frequent cross-border transgressions by both parties. While the Khmer Rouge felt compelled to combat what they considered territorial violations by Hanoi, the North Vietnamese were losing patience with having to commit larger and larger units to defending the border.

Historic resentment between the nations was further heightened when the Vietnamese government began to take note of the atrocities against civilians committed by the Khmer Rouge, especially when ethnic Vietnamese in Cambodia became targets. Some were forced into labor camps and barbed wire compounds. Many were reportedly "killed in the crossfire." The Cambodian government, fueled by the people's anger toward Vietnam, eventually instituted a pogrom in which thousands of civilians were massacred by Cambodian soldiers, police, and civilians. The government in Saigon pleaded with the government of Cambodia and the international community for repatriation of ethnic Vietnamese and intervention in the atrocities. Eventually, the Cambodian government, faced with international pressure, relented by evacuating 190,000 Vietnamese Cambodians to Vietnam. The Vietnamese, in turn, exacted random revenge for the massacres by torturing and executing Cambodian citizens under their control.[99]

In late 1978, Hanoi decided to mount a punitive expedition to Cambodia. To legitimize this incursion, the Vietnamese sponsored the establishment of an anti-Pol Pot movement called the Kampuchean (or Khmer)

National United Front for National Salvation, made up of fugitive Cambodians fleeing the Khmer Rouge. The attack was successful in dislodging Pol Pot's forces, and Phnom Penh fell in January 1979. The Khmer Rouge was not defeated, however. It retreated to its bases of power in the countryside and began an insurgency.

The Vietnamese occupied Cambodia for ten years despite international pressure. Eventually, changing international political conditions, including international pressure and sanctions on both countries, and the collapse of the USSR (Hanoi's benefactor) led Hanoi to consider compromise and withdrawal from Cambodia. Such a compromise required, in turn, that China and Vietnam end their proxy war in Cambodia and develop an acceptable solution to an interim government after Vietnamese withdrawal. The Vietnamese refused to leave until the Cambodian government agreed to exclude the Khmer Rouge from future political participation, which the Cambodians refused to do on the basis of the Khmer Rouge's considerable political support.

At the prompting of Indonesian leaders, in July 1988, heads of the warring Cambodian factions and of Vietnam met face to face and agreed to extend their meetings for "as long as it takes" to reach a solution to the issues of Vietnamese withdrawal and an interim government.[100] Vietnam had already agreed to withdraw 50,000 troops by the end of the year and pulled its military command staff from Phnom Penh in June. In 1989, it agreed to final withdrawal of its troops.[101]

A peace treaty was finally signed in October 1991. This reconciliation event allowed the Khmer Rouge to play a limited role in Cambodia's political structure. The quadripartite government allowed all major warring factions as well as Vietnamese-supported leaders a say in the future of Cambodian politics. This arrangement was obviously unsatisfactory to the millions of surviving victims of Pol Pot's atrocities as well as the Vietnamese, for it threatened to undermine the stability of all other arrangements, with the prospect of the Khmer Rouge returning to power.[102]

Neither the border issue nor the issue of the ethnic Vietnamese has been settled to either country's satisfaction, but the Vietnamese are hopeful that Cambodia's entry into ASEAN in 1997 would give the two nations a forum for diplomacy rather than hostile actions.[103] The United Nations recommended creating an international tribunal for the perpetrators of genocide but gave no specific recommendation as to what form this judicial process should take. Far from hailing Vietnam as their rescuers, many Cambodians suspect that Vietnam masterminded the Pol Pot genocide. The U.N. suggested a truth commission in Cambodia as well, but the Cambodian government has been unwilling to reopen that chapter of their history, so the truth remains untold and the perpetrators remain unpunished.[104]

Postreconciliation relations between the nations are cautious, formal, and wary. As recently as June 1999, Vietnam's Secretary General Le Kha Phieu paid a state visit to Phnom Penh aimed at reducing tensions between the countries and finding solutions to immigration and border issues, but the visit was plagued by anti-Vietnamese protests.[105] Although the countries signed a peace treaty in Paris, it failed to stabilize Cambodian politics or address the major issues of contention between Vietnam and Cambodia—the border dispute and treatment of ethnic Vietnamese in Cambodia.

Concerning the two contending hypotheses, this case corresponds more closely to the signaling model. The Paris accords generally lacked costly commitments, except perhaps Vietnam's willingness to accept a power-sharing arrangement that included participation by the Khmer Rouge. Concessions made were the product of substantial external pressure and were not irrevocable. It is not surprising, therefore, that little improvement in bilateral relations has occurred, as the negotiations neither fulfill the requirements of a costly bargain nor reflect any elements of forgiveness.

El Salvador–Honduras

El Salvador and Honduras were both colonies of Spain beginning in the early 1500s, and later members of the Central American Federation established in 1824 with Guatemala, Nicaragua, Mexico, and Costa Rica. By the 1860s, El Salvador's Liberal Party, in close collaboration with powerful plantation families, came to power and ruled the country for seventy years. This arrangement ended with the worldwide depression of the 1930s. A coup installed General Maximiliano Hernandez Martinez as president in 1931, beginning a succession of military governments that controlled the nation through 1979.

Honduras, fully independent since 1838, has had a stormy history of civilian, strongman, and military governments punctuated by United

States intervention in the early part of the twentieth century. At the time of the war with El Salvador, a military government headed by Colonel Osvaldo Lopez Arellano controlled Honduras.

The war of 1969 revolved around a long-standing border·dispute.[106] Hondurans also resented what they perceived as an inequitable distribution of trade benefits under the Central American Common Market (CACM) of which both countries were members. The most critical issue was the 300,000 Salvadorans who had migrated to Honduras in search of land or jobs and who, in 1969, found themselves threatened by an involuntary repatriation program begun by the Honduran government.[107]

The pattern of Salvadoran emigration to Honduras in search of land and employment led to increased pressures on the Honduran government by peasant organizations to enforce the 1962 Agrarian Reform Bill that called for repatriation of lands to Hondurans and a reversal in migration patterns. Adding to bilateral tensions, the ruling Honduran Nationalist Party tolerated vigilante tactics in evicting Salvadorans from land and stoked the anti-Salvadoran mood that prevailed throughout the country by the late 1960s. When El Salvador won a World Cup soccer match against Honduras in San Salvador, the mood worsened and thousands more Salvadorans were evicted from Honduras, thus destabilizing the political situation in El Salvador.[108]

El Salvador responded by sealing its borders with Honduras, hoping to force Honduras to resettle the migrant Salvadorans. The policy failed, and, spurred by reports of mistreatment of refugees, the Salvadoran government opened hostilities on July 14, 1969, sending troops into Honduras to "defend the human rights of their countrymen." The countries broke diplomatic relations, and hostilities lasted for four days.[109] El Salvador's goal was to capture territory quickly and use it as a negotiating tool. The Honduran armed forces held their own, however, as the conflict galvanized them in defense of their territory.

A cease-fire took effect on July 18, but El Salvador continued actions until the Organization of American States (OAS) threatened economic sanctions against the country unless fighting ceased. The brief war cost several thousand lives.

At the end of January 1970, tensions along the Honduran border again erupted into large-scale fighting. Honduras claimed that the Salvadoran army had attacked border villages. The OAS began talks with both sides in Washington, but these collapsed by May. There were additional clashes in 1971 and 1972. Newly elected governments in 1972, however, created an opportunity for renewed efforts for peace. A secret meeting between foreign ministers of the two countries produced an eight-point agenda for resolution of the conflict, but these negotiations also broke down in December 1972 over the issue of the boundary line. Sporadic fighting continued until 1976 when a series of violent incidents alarmed both sides, compelling the foreign ministers to meet in July of that year. On August 9, the two sides agreed to the Act of Managua that called for demilitarization of areas of conflict along the border. By the end of the decade, the borders had been reopened and Hondurans could move freely between the countries, but no Salvadorans could recross the border into Honduras.

In 1978, the two countries accepted a mediation effort by the International Court of Justice (ICJ) under the guidance of Jose Luis Busta-monte.[110] The mediation proceeded in fits and starts because of different conceptions of the scope of a treaty (Honduras favored a comprehensive solution that would resolve the border dispute, El Salvador was willing to leave the border issue for later) and because of the civil war in El Salvador. Nonetheless, by October 1980, the two sides successfully negotiated and quickly ratified a treaty. They were urged on by the United States, which was concerned about the occupation of demilitarized zones on the border by Salvadoran guerrillas. The treaty left the border to be defined at a later date.

Bustamonte insisted that both countries put aside their remaining differences and make a gesture of reconciliation. The reconciliation ceremony took place at the government palace in Lima, Peru, with high representatives from El Salvador and Honduras and several foreign ministers of the OAS. The two countries agreed to a joint commission to resolve the border dispute, reopen diplomatic consular missions, open border traffic, and maintain nonaggression in future relations. They also committed to revitalizing the CACM and to remilitarizing disputed pockets of territory. Both governments wanted to eradicate these areas as they were sanctuaries for Salvadoran guerrillas.[111]

In September 1992, the ICJ awarded most of the disputed border territory to Honduras.[112] In January 1998, the countries signed a border demarcation treaty that would implement the terms of the court's decree.

The treaty awaits ratification in both countries. To date, Honduras and El Salvador maintain normal diplomatic relations, but relations after the reconciliation event of 1980 have not substantially improved.

Recall that the events data picture for this case also offered little evidence of improvement in bilateral relations subsequent to the reconciliation event. El Salvador–Honduras is a case that adheres closely to a rational, negotiated bargain between actors. Although a settlement was negotiated, the process lacked successful elements posited in the signaling hypothesis. The negotiations and agreement were not especially costly to the parties, nor did they expose either country to significant vulnerabilities. Similarly, the agreement was not wholly voluntary, as both parties faced considerable pressure from the United States and other OAS members to find a negotiated solution. The agreement was not a surprise or a novel endeavor either, as it had been an effort that continued for a decade. Finally, it was not irrevocable, as it did not include the critical issue of land disputes at the border. Instead, it rested on a narrow base of shared interests: a desire for improved trade between the countries and among members of the CACM, and an attempt on the part of both governments to eradicate guerrilla strongholds in areas along the disputed border.

There is scant evidence of forgiveness in this case. Neither side acknowledged culpability for the war or sought to uncover the truth behind allegations and counter-allegations associated with the war. Honduras secured a measure of justice from the ICJ regarding the land dispute. Although bitterness between the countries subsided after the war as each was preoccupied with its own political stability during a time of regional upheaval, identities did not substantially change. The call for reconciliation and new relations was both superficial and largely coerced.

Findings

This brief review of international conflicts, reconciliation events, and outcomes leads to very different findings from those suggested by the civil conflicts. In the civil conflict cases the forgiveness model provided a strong explanation for why and how reconciliations succeed or fail. Specifically, when the belligerents underwent a process of national forgiveness characterized by truth telling, redefinition of identities, limited justice, and a call for a new relationship, they restored lasting social order. Parties that entered into a negotiated bargain only (even if the conditions for effective signaling were met) did not restore enduring domestic peace.

At the start of this chapter we posed the question, "does the process of societal forgiveness or costly signaling hypothesized in chapter 1 extend to explanations of postconflict reduction *between* states?" In light of the case studies above, the answer appears to be no and yes. No, in that there is scant evidence of forgiveness operating as a conflict resolution process in international society. Yes, in that international reconciliation events can be a powerful signal in a negotiated bargain that leads to improvement in bilateral relations. As predicted by the rational choice signaling model, in every case in which the reconciliation signals were costly, novel, voluntary, and irrevocable, the negotiated bargain resulted in substantially improved relations. In three of the four cases in which the signals met none of those criteria, however, no substantial improvement in relations occurred.

These results suggest that the role of reconciliation events as a means for conflict resolution is substantially different between nations than it is within nations. Factors associated with forgiveness that act to restore order in civil conflict cases are largely absent in international cases. Yet, unlike the civil conflict cases, negotiated bargains *can* work to restore order between nations when reconciliation events constitute effective signals of a desire for improved relations by their costly, novel, voluntary, and irrevocable nature.

What accounts for this marked difference in the role of reconciliation events between civil and international conflicts? A broader look reveals some crucial features.

Absence of Forgiveness Factors

The international cases suggest that national actors lack the motivation and mechanisms that would allow for exploration of truth; expeditious redefinition of the actors' identities through legal, constitutional, or institutional means; or application of limited justice. Table 3.1 summarizes the presence or absence of forgiveness factors in the eight cases. Although the parties may have called for a new relationship rhetorically, they generally did not take the difficult steps of forgiveness through public truth telling, redefinition of identities, or limited justice.

Table 3.1
Presence of Forgiveness Factors and Outcome

Country Dyads	Public Truth Telling or Acknowledgment	Redefinition of Identities	Partial Justice	Call for a New Relationship	Outcome
USSR–West Germany	No	No	No	Yes	Improved relations
India–China	No	No	No	Yes	Improved relations
Egypt–Israel	Partial	No	No	Yes	Improved relations
China–Vietnam	No	No	No	Yes	Improved relations
Poland–West Germany	Yes	No	No	Yes	Improved relations
U.K.–Argentina	No	No	No	No	No substantial improvement
Cambodia–Vietnam	No	No	No	No	No substantial improvement
Honduras–El Salvador	No	No	Yes	No	No substantial improvement

There are some limited exceptions to this rule. Two cases, Poland–West Germany and Egypt–Israel, evidenced some public truth telling through a dramatic act of acknowledgment by one of the national leaders. Even in those cases, however, no systematic investigation of the war or determination of culpability for acts committed during the war followed the initial gesture.

A fundamental redefinition of identities was lacking in virtually all of the cases, although Poland and Germany have inched toward such a transformation. Often, identity change was limited by the dictates of overriding regional or international roles of the conflicting parties. For example, the competition for influence over Cambodia between China and Vietnam or for regional supremacy between India and China limited the extent of potential cooperation.

The Honduran–Salvadoran dispute had a measure of justice. The OAS threatened sanctions against El Salvador for failure to comply with terms of a cease-fire, and the ICJ resolved certain territorial disputes in favor of Honduras.

At most, in some cases an element of forgiveness may have contributed indirectly to a successful bargain leading to a pattern of improved relations between belligerents. For example, Brandt used the tool of public acknowledgment and apology (the initial step in truth telling) to underscore the costly, novel, and credible nature of his commitment to improved German–Polish relations. Sadat's dramatic address to the Israeli Knesset produced a similar effect. Both of these important symbolic acknowledgments of harm took place at the beginning of the reconciliation process, much like the civil conflict cases. We can assume that they performed a similar function too, that is, to open a space for the possibility of additional steps toward reconciliation. As noted, however, these gestures did not become part of an extensive truth-telling process or become part of a larger forgiveness procedure.

In these two examples and in the other international cases, there was insufficient motivation, inadequate mechanisms, or insurmountable obstacles for a sustained and constructive exploration of the truth, redefinition of the actors' identities, and resolution of guilt and the application of limited justice. With regard to motivation, it is revealing, perhaps, that all but one of the international cases (U.K.–Argentina) that emerged from our survey as including a reconciliation event involved nations that are geographically contiguous. In addition, in all cases, territory and border disputes were important causes of war. These observations imply that only nations that must share space with another nation, much like groups within a national territory, even attempt to reconcile. The sense of shared society or affinity that exists within a country is much more limited in international society. It appears that a natural affinity does not yet extend to people of all nations as Darwin hoped, at least not enough to permit forgiveness to operate. Although bordering nations often share space, the intensity of the contact is less than that of groups within nations, and they may move at a much more protracted pace in addressing borderland disputes. As the El Salvador–Honduras case suggests, domestic concerns take precedence over international disputes, which can linger unresolved for decades as internal affairs become priorities.

Concerning mechanisms for reconciliation, this study suggests that international society, although a society of sorts, is not the kind that prevails in most nations, even those that temporarily resemble international anarchy during civil war. International society is qualitatively different from national society in its institutional and legal structures. Its institutional and legal shortcomings may make the pursuit of truth and justice largely unavailable to international belligerents. For example, the Vietnamese had nowhere to turn to get to the truth about the genocidal activities of the Pol Pot regime or to seek redress for Vietnamese citizens in Cambodia who suffered at the hands of that regime. Both realist and idealist interpreters of international relations can find solace in this finding. For realists, it confirms the distinctive institutional anarchy of international relations. For idealists, lack of institutions to secure some measure of truth and justice and the utility of these processes in resolving conflict at the national level point to the need for new institutions to resolve international conflicts; an international criminal court, for example.

Belligerents' identities evolved over time in international cases, but lacking the need to redefine themselves formally in a new or amended constitution, and having fewer legal and institutional forums for their role redefinition generally, this process appeared to occur extremely slowly, if at all. In the German–Polish case, the long-time aggressor and victim are only now, after more than fifty years, about to embark on relationship as partners and peers through institutions such as NATO and the legal and institutional framework of the European Union. Although not a case study here, the Franco–German relationship in the last half of the twentieth century also illustrates both the possibility and the protracted nature of identity redefinition between nations formerly engaged in war. Furthermore, comparison between Germany's postwar relations with its former European adversaries and Japan's relationship with its Asian adversaries suggest that acknowledgment of harm and attempts at atonement may be important aspects of the painstaking process of redefining identities.

Obstacles facing national and international belligerents may be somewhat different also. For subnational belligerents, the intimacy and inescapability of the relationship appear to create, simultaneously, a barrier and an impetus to settlement because of the actors' intense vulnerability. Paradoxically, perhaps, civil war disputants may find it both more difficult to negotiate a settlement through sending costly and credible signals and more necessary and possible to forgive as a way out of conflict, compared with international, disputes. Barbara Walter identified what may be a critical deterrent to a negotiated solution to civil conflicts—the ability to make credible commitments. She maintains "that civil war negotiations rarely end in successful peace settlements because credible guarantees on the terms of the settlement are almost impossible to arrange by the combatants."[113] Ultimately, negotiations fail because the adversaries cannot maintain their independent armed forces, and they face unacceptable vulnerability if they lay down their weapons at a time of great uncertainty. Walter stated:

In the end, negotiated settlements in civil wars perish under their own unique demands. Incumbent governments and rebels cannot structure the agreement so that it will, at worst, allow each side to return as close as possible to the status quo should one party decide to cheat. And as long as both factions understand that cooperation will leave them vulnerable and they have no means to avoid this condition, they will prefer to continue fighting rather than risk possible attack.[114]

Yet, as chapter 2 suggests, at the same time, civil war combatants, because of the longevity, intimacy, vulnerability, and inescapability associated with the relationship, may have greater motivation and preexisting institutional mechanisms to forgive as a means of settlement. Our case studies suggest that the step-by-step process of forgiveness can overcome the acute cooperation dilemma in this situation precisely because of the shared sense of society and desire for affinity.

Nation-to-nation reconciliation was often obstructed because it was embedded in a larger international context that included third-party allies and adversaries, systemic features, and because of civil conflicts within the nations. Third-party nations were important in nearly all the cases; for example, Russia's role in the India–China relationship and China's role in the Cambodian–Vietnamese conflict. International system constraints were most evident in the Cold War cases of the USSR–West Germany and Poland–West Germany. Furthermore, both of those cases and the El Salvador–Honduras and Cambodia–Vietnam cases illustrate that internal conflict or division within one of the parties to a bilateral relationship often complicates and constrains the process of reconciliation. Analogous problems exist in some participants to civil conflict reconciliation. For example, the civil war in El Salvador was influenced by the wider conflict in the region and the intervention of the United States. Also, many civil conflict cases face factional infighting within the ranks of one of the parties. But the subnational and supranational stresses were less ubiquitous than in the bilateral disputes.

The Relevance of Reconciliation Events as a Costly Signal in International Disputes

Although the forgiveness model does little to explain the outcome of international cases, the rational choice, signaling model is useful in identifying which reconciliation events are likely to lead to improvement in bilateral relations. Table 3.2 summarizes the presence or absence of those factors and the actual outcome in each case.

In cases in which reconciliation was a costly, novel, voluntary, and irrevocable signal, relations substantially improved after the reconciliation event. Similarly, with only one exception, when the signaling process was *not* marked by such actions, relations showed little or no substantial improvement. The one exception is China–Vietnam, where commitments failed to meet all the tests for an effective bargain, yet the two parties appear, thus far, to have established a better relationship. The caveat is that only a relatively short period of time has transpired since the reconciliation event. The fact that costly commitments were not made and that underlying issues remain unresolved suggest that improvement in relations between these countries should be closely watched for future stresses.

In sum, international conflict case studies support the relevance of the rational, signal-sending, bargaining explanation for why and when

Table 3.2
Presence of Signaling Factors and Outcomes

Country Dyads	Costliness/ Vulnerability	Novelty	Voluntary	Irrevocable/ Noncontingent	Outcome
USSR–West Germany	Yes	Yes	Yes	Yes	Improved relations
India–China	Yes	Yes	Yes	No	Improved relations
Egypt–Israel	Yes	Yes	Yes	Yes	Improved relations
China–Vietnam	Yes	No	Yes	No	Improved relations
Poland–West Germany	Yes	Yes	Yes	Yes	Improved relations
U.K.–Argentina	No	No	Yes	No	No substantial improvement
Cambodia–Vietnam	No	No	No	No	No substantial improvement
Honduras–El Salvador	No	No	No	No	No substantial improvement

reconciliation events lead to improvement in postwar relations in some, but not all, instances.

Why are international reconciliation events likely to be part of an effective bargaining process and not part of a forgiveness process? Ironically, perhaps, the less intimate, more arms'-length negotiations between, as opposed to within, nations reduce the immediacy of the vulnerability the parties face and thus make credible commitments in an international environment *easier* to secure than in civil conflicts. Commitment problems facing disputants may be more surmountable because the parties are more distant and, although international war raises the passions at one level,[115] it does not compel the parties to share one space with one military force. Therefore, conflicts between nations are more likely to overcome the cooperation-commitment problem necessary to move from belligerency to normal relations through negotiated settlement. On the other hand, lack of intimacy and inescapability in the relationship and dearth of international legal and institutional means for conflict resolution undercut motivations and reduce the mechanisms available for forgiveness to operate meaningfully in international disputes, except in a diluted and deliberate fashion.

Conclusion

These case studies and findings add fuel to the fire of the debate among international relations scholars over the existence, robustness, and potential of international society. For realists, the very different role of reconciliation events between national and international disputants and the lack of motivations and mechanisms for the operation of forgiveness at the international level confirm their belief in the existence of an international system, rather than society. For proponents of international society, the cases and findings of this chapter suggest that elements of society exist in both settings, but are generally far weaker or more immature at the international level. Idealists, in turn, can take heart in the power of forgiveness at the level of civil conflict and extrapolate its institutional and legal mechanisms for truth telling, justice, and actor redefinition of self and other to the international level where, presumably, one day, it will operate to reduce conflict. In short, the debate about international society is stimulated but not swayed by the findings in this chapter.

More important, one can see that the significance of reconciliation events extends to international relations, although for different reasons than in domestic national relations. Reconciliation events in international society often represent turning points in the relations of the belligerents. They are likely to constitute a meaningful signal of a desire for improved relations that breaks through past animosity and sets the stage for better future relations when they are costly, novel, voluntary, and irrevocable. This outcome is markedly different from civil conflict cases in which reconciliation events succeeded in reducing conflict, not because they operated as an effective signal in a negotiated bargain, but because they were part of the process of forgiveness characterized by truth telling, partial justice, and redefinition of identities.

4

Rethinking Rationality in Social Theory

Reason alone can never produce any action or give rise to volition. . . . Reason is, and ought to be, the slave of the passions, and can never pretend to any other office than to serve and obey them.[1]
—David Hume

A rational choice signaling model does a good job of explaining why and how international reconciliation events often, but not universally, lead to an improvement in relations between belligerents. We also saw in chapter 2, however, that this model failed to explain why and how reconciliation events produce a similar effect within countries. In civil conflict cases, a forgiveness model was more useful.

There is a reason rational choice cannot grasp the forgiveness process. Its foundational assumptions about what constitutes rational problem solving does not include the emotive dimension of the mind and of human behavior. For all its strengths and many uses, rational choice rests on a microfoundation that is, essentially, folk psychology. That is, it assumes, but does not examine, that the mind is a general-purpose, universally logical, problem-solving mechanism. The human mind allegedly applies the same rational processes to all problems. The origins of this marvelous apparatus and its actual structure and functions are not questioned. Furthermore, rationality is defined to include conscious reasoning processes only and to exclude emotion or emotional processes and any processes that take place outside conscious awareness. Indeed, emotion is seen as an impediment to rational decision making and problem solving.

In light of both the surprisingly strong fit between the forgiveness model and civil reconciliation cases and a wealth of recent research on the nature and operation of the mind in the natural sciences, this chapter suggests that it is time to examine those rational choice microfoundational assumptions. It is time to ask whether there is another way to think about the underlying assumptions of social theory that would allow rationality to include both emotion and cold-blooded calculation. To do so requires reaching beyond the discipline of political science to existing and emerging findings in biology and neuroscience.

Using a biologically based understanding of the human mind in place of general rationality assumptions offers certain advantages and disadvantages as an approach to social theory. Perhaps the greatest advantage of such a perspective is that it can include emotion in rationality rather than excluding it. As discussed below, an evolutionary, biological understanding of the mind (although itself beset with problems and challenges) integrates emotion and logic in a different, sometimes more useful, and more scientifically sound definition of rationality.

Returning emotion to rationality is not a panacea for social theory, however. This chapter, in addition to explaining how the natural sciences can help us overcome certain limitations of rational choice by integrating emotion with logic, also discusses how this biologically based microfoundation of the mind shares certain theoretical and methodological challenges with rational choice assumptions. It assesses the differences and possibility for effective partnership between this new perspective and social constructivism.

Finally, this chapter frankly assesses problems and perversions associated with bringing a biological dimension into social science theory. Many such attempts were deeply flawed and unquestionably dangerous when applied to policy. These failings are not *inherent* in the integration process, however. Rather, they stem from misapplication of biological ideas or disregard of cultural and social explanations. These failings warn us to tread carefully when applying natural science findings to social science. Conversely, however, rapid developments in neuroscience and biology make it problematic for social scientists to ignore developments in those fields and the relevance they may have for assumptions about rationality and human nature and the models and hypotheses that flow from such assumptions. Although social scientists must be extraordinarily careful in integrating other scientific insights into their work, the greater danger may be to continue to operate apart from, or contrary to, findings in other scientific disciplines.

Rethinking Rationality: Once More, with Emotion

As discussed in chapter 1, evolutionary psychology introduces the notion of specific rationalities or problem-solving circuitry in the human mind. This characterization is consistent with both the brain's evolutionary development and a growing body of scientific evidence that suggests modularity in the brain.[2] Equally important, an evolutionary perspective, unlike rational choice, allows for integration of emotion with reason in purposeful decision making and behavior. This inclusion is critically important because, we may, as shown in chapter 2, generate new models to explain important social puzzles and arrive at a more realistic understanding of human motivations that is consistent with an expanding body of knowledge in other scientific fields.

The Enlightenment is largely responsible for separating emotion and reason in our current understanding of the human mind. Drawing on classical Greek notions of a struggle within the mind between emotion and reason, philosophy made emotion inferior to logic. This alleged antagonism can be traced most directly to Cartesian dualism. Descartes saw reason as a specific manifestation of the human soul, whereas emotions were the expression of bodily processes we shared with animals. The goal of reason was to oppose and control emotion. Descartes also defined the mind's operations to include conscious thought only, thought of which we are aware.

By the start of the twentieth century, Charles Darwin, William James, and Sigmund Freud had suggested the possibility of holding emotion in rationality and expanding the realm of the mind's operation beyond conscious reasoning.[3] But, David Hume notwithstanding, these insights were largely ignored in philosophy, psychology, and social theory. Behaviorism and later cognitive science, both with exclusive emphasis on logic, dominated the field of psychology, and the Smithian notion of a rational utility maximizer prevailed in much of the social sciences. In international relations theory, "emotions virtually dropped from the radar screen" by the 1950s.[4]

At the start of the twenty-first century, rapprochement between cognition and emotion is again possible. Assisted by new technologies, such as functional neuroimaging and neural track tracing methods, questions of the interplay of emotion and logic in rationality are amenable to new forms of empirical research.[5] Although we stand on the near shore of these discoveries, results of much of this research suggest that emotion and logic are inextricably linked, and that appraisal can occur outside conscious awareness. Mounting evidence about the architecture, chemistry, and electrical pathways of the brain undermine the notion of separation of emotion and reason. Rather, as discussed below, recent research indicates that emotion and reason cooperate and that "cognition would be rudderless without the accompaniment of emotion, just as emotion would be primitive without the participation of cognition."[6] It appears that emotions assist reasoning in several distinctive and critical ways, especially in areas of personal and social matters involving risk and conflict. This assertion is not to maintain that emotion is somehow a substitute for reason, that excess emotions cannot lead to problems in making decisions, or that emotions govern our decision making. Instead, we suggest that growing evidence points to the likelihood that "well-tuned and deployed emotion . . . is necessary for the edifice of reason to operate properly."[7] Emotion and reason are not generally antagonistic; they are complementary, interactive systems of a problem-solving brain. Emotions may make us better problem solvers and generally more, not less, rational in the sense of identifying and securing our preferences. Furthermore, making decisions with emotions is not an unfortunate exception; it may be the rule.

Specifically, current research suggests that emotions, in the right measure, facilitate, and, indeed, may be necessary for rational decision making because they:

1. Give priorities to sensory data and sustain attention
2. Identify problems and preferences and create meaning
3. Motivate, direct, and accelerate strategic reasoning[8]
4. Help store and retrieve memories

Before discussing each of these functions in some detail, we explain briefly what emotions are in a biological sense and how they operate in the brain and body.

What Are Emotions?

Physiologically, emotions are dispositions to action.[9] They are part of the bioregulatory devices that enable us to survive.[10] Emotions are generated from biologically automated pathways in the brain. They are functions of our nervous system. They are complicated systems of chemical and neural responses in the brain and body whose physiological role is to anticipate and respond behaviorally to various, archetypal, life-challenging situations emanating from the environment. *External stimuli do not create emotions, per se;* rather they trigger neurophysiological processes in the brain.

Emotions have a profound influence over a person's behavior and mental activity by changing sensory, perceptual, and cognitive processing and by initiating a host of synchronized physiological tendencies that energize and guide behavior. "Emotion," said Antonio Damasio, "is about movement, about externalized behavior, about certain orchestrations of reactions to a given cause, within a given environment."[11] Indeed, the word "emotion" stems from the Latin verb *motere*, "to move," suggesting that action is implicit in every emotion.[12]

Neuroscientists usually distinguish between emotions and feelings. Feelings are our conscious thoughts about our emotions.[13] They consist of mental images arising from neural patterns that represent changes in body and brain that make up an emotion. Feelings alert us to problems our emotions have already begun to solve and they "extend the reach of emotions by facilitating the planning of novel and customized forms of adaptive response."[14] Unlike conscious awareness of our emotions (feelings), emotions are, for the most part, generated unconsciously. This distinction is important. For neuroscience, emotion is not merely a collection of thoughts about a situation; it is a biological process triggered by our environment that we might, or might not, consciously recognize as feelings.[15] Emotions can be defined by their neural attributes, not simply by descriptions of their external manifestations or our conscious awareness of them.

At the neural level, each emotion system consists of a set of inputs, an appraisal mechanism, and a set of physical and chemical outputs.[16] Some would add to these a fourth component in humans: conscious recognition of an emotional state in the brain and body (i.e., feelings). Emotions begin with a cognitive component: detecting certain input or trigger stimuli that are relevant to the functioning of the emotional network. The cognitive detection mechanism can also learn to respond to stimuli *associated with* natural triggers, so-called learned triggers. Both types of triggers elicit behavioral and physiological responses. The triggers can lead to the second component: a patterned, coherent action plan, or appraisal, useful in addressing such situations.[17] Third, emotions involve a somatic component: activation of the autonomic and central nervous systems with their visceral and musculoskeletal effects. It should be noted that a whole range of neurochemical and neuroanatomical processes is necessary to make emotions possible. Finally, emotions may include a subjective-experiential component: conscious awareness of a change in the body, or the feeling of an emotion.[18]

Although the human mind is capable of recognizing and describing subtle emotional states that reflect one's particular society and culture, so-called basic emotions may be universal. Some neuroscientists, psychologists, and biologists suggest that humans possess a suite of emotions that are expressed in a similar fashion, in the nature of the antecedent events that call them forth, and perhaps, in the appraisal process, across cultures.[19] Basic emotion theorists do not deny that emotions are labeled or expressed differently across cultures and among individuals within a culture. Simply, some emotions and their expressions are relatively constant in all persons. The exact number and terminology used to describe these universal emotions vary by study[20] but generally include joy (pleasure), fear, anger, and sadness. Each of these appears to be mediated by a separate neural system that has evolved for a particular reason. "The system we use to defend against danger is different from the one we use in procreation, and the feelings that result from activating these systems—fear and sexual pleasure—do not have a common origin."[21] We cannot be certain how many basic emotional systems exist in the brain, but neuroscience has identified several distinctive ones and their proximate locations and neural pathways.[22] The existence of several emotional systems rather than one should not be surprising. The brain, for example, does not have one system dedicated to perception. We see, hear, and smell through different visual, auditory, and olfactory systems. Each of these systems solves different sorts of perceptual problems, and similarly, each emotional system has a different functional purpose. As neuroscientist Joseph LeDoux concluded, "The most practical working hypothesis is that different classes of emotional behavior represent different kinds of functions that take care of different kinds of problems . . . and have different brain systems devoted to them."[23] Although distinctive in their neural pathways, emotions have numerous features in common that are useful to group together for this discussion.[24]

As adaptive mechanisms that help us deal with important events,[25] the function of emotions is twofold: to induce a specific reaction to a situation, and to regulate our internal state so that we can be prepared to act.[26] An emotional system, on detecting a significant event, narrows the range of response options available to a few—freeze, fly, or fight in response to a fear stimulus, for example. This link from appraisal to response is rapid, tightly coupled, and relatively automatic. These features contrast with brain systems involved primarily in reasoning, which are not as tightly coupled with response control systems. Cognitive reasoning follows the emotions, but it presents us with more choices and greater response flexibility.[27]

This difference makes good sense when you think about it. In a dangerous environment, time can be of the essence, and you may have to make split-second decisions; prolonged evaluation and contemplation could cost you your life. LeDoux argued that, in biological and evolutionary terms, emotions as such, are "the distillation of wisdom; the critical survival lessons of life hardwired into our DNA over evolutionary time. Humans have been biologically shaped to be fearful, sad, angry, and joyful. Emotions are a critical source of information for problem solving and learning," processes previously thought to be exclusively cognitive.[28] Emotions guide us in facing important, recurrent predicaments: reacting to potential physical danger, bonding with a mate, raising children, and, perhaps, settling societal disputes. Different emotions prepare us to act in efficacious ways to life's recurrent challenges.[29] "What," asked LeDoux, "is irrational about responding to danger with evolutionarily perfected reactions?"[30] Derailed emotions (those unmediated by reason) could be irrational and harmful, but emotions generally are an aid to rational decisions. Although we are aware of them by our conscious feelings, our emotions did not evolve as feelings; they evolved as behavioral and physiological responses controlled by our brain.[31]

This emotional appraisal and response system, although acting independently, rapidly, and largely unconsciously, also acts cooperatively with our cortex, the locus of our conscious reasoning processes. Emotions animate and inform our reasoning, which refines, strategizes, and sometimes vetoes the inputs of emotions. It appears that the thinking cortex creates greater response flexibility and prevents the inappropriate response more than it acts to initiate the appropriate response.[32] For example, our fear response may tell us to freeze while hiking when we suddenly discover a long slender object in our path, but our reasoning may tell us, on a moment's reflection, that the object is a stick not a snake, and that we need not flee, but can step safely over it. Our best current understanding is that emotional and rational appraisals are semiindependent but interconnected functions of the brain.

How Do Emotions Arise in the Brain-Body?

Paul MacLean used the concept of a "triune brain" as a didactic device for understanding the evolutionary progression of three strata in the brain.[33] In simple terms, the human brain was built in three stages: first, a primitive brain stem at the top of our spinal cord, which we share with all species that possess a central nervous system. Its role is to control basic life functions such as breathing and metabolism. From that stem emerged the brain's emotional centers, clustered in what is sometimes called the midbrain or limbic system (a misnomer because, as noted, it is not one system, but many). The emotional brain systems are localized and organized primarily *subcortically*, with strong links to the cortex and weaker feedback links from the cortex to these emotional regions. These regions include the brain stem, hypothalamus, amygdala, periaqueductal gray, and others. Millions of years later, our neocortex ("neo" because it evolved later), the so-called thinking brain, literally grew atop our emotional brain centers. An emotional brain existed long before higher reasoning developed. Thus the brain's emotional systems are interposed between basic regulatory devices and high reason.

How do emotions work? Typically, certain preset neural systems related to emotions send commands to other regions of the brain and throughout the body in reaction to an environmental trigger. The commands are sent out electrochemically along neural pathways that act on neurons,[34] muscle fibers, or organs and through the blood stream in the form of chemicals that act on our tissues' receptor cells.[35] The sum of these neural and chemical commands is a global change in our physical state and in the subsequent operations of our brain.[36] Although billions of neurons in the brain make trillions of connections, scientists have detected and traced very systematic patterns of interactions between neurons in various brain areas.[37] These natural patterns are the inner cause of behavior.

The neocortex adds conscious reasoning about external stimuli, including thoughts about emotions (feelings), the use of complex ideas, images, and symbols, and the ability to generate a range of possible responses to problems. These capabilities made enormous advancements in our ability to solve problems and to survive and flourish as a species. But they did not divorce us from our basic emotional repertoire and reactions and our emotional appraisal and problem-solving capabilities. Instead they enhanced and refined them.

Research on fear helps us see the interaction of emotion and reason. LeDoux found a dual neural path for fear stimuli, one cortical (involving the cortex) and one subcortical (focused in the emotive brain centers). Specifically, with regard to fear, the sensory thalamus activates the amygdala (a midbrain emotive center) at about the same time as it activates the cortex. In addition, this thalamic pathway is far faster than the linkage to the neocortex, permitting an emotional response to begin before the cortex can resolve completely what it is reacting to. Some sensory information will receive emotional priority before measured thinking takes place. Neural fibers from the amygdala activate the brain's sympathetic, autonomic system and release chemicals such as epinephrine, vasopressin, and cortisol. This potent chemical bath, in turn, immediately changes the way we think and feel.[38] These chemicals linger and dominate our system, often as moods or affective states.[39] This subcortical fear system allows the defense networks of the amygdala to influence attention, perception, and memory in situations posing danger.

LeDoux found that there are far more neural inputs from the amygdala into the cortex than the reverse, although information flows both ways. Thus, in responding to a fearful stimulus, mental design ensures that the impact of emotion on conscious reasoning will usually be greater than lesser. It is emotional stimuli that color and animate our thoughts. It is not easy for the cortex to shut off these influences. You can experience this set of priorities the next time a strong emotional response such as anger or fear is triggered. Note how difficult it is and how long it may take for cognitive messages to assuage these emotional appraisals and the physical states they create. Conversely, it is laborious to summon a strong emotional state through conscious thoughts about such emotions; that ability we associate with actors who move us.

This dual system, with greater speed and strength emanating from the emotional centers, makes evolutionary sense in a fearful situation: it permits rapid, if not fully thought-out responses. LeDoux surmised that this dual system is useful because "Failing to respond to danger is more costly than responding inappropriately to a benign stimulus."[40] But we are not limited to an emotional response. Our reason works on problems our emotions first identified and animated us to solve.

How Do Emotions Aid in Decision Making?

Emotions are not divorced from reasoning. They have important functions that are indisputably cognitive, related to activities such as attention, perception, planning, and memory.[41] It is important to appreciate their extensive involvement in these elements of rational decision making.

The Role of Emotion: Focusing Attention and Creating Meaning   Emotions help us give priorities to data from a universe of stimuli. They propel our attention, focusing and sustaining our concentration on selected stimuli relevant to our drives and goals.[42] In complex cognitive tasks, people often experience information overload and have to select a narrow subsample of the range of information available for further processing. Emotion helps us narrow our choices to significant aspects of our environment so that reason can operate selectively on a manageable task.[43] Emotionally significant data take priority, bumping mundane events out of awareness at an early, preattentive state of processing.[44] As Richard Lazarus explained, "emotions *focus attention* on some concerns and, by the same token, *distract attention* from other concerns."[45] The converse is not true, mere thoughts do not as easily displace emotions from awareness—"wishing that anxiety or depression would go away is usually not enough."[46] Hence, emotions significantly determine the focus of our attention.

Furthermore, emotions are one, nearly instantaneous, source of meaning; fear generated by the rapid approach of a large predator, even before the approaching object can be identified, for example. In ancient times, humans who responded appropriately with a fearful freezing and then flight or fight reaction probably had a much greater survival rate than those who waited for conscious appraisal and reason to guide their actions. Chemicals released in an emotional reaction carry an important, meaning-creating signal: they tell us "this is important," "pay attention," "keep this."[47] Emotions begin to create meaning and animate us, and set the motivational tone for the kinds of experiences we expect and seek. They communicate these intentions and expectations simply, efficiently, and accurately, despite their limited vocabulary relative to thought.

The Role of Emotion: Identifying Preferences and Directing the Selection of Strategies   As noted, the emotional meaning of a stimulus can be appraised by the brain's emotional circuitry before the perceptual systems have fully processed the stimulus. Strange as it might sound, the brain can begin to tell you something is good or bad, dangerous or desirable, before it is certain what that something is.

Emotions recognize challenges and opportunities in our environment, and they identify our preferences. Rational choice tells us that individuals pursue preferences logically, but it does not tell us, at an individual level, what preferences are or where they come from. This void exists because emotion is left out of the mix. Preferences begin as emotional reactions that can be formed with little conscious registration of the stimuli. Experiments by Robert Zajonc led him to conclude "affective judgments may be fairly independent of, and precede in time, the sorts of perceptual and cognitive operations commonly assumed to be the basis of affective judgments. Emotional reactions to stimuli are often the very first reactions of the organism. . . . [They] can occur without extensive perceptual and cognitive encoding, are made with greater confidence than cognitive judgments and can be made sooner."[48] This early emotional appraisal is gross and vague (approach-avoidance distinctions, for example), but it substantially influences ensuing cognitive processes. In short, thanks to our emotional circuitry, we may actually begin to know what we want before we know fully what that is.[49]

Emotions not only animate us and guide preferences; they also make devising strategies to achieve those preferences manageable, helping solve the dilemma of combinatorial explosion noted in chapter 1. Researchers have found that the prefrontal cortex—the area of the brain linked to planning, reasoning, and decision making—relies on matches between complex external stimuli *and* the emotional state associated with those stimuli (the somatosensory pattern) in making decisions. Specifically, the somatosensory pattern constrains the process of reasoning over multiple options and multiple future outcomes. Images of future examples are marked, and thus "qualified" or "judged" by the juxtaposed images of the somatic state. In complex decision making, this process greatly facilitates the operation of logical reasoning. So-called somatic markers allow certain option-outcome pairs to be rapidly endorsed or rejected, rendering the decision-making space more manageable for a subsequent cost-benefit analysis based on overtly logical reasoning. In situations with a high degree of uncertainty as to the future and/or the optimal course of action, constraints imposed by somatic markers allow individuals to decide within reasonable time intervals. This advantage would apply to many complex social situations and to the mental processing required for navigating them.[50] For patients with damage to their emotional centers and impaired somatic marking capability, response options and outcomes are more or less equal. Decision making in subjects unable to use their affective experience becomes extremely slow and laborious, limited to logical consideration over many potential alternatives, themselves lacking somatic markers. "As a result, decision making may fail to be timely, accurate, and propitious," or, lacking affective guidance, "it becomes random and impulsive."[51]

The Role of Emotion: Memory Storage and Retrieval   Emotions generally assist us in storing and retrieving memories required for making decisions. Memory is the creation of persistent change in the brain by a transitory stimulus. Most researchers believe the physical evidence of memory is stored as changes in neurons along specific pathways in the brain. Mechanisms through which memories of emotional significance are registered, stored, and retrieved are different from those through which cognitive memories of the same stimulus are processed and stored. The brain has many memory systems, each dedicated to a different kind of learning and memory function.[52] Numerous studies demonstrate that we tend to remember what is most emotionally laden because all emotional events receive preferential processing.[53] Our vernacular reflects these priorities when we speak of knowing (remembering) something by heart. Emotional events carry greater implications for an individual's sense of self and integrity than nonemotional or neutral events. It is no coincidence, therefore, that one often remembers an emotional experience vividly or in great detail. Many Americans, for example, inevitably know when and where they learned that President Kennedy had been shot.[54] Generally, the more intense the emotional arousal, the stronger the memory imprint.[55] This is not to suggest that emotional memories are flawless, only that certain core information, the gist of the event, and perhaps certain collateral details are likely to be imprinted and sustained in memory.[56]

Emotion and Logic Together

The idea of separation of logic and emotion is yielding to experimental facts pointing to the importance of emotional structures and processes as critical to reasoning.[57] Work by Antonio Damasio and others suggests that emotion is necessary to the proper function of our logical capabilities. Patients in whom the frontal lobe (the area of highest reasoning) is removed to extract an invasive tumor, generally recover well and retain their thinking skills as measured on standard tests of intelligence. In contrast, patients who had their amygdala (a seat of many emotional appraisals) removed fared far worse, losing the capacity for imagination, decision making, creativity, and emotional expression and nuance.[58] Although still capable of using the instruments of their rationality in logical applications, those with damage to their emotional centers repeatedly made irrational and disadvantageous personal and social decisions in situations involving risk and conflict.[59] Damasio concluded that "selected reduction of emotion is at least as prejudicial for rationality as excessive emotion," and "reason does not stand to benefit from operating without the leverage of emotion."[60]

In sum, separation of emotion from decision making and denigration of emotion as an impediment to reason are increasingly suspect as foundations for scientific social theory. Affective reactions are primary in philogeny (our brain's evolution) and in ontogeny; children express emotion long before they express the instruments of their reason.[61] Emotions were and are useful to our survival; thus, in biological terms, it is improbable that reason operates independently and without their aid. When some preexisting system is useful, evolution does not make it indirect or entirely dependent on a newly evolved capability. Rather, it is much more likely that our affective system allies with our later-evolving reasoning capabilities to carry out problem-solving functions jointly.[62] The neocortex and its profound reasoning ability open our emotional circuitry to alternative behavioral responses and conscious choices.[63] But, as David Hume suspected, these strategies serve an emotional master. Emotions are fast, effective guides to behavior that are part and parcel of what people think or do. Contrary to rational choice theory, Zajonc maintained, "people do not get married or divorced, commit murder or suicide, or lay down their lives for freedom upon a detailed cognitive analysis of the pros and cons of their actions."[64] Leaving emotion outside decision making makes little sense.

Moreover, leaving emotion out of rationality defies our human nature. As one pair of researchers from neuroscience and the humanities warned: "Nature is more ingenious than we are. And we stand to miss all that power and ingenuity unless we attend to neurobiological plausibility."[65] We suggest that it is plausible that a new model of rational decision making merging emotion and reason could result in useful social science hypotheses in some cases.

Commonalties of Rational Choice and Evolutionary Psychology

For better or worse, rational choice and evolutionary psychology have a great deal in common. Like rational choice approaches, a hypothesis grounded in evolutionary psychology is deductive and permits free interchange of human actors. Evolutionary approaches share with rational choice the scientific pursuit of patterns and probabilities in human interaction.

On the other hand, evolutionary approaches are less concerned than rational choice with applying equilibrium analysis to human interaction and more interested in identifying probabilities or frequencies of potential outcomes. The analogy would be to say evolutionary thinkers are more like geneticists and less like physicists. According to rational choice, social equilibria result when individuals choose an outcome they would not wish to depart from, given available information and choices of other actors. Unless such equilibria can be discovered, "law-like statements— from which predictive hypotheses are derived—cannot be developed."[66]

Without a specific equilibrium, rational choice models become indeterminate.[67] Evolutionary analysis is more comfortable with the possibility of multiple equilibria in interactions, searching for patterns and probable outcomes or paths rather than specifically correct predictions.

Although scientific in approach, an evolutionary perspective, by raising a new, biological dimension in explaining human behavior, may be less parsimonious than rational choice models.[68] Moreover, its application to social theorizing is new, and our understanding of the human mind is rudimentary. Thus an enormous amount of work is required to see what insights, if any, an evolutionary perspective can produce about how the nature of humans' adapted reasoning interacts with today's social and political environments. It is fair to ask, is the candle worth the contest?, especially given the legacy of past attempts to align social theory with developments in the natural sciences, an issue we consider later in this chapter. Below, we present several theoretical challenges that an evolutionary approach shares with rational choice models.

Theoretical Challenges Shared with Rational Choice: Explaining Altruism

Like rational choice, the assumptions of human motivation used in evolutionary psychology must wrestle with the dilemma of altruistic behavior despite the assumption of self-interested individuals. That is, evolutionary theory posits that organisms are selfish in a biological sense,[69] reproduction maximizers rather than rational choice's utility maximizers. If so, individuals should not perform any behaviors that are altruistic, that are for the good of other members of the species rather than for themselves.[70] An individual organism competes primarily with others of its own species for "scarce resources that are convertible into the ultimate currency of biological evolution: fitness—defined as reproductive success."[71] Natural selection favors selfish behavior because any truly altruistic act increases the recipient's reproductive success while lowering the donor's. If the organism is the exclusive unit of natural selection, then evolution should work against the development of altruism.[72] If cooperation generally entails some cost to the individual, how can we show that individuals might actually gain from cooperation rather than from unbridled self-interest?

The evolutionary perspective addresses this problem in several ways. Perhaps the dominant approaches are through concepts of inclusive fitness and reciprocity. Fitness, the ability to transfer one's genes to posterity, can sometimes be furthered not simply by mating or seizing resources that will make this possible, but by assisting others. William D. Hamilton pointed out that reproductive success must be expanded to include benefits to related organisms, close kin who share part of one's genetic makeup, discounted by their coefficient of relatedness. For Hamilton, the measure of reproductive success is described as "inclusive fitness," that is, reproductive success including both an individual and that individual's close kin.[73]

Work by Robert Axelrod and Hamilton,[74] Robert L. Trivers,[75] and others explains how, through the mechanism of reciprocity, this domain of cooperative relations might expand beyond kin to other individuals. Social cooperation can occur in cases of mutual benefit, such as those marked by reciprocity in relations. Thus, despite egoistic motivations, if cooperation by two or more organisms could be mutually beneficial, evolution might select for a capacity to make, in effect, cost-benefit calculations in social exchange.[76] Inclusive fitness and reciprocity provide some support for a countervailing tendency away from competition and toward cooperation that might have evolved in a species that experienced prolonged helplessness in infancy, poor defenses against predators, scarcity of food requiring cooperative hunting and food sharing, and similar environmental challenges.[77]

Theoretical Challenges Shared with Rational Choice: Reifying Collectives

Another shared difficulty is that evolutionary psychology and rational choice reify collectives; that is, they assume that group actions, like reconciliation, can be explained from assumptions about individuals' decision-making processes. Treating the polity as a unitary rational actor is widespread in international relations theory, for example.[78] In this study, both signaling and forgiveness models assume that subnational or national entities can be expected to behave like rational individuals (although they differ regarding the underlying assumptions about what constitutes rationality).

Both approaches treat large groups as unitary actors or assume that individuals ultimately make decisions for a larger group. But to the extent that one concludes that organizations, bureaucracies, cultures, societies, or nations have their own attributes, an aggregation problem arises in moving from individual choice to policy outcomes of larger groups. Generally, there are three broad critiques: rationality becomes bounded and imperfect as one moves from individual choice to organizational procedure[79]; personal choice may be dictated by external cultural norms; and individual agents are shaped by their institutional and societal settings, thereby altering preferences and choices.[80] Thus, it is legitimate to question whether rational choice and evolutionary psychology models of choice hold more relevance for individual rather than group behavior.

Rational choice theorists have wrestled with this dilemma and offered a number of useful but not wholly satisfying solutions. One approach suggests there is no way to build theory *other* than to reduce to individual choice. James M. Buchanan and Gordon Tullock, for example, held that collective action is only "the action of individuals when they choose to accomplish purposes collectively rather than individually."[81] Because groups, whether a family, society, or state, cannot have preferences, theorists *must* assume the existence of individual preference orderings and choice.[82] This does not fully solve the conundrum of explaining collective outcomes by reference to the maximizing actions of individuals, nor does it rebut the charge of reductionism in theorizing.

Several literatures attempt to fill the gap between the individual and the collective in explaining policy choice. To make the leap from individual to collective, some contend that organizations also operate rationally.[83] Indeed, some maintain that certain decisions can be made more efficiently by organizations rather than by individuals because of reduced transaction costs.[84] Others developed nonrational models of organizational or bureaucratic behavior. In foreign policy, Graham Allison's may be the best-known.[85]

This theoretic challenge clearly faces an attempt to explain reconciliation among groups. Forgiveness and reconciliation between political collectives is generally thought to require the active intervention of a principal, an authoritative deputy who represents the collectivity because, however real and powerful a collective entity, it cannot speak or act on its own. Such deputies, however, serve not only as autonomous individuals, as Buchanan and Tullock would have it, but as agents or emissaries of the larger group. By virtue of their institutional office or position, these individuals are both empowered to speak for the many and circumscribed by collective goals and interests. In affecting reconciliation, therefore, their role may be less a sincere expression of personal views and more public acknowledgment of the conflict, promise that similar acts will not be repeated (forsaking revenge), and commitment on behalf of the many to the future of the relationship. As such, the deputies embody collective decisions in part.

Nonetheless, Buchanan and Tullock and others raise a good point. In articulating and affecting the pattern of intergroup relations, leaders also have the power to shape the beliefs of the group they represent as part of an iterated process of change.[86] Furthermore, to the extent authoritative policy decisions are delegated to an individual or a relatively small elite, the assumption of individual rationality may be appropriate. In considering this question, Jack S. Levy conceded that the unitary rational actor model also applies to more pluralistic regimes on crisis issues "in which threats and interests are unambiguous."[87]

Our study cannot fully resolve the reification question. It can only acknowledge that both approaches must, at a minimum, recognize this feature, question its appropriateness to particular situations, and, at some point, develop better understanding of how theories of individual rationality translate into collective policy choice.

Theoretical Challenges Shared with Rational Choice: Falsifiability

Another problem of evolutionary psychology is that its motivational assumptions are not immediately falsifiable. If the mind is viewed as a final cause of behavior and its shape the product of an ancient evolutionary history, neither its particular effects nor its origin is directly visible.[88] Alexander Rosenberg stated that an evolutionary perspective on human behavior is silent on immediate or proximate causation. Particular behavior may be the result of intentions, socialization, conditioning, or deep psychological design. "The evolutionary perspective is that of ultimate causes . . . leav[ing] to others the proximate explanation of how the rule gets expressed and how it gets enforced from society to society."[89]

This critique is true, but it is equally valid as applied to the underlying assumptions of most broad deductive theories such as rational choice models. The motivational and behavioral assumptions of evolutionary psychology are merely a paradigmatic foundation for generating hypotheses in a scientifically consistent way; they are not, in themselves, an explanation for anything. Rather, like rational choice assumptions, evolutionary, biological theories of the mind are necessary to provide a complete explanation of social behavior and are not narrowly falsifiable.[90] Rosenberg's point is a good one because it reminds us that before an evolutionary paradigm bears fruit in explaining social phenomena, the hard work of generating useful models and hypotheses for important problems is required (including specifying the role of cultural and institutional variables). Tests must be devised and implemented, results must be assessed and reassessed, et cetera, all before one makes a claim of explanation.

Constructivism and a Biological Perspective: Common Ground?

A social constructivist viewpoint (one that explains phenomena by reference to social interactions) would appear to start from a very different vantage point than that of evolutionary psychology in searching for explanations. In the extreme, a constructivist explanation would maintain that society and societal phenomena, like the resolution of conflict through reconciliation, can be understood solely as *inter*subjective reality; that is, a product of social interaction. Similarly, emotions and behavior associated with them are social constructs, infinitely labile, learned, and reinforced through social discourse.[91] In contrast, evolutionary psychologists maintain that an important component of emotion and behavior is universal, biological, and *intra*subjective; that is, partially a function of biology. Unlike constructivists, evolutionary theorists assume a world of extant phenomena that presents organisms with certain cognitive challenges that must be understood to reproduce and survive. This perspective can accept the constructivist insight that human symbolic representation of reality is subjective and may be posed in alternative forms. Unlike constructivists, evolutionists would not go so far as to say that the structure of all phenomena is primarily or solely dependent on the cognitive system that developed it, that our thinking about material reality (including the mind) is necessarily transcendent to that reality. Rather, our thoughts, in part, are a response to certain material, environmental conditions and challenges facing the organism itself.

Neta C. Crawford's work on emotion and politics posits a balance between the approaches, noting that biological and constructivist explanations are not necessarily mutually exclusive. Instead, "biological, cognitive, and social constructivist approaches to emotion account for findings at different levels (cellular, behavioral, social, etc.) . . . no one theoretical approach will likely be able to account for the complex relationships between experience, perception, cognition, culture, and biology."[92] This ecumenical approach is laudable and workable.

To illustrate, our study places great emphasis on the role of identity and identity change as an essential component of forgiveness. Identity—"the state of being similar to some actors and different from others in a particular circumstance"[93]—is best understood as having both internal and external dimensions. It is possible, of course, to argue that identities are given and immutable or, alternatively, that they are constantly changing products of social interactions. But these extreme positions would do better to acknowledge that identities are both susceptible to social molding and, nonetheless, relatively stable. Identity is a tool for managing and organizing information about oneself and one's relationship to the environment. As such, it must be resistant to constant change to be internally cohesive and useful. At the same time, it must be susceptible to modification in reaction to its environment to be efficacious. Identity is shaped by internal cues such as perception and emotions and by environment and social artifacts such as roles, norms, and values. The interaction among these factors is extraordinarily complex.[94]

Similarly, emotions have a clear biological basis but are not limited to biology. Although the machinery for emotional appraisal is largely preset, inducers or triggers for emotional arousal are not part of it. Some emotional triggers are clearly the result of conditioning or learning. Most important, social and cultural environments strongly influence aspects of emotional *expression*. Environmental forces shape the cognition and behavior that follow deployment of emotion.[95]

Some Additional Cautions before Using an Evolutionary Perspective in Social Theory

Many problems of adding a biological, evolutionary perspective to social theory are the result of self-inflicted wounds. Adding a biological element to the study of politics has a dark history. As a result, this perspective is taboo in most social science and will typically provoke certain accusations that have to be acknowledged but are not, per se, a failing of the perspective, only its past applications.

Biological theories and concepts have been used from the midnineteenth century to the present in nefarious ways to promote or justify social pathologies such as colonialism, racism, and fascism. In the 1920s, for example, genetics was used to support racist immigration policies in the United States. The Nazis carried the notion of genetic superiority to its greatest extreme beginning in the 1930s with its eugenic programs of sterilization and extermination.[96] It is understandable that for the past fifty years social scientists have avoided the natural sciences in part because of the pseudo-certainty these approaches bestowed on several social evils. This experience encouraged social science to divorce itself from natural science. In anthropology the prevailing view is that humans are "cultural animals," with virtually all emphasis on culture and its variability[97] and little or no consideration of the animal with its patterned responses and universal characteristics.[98] The divorce from the natural sciences also prevails overwhelmingly in international relations theory, whether constructivist or rational-realist. The rational choice conception of the human mind as a blank slate composed of certain elemental drives and an ability to learn or think rationally is consistent with this separation of the natural and social worlds. Most social constructivists go even farther. In the extreme, they contend that emotions are solely the products of society, not biology.[99]

Thus, although the human organism clearly is not exempt from the evolutionary process, virtually all social scientists study humans as cut off from their biological inheritance. The resulting explanations for social behavior thus focus on the importance of culture, learning, institutions, language, and other human artifacts (although recent work questions humans' monopoly over some of these attributes). Evolutionary principles are seen as having minimal relevance to understanding the structure and operation of society (or culture). Social phenomena, therefore, can be understood from the outside in, as a product of changing environmental conditions or cultural factors. As for the possibility of an internal biological dimension to human motives or behavior, it is easier to avoid, deny, or assume it away because of historically based antipathies that it provokes.

We raise doubt as to whether, in divorcing itself from other scientific disciplines, political science may be missing important insights. It may be time to ask whether developments in understanding the mind from biology and neuroscience intrude on rational choice premises that the mind is an all-purpose logical calculator, or the constructivist assumption that social expressions are infinitely plastic. What if important patterns of human behavior, such as reconciliation, can, in some social-cultural settings, be better understood through hypotheses that draw on neuroscience findings of the constructive role of emotion in decision making and the patterned, evolved, specific problem-solving capabilities of the human mind? What if fears and misconceptions surrounding the implications of integrating biological notions into social science could be held at bay long enough to consider the relevance of such an approach? This requires rejecting several failings of those who attempted to raise biological factors in social explanations that we consider next.

Reductionism

Deriving social hypotheses consistent with modern biology should not be biologically reductionist. Integrating biological, behavioral, and social sciences in a consistent way should not imply reduction in the complexity of explanation through assimilation of one field by the other. Recognizing that evolutionary pressures may have sculpted our minds is not in itself a theory of psychology, much less one of politics. In fact, rather than reducing explanations, by tracing the principles of one field to those of another, additional principles may be suggested; in this case the model of reconciliation as forgiveness.[100] Suggesting an evolved component of human motives does not necessarily preclude or denigrate other cultural or social structural factors.[101] Attempts to link biology and social theory by Edward O. Wilson and other sociobiologists have often been criticized, perhaps correctly, for stressing the centrality of genetics in determining human social behavior.[102] Although efforts that included biological factors in social theory may be guilty of reductionism or genetic determinism, reductionism vulgarizes an approach that is willing to consider the possible relevance of those factors.

Whereas this approach does not imply a reduction in variables or disciplinary imperialism of the natural sciences, it also does not accept that all societal outcomes are equally possible (an interpretivist-constructivist approach) or that they are solely the subject of conscious, contemporary human reasoning (rational choice model). Instead, it asserts the possibility of uncovering certain predictable relationships between individuals and their environments traceable in part to the mind's emotive, adaptive, problem-solving capabilities.

Simple Dichotomies

Second, an evolutionary psychology approach should not become another iteration of the popular nature versus nurture debate, or academic dichotomies such as instinct versus reasoning, biology versus culture, or innate versus learned. These simple dualities should be rejected in favor of a search for complex interactions among biological, institutional, political, economic, social, cultural, and other variables. Any particular manifestation of social behavior is a product of basic motivations and the environment. Nature and nurture, biology and society, provide different skills for addressing life's challenges. Nature can provide us with intrinsic potentials and nurture the opportunity to manifest these potentials in various ways. Personality research involving identical twins, for example, supports the notion of heritability and learned traits as roughly equal in shaping behavior.[103]

Oversimplifying Human Nature

Third, an evolutionary perspective should not be an argument that humankind is basically aggressive or fundamentally cooperative. Instead, as this investigation of reconciliation reveals, aggression and cooperation can be viewed as recurrent social behaviors, and we can safely assume that both are partly innate and partly learned. Joshua S. Goldstein captured this point in his rejection of sociobiological assertions of human's aggressiveness: "Human beings have both nonviolent and aggressive behavior in their repertoire, and both behaviors probably have biological roots. We all have both capacities—to cooperate and to kill—and we have minds to think about such choices."[104] Furthermore, there is every reason to believe that our early ancestors lived in small groups characterized by a similar combination of cooperation and rivalry. As suggested in the introduction of this book, the more relevant question is, how is social cooperation restored despite aggression?

Genetic Determinism and Behavioral Genetics
Fourth, an evolutionary perspective should not be conflated with an argument for genetic determinism or an ideological justification for the status quo. Instead, by recognizing the interplay of culture, social structures, and other variables with evolved habits of mind, "one can therefore avoid the twin dangers of assuming either that humans are merely animal or that we are in no way an animal species."[105]

Furthermore, this approach should not be confused with behavioral genetics, which, in contrast, is "interested in the extent to which *differences* between people in a given environment can be accounted for by *differences* in their genes."[106] Although no two individuals share the exact same genetic makeup (except for identical twins), the genetic basis for the human mental architecture is *universal*. An evolutionary perspective suggests what these universal, shared features of the mind might be; for example, the emotion fear or the ability to use language. It then examines how these features might help us understand certain social phenomena, not to search for imagined genetic differences. For the same reason, an evolutionary perspective should not support genetic racism. Viewed in evolutionary terms, we are one species. Variations in morphology, such as skin color, are inconsequential, a product of 0.01 percent of our genetic makeup. As leading genetic researcher J. Craig Venter explained: "Race is a social concept, not a scientific one. We all evolved in the last 100,000 years from the same small number of tribes that migrated out of Africa and colonized the world."[107] Although we may be keenly attuned to differences in appearance, we all have the same species-specific biological endowment.

Sociobiology
Finally, an evolutionary perspective *should not* become synonymous with sociobiology as that term is generally applied or adopted. Although a sociobiologist might be comfortable with evolutionary biological ideas, the converse is not necessarily true. Many works that are called or call themselves sociobiological are biologically reductionist; they ignore or slight the role of culture and society, make erroneous claims about the biological essence of human nature as inherently aggressive, or worse still, subdivide the human species into racial categories or other biologically unsupported subgroups. An evolutionary perspective shares with

sociobiology a belief that human adaptation is an important factor in shaping the mind, but it does not, and should not, repeat the errors of sociobiologists.

Specifically, evolutionary perspectives should not embrace the claim of some sociobiologists that today's individuals in their contemporary society are "fitness maximizers" or "inclusive fitness maximizers"; that is, the goal of extant human behavior is to maximize gene representation in subsequent generations relative to our contemporaries. David Buss labeled this assertion the "sociobiological fallacy" because it conflates a theory of the origins of mechanisms (inclusive fitness theory) with a theory of the nature of those adaptive mechanisms.[108] Instead, he recognized that "once those [evolved] mechanism are in place, they can be activated or executed in ways that may or may not lead to inclusive fitness in current environments."[109] To illustrate, our evolved ability to taste sweet foods may have been adaptive because it helped early humans to identify safe, ripe, and nutritious fruits. In today's environment characterized by an overabundance of processed sweet foods, this preference may be maladaptive to the extent that it leads to obesity or diabetes. In short, the contemporary value of adaptive mechanisms should not be confused with the causal process that created them. Some sociobiologists make this mistake, however, going "directly from principles of evolution to patterns of [contemporary] social organization."[110]

Conclusion

It is critical to understand what evolutionary psychology is and is not. It suggests that all humans have an evolved brain that integrates emotion and logic, and that it is capable of identifying certain problems and deploying reasoning and emotional abilities to resolve these problems in certain ways. Chapter 2 presents intriguing evidence of the possibility that forgiveness and reconciliation is one such evolved mechanism that, in some settings, allows humans to address the fundamental problem of sociality; that is, how to restore order and beneficial relationships in a society after conflict. It is also possible that this mechanism operates at many levels of social organization in certain patterned and predictable ways, and thus may help us understand some cases of conflict and its resolution.

More broadly, an evolutionary approach has several strengths as an orientation to generating social explanations that are useful to exploring not only reconciliation, but also other important social puzzles. Its greatest strength, we suggest, may be its ability to capture, again, emotion in rationality and to bridge findings in the natural sciences with social science theory. It has certain weaknesses, too, many of which are challenges shared with rational choice models. Finally, it has an intellectual and policy history that can at best be described as unfortunate, and at worst abhorrent. Nonetheless, because something has been and can be misused does not mean it cannot or should not be used in a manner that is constructive and cautious. An evolutionary approach may be applicable to a variety of political questions as well as those in other social disciplines, a topic we consider in the next chapter. But, it can be dangerous as applied to policy prescription if not handled with care.

5

Implications for Policy and Practice and Avenues for Further Research

Many receive advice, few profit by it.
—Publilius Syrus (~100 B.C.)

This chapter offers concise and modest advice on the role of reconciliation as a conflict-resolution tool for conflict resolution practitioners and policy makers. It summarizes generic features, drawn from case studies, of factors associated with successful and unsuccessful reconciliation at the national and international levels. The chapter identifies avenues for future research on reconciliation and conflict resolution, and suggests other political questions that might be amendable to the development of explanations founded on a different view of rationality.

Implications for Policy

As noted in chapter 1, reconciliation is an undertheorized phenomenon in studies of civil and international conflict resolution. This is unfortunate because resolution of civil conflict is a more pronounced and critical policy issue today than ever before, and despite hopes for a new world order, international war is still very much with us. This study offers a systematic, theoretically informed, and theoretically innovative analysis of reconciliation. But can it speak meaningfully to policy makers and practitioners facing the challenge of resolving civil or international conflicts? Well, yes, but only in a general way.

Alexander George cautioned us to recognize that theoretical knowledge is an aid to, not a substitute for, policy judgments that must be made in the context of a particular situation.[1] Policy makers and practitioners and their judgments can benefit from scholarship to the extent that research provides a conceptual framework for different strategies and "generic knowledge"[2] of strategies that identifies their uses, limitations, and conditions required to implement them effectively.[3]

Although identifying numerous favoring and disfavoring conditions runs contrary to the theorist's search for parsimony, wrestling with such complexities and ambiguities is a way of life for applied conflict resolution. By identifying conditions important to the success or failure of a strategy as suggested by the case studies, the scholar can help the policy maker assemble a list of considerations for assessing the feasibility or desirability of that strategy in the policy maker's present situation. That list will be useful even if its conclusions are merely plausible (rather than scientifically certain) and the analysis from which it is compiled is complex or rich rather than parsimonious.

Civil Conflict

Conventional scholarly wisdom holds that civil conflicts rarely end in peaceful settlement.[4] Our study, which includes more recent data, also found that most civil conflicts do not result in restoration of enduring social order: the rate of recidivist conflict in nonreconciled cases exceeded 90 percent. But this study does provide new information that offers an important and hopeful caveat to this conclusion, and it qualifies certain previous judgments about the essential involvement of third parties.

Chapter 2 states that over the last two decades, countries wracked by civil conflict, often protracted and horrendously violent, can peacefully reach an enduring settlement through forgiveness and national reconciliation. In seven of the eleven cases involving a reconciliation event, through forgiveness, the combatants reached a peaceful solution that produced lasting social order and did not devolve into further conflict. This result is a significant and very positive qualification to the general notion that peaceful resolution of civil conflict is extraordinarily rare.

Each of those conflicts that succeeded in a peaceful and enduring resolution went through a similar process of national forgiveness that almost universally included four specific phases. First, a stage of truth telling, public acknowledgment of the harms inflicted by the war, that serves as a means of recognizing the humanity and legitimacy of both parties. Official acknowledgment of injuries appears to carry greater force than private or unsanctioned efforts at reaching the truth. Truth telling, although potentially socially destabilizing, contributes to other factors associated with successful national forgiveness—redefinition of the identities of the belligerents, limited justice, and the call for a new relationship. When the pursuit of justice is constrained, officially sanctioned truth can serve, to a degree, as a substitute for the realization of justice. Furthermore, by recognizing the right of the other to the truth, it begins a process of re-definition of identity of the other from enemy to potential partner in a negotiated settlement and a new common future. Truth telling also strips away the impunity of some individuals or groups and begins a reorienta-tion of their role in a reconciled society. In fact, it is usually one of the first, and most indispensable, elements of successful civil reconciliation.

Second, national reconciliation requires redefinition of the identities of the belligerents. Each party has to restore a sense of self and a sense of the other that are different from those of the war years. In the end, the parties must see themselves and the other camp in a more holistic and valued way. The method of changing identity varies. It often begins through recognition necessary to conduct negotiations. Truth telling, in turn, provides for a redefinition of identity. It allows the injured to tran-scend the role of victim and assume a more complete identity as citizen, and it punctures the aura of impunity of aggressors, thus beginning a process of redefining their role.

Successful reconciliation also continues to redefine the roles and rela-tionships of important social groups and institutions. Existing institutions are rarely eliminated. Typically, certain prerogatives of the military or other armed groups are constrained and the institutions of civil society strengthened (especially the judiciary) through long-run legislative, con-stitutional, or institutional reforms.

Third, national reconciliation typically includes limited justice, some-thing less than full retribution for harms committed during the conflict. Although frustrating to some, incomplete justice (often limited by a form of amnesty to certain groups or individuals) reforms society and reaffirms justice as a value without repeating the cycle of violence and retribution. Often the inability to secure justice in full measure is a practical necessity because of the weakness of judicial institutions after a civil war and the residual power of particular groups implicated in the violence. But limited justice may have hidden virtues. Limiting retribution for wrongs may be valuable for the society as a whole when so many share guilt for their actions or inaction in wartime. To prosecute fully all the sins of omission and commission committed during a civil conflict could destroy the society it seeks to restore. Furthermore, in the fog of war, there will be situations in which culpability cannot be fully resolved, and more injustice than good can result from attempts to punish the guilty. Finally, limited justice encourages individuals or groups who have suffered to consider extending the gift of mercy to former enemies as a powerful contribution to a new social order.

Many practitioners ask, How much justice is enough? Our case studies cannot answer that question in the abstract because the issue we are concerned with is not justice qua justice, but restoration of social order. Therefore, that is not a relevant question for this study because, considered alone, no injustice is tolerable. Rather, the question is, how much justice is enough to contribute to lasting social order? The answer appears to be enough to reestablish justice as a viable element of the new society but not absolute justice, because, however desirable in theory, in practice it either cannot be secured or seeking it would destroy the emerging social order. The actual level of justice secured between this minimal and maximal point varies considerably from case to case, as do mechanisms and obstacles for securing it.

Finally, at some point along the way, or at the end of the process, the parties (typically their official representatives) call for a break with the past and dedicate themselves to a new relationship. In this phase symbolic words and gestures help mark the trajectory, but not the end point, of the relationship.

Contrary to some findings on the possibility for peaceful termination of civil war, these forgiveness processes were substantially "home grown" rather than imposed from outside or under the tutelage of a more powerful third-party nation or organization. Drawing on earlier data, Barbara F. Walter concluded that third-party intervention is both a necessary and sufficient condition for the negotiated end to civil conflicts. She maintained

Groups fighting civil wars almost always choose to fight to the finish unless an outside power stepped in to guarantee a peaceful agreement. If a third party did not intervene, these talks usually failed. If a third party agreed to enforce the terms of a peace treaty, negotiations always succeeded regardless of the initial goals, ideology, or ethnicity of the participants.[5]

Based on a reading of an earlier set of cases, she explained this result using a rational choice, bargaining assumption. According to Walter, negotiations in civil conflicts are *more* prone to failure than international conflicts because the warring parties cannot make "credible commitments" to disarm and share power without the guarantee of future security by an outside party. Simply put, they cannot both maintain their independent armed forces if they decide to reconcile, and if they disarm, they face unacceptable vulnerability at a time of great uncertainty. In short, civil wars, with their acute anarchic conditions, pose a greater cooperation dilemma than international wars.

Yet, in Argentina, Uruguay, Chile, Mozambique, and South Africa, belligerents did reconcile without a guarantor of peace. Third-party involvement from a larger power was a critical factor only in the Honduran and Salvadoran reconciliations, although it was helpful logistically in others such as Mozambique. Furthermore, extensive and repeated third-party involvement in the Chadian case did not lead to a negotiated solution that created a lasting peace. Thus, the notion that third-party guarantees are necessary and sufficient for negotiated civil war settlements is not supported by these more recent cases. Third-party intervention appears to be helpful either for reasons of making credible commitments often through economic inducements or sanctions against the parties, or because it supplies critical resources and expertise to implement commitments; that is, it bolsters capabilities more than intentions. International support of Honduran efforts at truth telling and justice perhaps best illustrate this point.

For policy and practice, the civil war settlement cases presented here are both hopeful and cautious. Hopeful, in the sense that the process of national forgiveness holds great promise in resolving such conflict, and although the steps involved are extraordinarily difficult, they are both knowable and possible. The findings are cautious in the sense that third-party intervention may be less important than previously believed. The belligerents themselves must do the heavy lifting to reach the truth, redefine themselves and the other, and step back from vengeance. Third parties can help, but they primarily can help those that help themselves.

These insights may be of interest both to parties directly involved with, and third parties interested in, continuing or incipient cases of national reconciliation. Although some believe we are entering an age of declining civil and ethnic conflicts,[6] there are likely to be many challenges ahead from northern Ireland to Korea to sub-Saharan Africa where the general patterns emerging from these cases may be a general guide to policy.

Although parties to conflict have the chief burden of reconciling through forgiveness, third parties and the actions of conflict resolution government and nongovernment organizations (NGOs) can and do play critically important roles in encouraging, facilitating, and supporting each step in the process. In truth telling, for example, internal and external human rights organizations often play an important role in ferreting out the truth. Argentina exemplifies the importance of internal groups; in Uruguay, the importance of external human rights organizations is seen. In redefining social identities, governments can encourage recognition and acknowledgment in convening negotiations through external pressure on warring factions as in El Salvador and Honduras. They can provide expertise and financial support to build or rebuild certain social institutions and to decommission others, as in Mozambique. In achieving a measure of justice, international judicial organizations can support or temporarily supplement weakened judicial systems. Honduras best illustrates this point.

Civil reconciliation often involves the role of grass-roots organizations (religious bodies and civil society groups) in initiating, sustaining, and/or consolidating stages of national forgiveness. Mozambique's reconciliation could not have been effected without the active role of organized churches and village spiritual leaders; and civil society groups were critical in urging domestic leaders to undertake reconciliation efforts in El Salvador and Argentina. Enlightened and often courageous leadership by national elites can also be critical. The role of South Africa's leadership, particularly that of Nelson Mandela, may be the most compelling example, but national leadership was also important in Argentina, Chile, and elsewhere.

International War

Reconciliation events occur at the international level where they often mark a turning point in relations, resulting in improvement in interactions. But conflict resolution in these cases should *not* be understood as forgiveness. There is little evidence of international forgiveness defined as a process that includes truth telling, redefinition of identity, limited justice, and the call for a new relationship.

Instead, reconciliation events in international relations demarcated and buttressed effective signal sending and negotiated solutions in bilateral disputes. In cases in which relations improved after a reconciliation event, it was because the event was part of an effective signaling effort of a credible desire for improvement. Reconciliation events worked by helping to improve relations between national belligerents when they were costly, novel, voluntary, and irrevocable. They generally failed when they lacked these four characteristics.

This finding is a cautiously optimistic one for policy makers and negotiators. It is encouraging that negotiated bargains can end disputes between former belligerents and lead to improved relations. The finding also suggests that there is no free lunch: to make credible and effective signals capable of furthering peacemaking and peacekeeping requires that the parties voluntarily and irrevocably make novel and costly concessions.

A second caution is suggested by the absence of forgiveness factors in international disputes. Namely, it would be naïve to attempt to recreate the forgiveness process that worked so well in resolving civil conflicts, at least for the foreseeable future. That is not to say that the four elements of the process are not partially apparent or potentially helpful. Rather, the cases suggest that the presence of these factors—public acknowledgment of harm, for example—helps to reinforce the costly, novel, and irrevocable nature of the signal and thus makes it more reliable. This contribution is an indirect benefit to signaling and negotiation but is not directly part of a forgiveness process. The international system generally lacks institutional and legal mechanisms necessary to translate acts such as acknowledgment into truth telling, redefinition of identity, and justice. This fact, coupled with limited motivation to take such steps in international society because of lower levels of affinity (what Arnold Wolfers long ago identified as the lower level of amity in international relations),[7] and the weaker nature of international society relative to domestic ones, means that forgiveness is not yet a meaningful goal in international relations. It evolves only over long periods of time not available to policy makers, if it occurs at all.

This conclusion implies that the role of NGOs and private actors may be more diffuse or attenuated in restoring order than in civil conflicts.

There is evidence of the beneficial role of NGOs in people-to-people reconciliation efforts after international wars as a buttress to, or a precursor of, a negotiated solution. Nonetheless, international reconciliation events appear to originate more from elite initiatives rather than from grass-root efforts. The most well-known of these were Brandt's Ostpolitik and the dramatic visit by Sadat to the Israeli Knesset.

Finally, the effects of third-party governments are equivocal in international cases. Third-party actors often complicate conflict resolution by limiting the variety or the value of concessions that disputants can make and are generally less beneficial than in civil conflict reconciliation. Regional roles or alliance commitments can prohibit the possibility of negotiations or concessions open to negotiators. This restraint was evident in the Cold War cases such as Russian constraints on Polish–German normal relations, for example. This is not always the case, however. The role of the United States in providing resources necessary to conclude the Egypt-Israel peace treaty is a case in which third-party participation expanded the range of possible solutions. Third-party pressure was also helpful in bringing national belligerents to the negotiating table in Honduras–El Salvador.

Avenues for Future Research

On Reconciliation
Several avenues for additional research on reconciliation are suggested by this study. In the international arena, recall that forgiveness was generally absent in the time frame of our cases, but it is possible that it does occur over longer periods of time. Dyadic relationships such as Germany and France or Germany and Israel that, for one reason or the other, do not fall within the selection parameters of our study may provide evidence of this. Additional work on the role of forgiveness factors in international conflict resolution and the interplay of forgiveness factors with signaling may be warranted.

With regard to civil conflicts, additional case studies will likely qualify and refine the findings presented here. The case studies suggest other variables—leadership, third-party intervention, the strength of preexisting national institutions and social bonds, and a host of others—that may be important determinants of the outcome of reconciliation attempts.

Multivariate analysis might clarify which of these factors are important to successful reconciliation and in what combinations. Policy makers and practitioners will require more fine-grained study of individual civil conflicts and their resolutions, and will have to draw from country-specific expertise to determine how certain factors, such as the quality of leadership or leadership transitions, interact with the general forgiveness process in producing successful reconciliations.

On Emotion as Part of Rationality in Generating Hypotheses in the Social Sciences

Chapter 2 suggests that social scientists may be missing something by excluding emotion and the possibility for specific, rather than general, problem-solving capability in the study of reconciliation in conflict resolution. If this is true, it is reasonable to ask, What other areas of political inquiry might benefit from an evolutionary perspective on rationality; one that includes emotion and does not assume that we solve all problems the same way?

The possibilities are numerous, but we suggest a few in the areas of foreign affairs and diplomacy. First, and perhaps most obvious, an evolutionary perspective on rationality may explain the flip side of reconciliation and conflict resolution: recidivist violence and the underlying emotional forces of shame, anger, and aggression. It is time to ask how these powerful emotions interact with reasoned choice in decision making among groups or between nations. Although the emotional dimension of vengeful violence is palpable, it is traditionally treated as an "irrational" factor and is excluded from social scientific analysis.

There may be other ways to understand the role of anger in violence or the desire for revenge in recurrent conflicts, however. Emile Durkheim hinted at a deeper rationality of revenge when he wrote

It is an error to believe that vengeance is but useless cruelty. It is very possible that, in itself, it consists of a mechanical and aimless reaction, in an emotional and irrational movement, in an unintelligent need to destroy; but, in fact, what it tends to destroy was a menace to us. It consists, then, in a veritable act of defense, although an instinctive and unreflective one.[8]

In the future, we might explore how this emotionally led instinct interacts with reason, when vengeance is and is not rational, what factors cause the emotions associated with vengeance to overwhelm reason, and what factors contribute to reasoned mediation of this emotion.

Similarly, Robert Frank's integration of emotion and reason argues for long-term rational advantages of vengeance in solving commitment problems and avoiding cheating.[9] If so, it is important to determine when and how the possibility of vengeance facilitates reliable commitments, and when it merely damages the trust and understanding necessary for reliable commitments.

In general we can ask, How might our approach to the issue of vengeful violence change if its emotive dimensions were integrated into a theory of rational decision making? What new models can we form to account for anomalies in existing explanations? How too would our proposed solutions for avoiding or ending the cycles of violence and revenge change in light of possible new insights?

Vengeful violence is but one of numerous other puzzles and concepts in the study of politics that might benefit by hypotheses founded on an alternative notion of rationality. An evolutionary perspective may be particularly appropriate and useful in areas in which the subject under consideration has a pronounced emotive component; issues such as loyalty, patriotism, nationalism, or, as discussed in chapter 4, identity. Similarly, several literatures should reconsider the role and the power of fear in rational analyses of security, insecurity, threat perception, and deterrence.

Those areas closer to individual or small groups decision making also may be particular fruitful areas for including the emotional dimension of politics. Crisis decision making may be an arena in which emotions play a critical role. Emotions are also likely to be important aspects of negotiations between small groups or person-to-person interactions and efforts to persuade.[10]

More fundamentally, emotion appears to be critically important to issue identification, preference formation, choice, and memory. If so, what constitutes rational problem solving would at least have to consider the possible role of emotion and problem-specific logic in decision making in most situations. To give one example, reasoning by analogy and the role of memory in collective judgments may be understood differently if emotion is included. As noted earlier, our minds tend to remember what is most emotionally laden, and emotional events may be processed and stored differently than nonemotional ones. How, then, does this fact determine which collective memories are established and how historical memories are applied to new situations?

Conclusion

We hope that this book raises questions larger and more numerous than it answers. If so, that is a good and useful contribution to inquiry. Our study does not pretend to be the last word on the infinitely complex problems of reconciliation processes, civil and international conflict resolution, or the interplay of reason and emotion in rational human problem solving.

Instead, it ranges broadly, looking at a critically important problem—civil and international conflict resolution—and the possible relationship between reconciliation events and resolution of these conflicts. It found that reconciliation events are important to restoration of both civil and international order, but for different reasons. When these events are part of a four-part forgiveness process they can contribute to successful termination of civil conflict and social reconstruction. This finding is of great importance theoretically and practically.

Reconciliation events can also contribute to international dispute settlement when they are part of a negotiated bargain characterized by signals that are costly, voluntary, and irrevocable. Although less startling than the finding of the importance of forgiveness in successful civil war reconciliations, this is important in itself and for the distinction it draws between national and international societies.

In a broader contribution, this book uses two different notions of rationality in wrestling with the critical question of how to restore sociality after conflict. One set of assumptions—rational choice—is well known and its utility as a foundation for social theory is widely accepted. In this study, for example, it provides foundational assumptions for the signaling model that was useful in understanding the process of international reconciliation.

More controversially, this book also demonstrates the utility of a different concept of rationality, one consistent with evolutionary psychology. This approach differs from rational choice in two key ways: it maintains that the mind has many different problem-solving mechanisms · with different inferential patterns, not one general, universally logical decision-making capability; and it integrates, rather than separates, emotion and reason in rationality. As discussed in chapter 4, this approach has a sound basis in the natural sciences and, as shown in chapter 2, it can be a viable foundation for generating useful social explanations—in this case, understanding civil reconciliation through forgiveness. For those interested in broader questions about rationality assumptions in social theory, this careful articulation and use of this new approach to rationality may be an equally or more important and interesting contribution of this book. As noted, importing findings from the natural sciences to social science is fraught with problems, some theoretical, others historical. Whether and how these problems are surmounted and to what extent useful understandings of social phenomena emerge from reexamining rationality in this way remain to be seen. In the near term, the need to reconsider rationality is likely to be treated as an unwelcome burden for many seeking a scientific understanding of politics. But good science must always be willing to challenge its assumptions based on findings in other scientific fields if it is to advance.

Appendix A
Civil War and Reconciliation

Country	Reconciliation	Date	Recurrent Conflict
Afghanistan			Yes
Albania			
Algeria			Yes
Angola			Yes
Anguila			
Argentina	Yes	1984	No
Austria			
Bangladesh			Yes
Bolivia			
Bosnia			
Brazil			Yes
Brunei			
Bulgaria			
Burma			Yes
Burundi			Yes
Cambodia			Yes
Cameroon			
Chad	Yes	1971–1992	Yes
Chile	Yes	1991	No
China			Yes
Colombia	Yes	1957	Yes
Comoros			
Congo			Yes
Costa Rica			

Country	Reconciliation	Date	Recurrent Conflict
Cuba			Yes
Croatia			
Cyprus			
Djibouti			
Dominican Republic			Yes
East Germany			
Ecuador			
Egypt			
El Salvador	Yes	1992	No
Equatorial Guinea			
Ethiopia			Yes
Finland			
France			
Gabon			
Georgia			Yes
Germany			
Ghana			
Great Britain			
Greece			
Guatamala			
Guinea			
Guinea–Bissau			
Haiti			Yes
Honduras	Yes	1993	No
India			Yes
Indonesia			Yes
Iran			Yes
Iraq			Yes
Ireland			
Italy			
Jordan			Yes
Kenya			
Korea, North			
Korea, South			
Laos			Yes

Country	Reconciliation	Date	Recurrent Conflict
Lebanon			Yes
Lesotho			
Liberia			Yes
Mexico			Yes
Moldova			
Morocco			
Mozambique	Yes	1992	No
Nepal			
Netherlands			
Nicaragua			Yes
Niger			Yes
Nigeria			Yes
Oman			Yes
Pakistan			Yes
Panama			Yes
Paraguay			Yes
Peru			Yes
Philippines			Yes
Poland			
Portugal			Yes
Romania			
Russia			Yes
Rwanda			Yes
Saudi Arabia			
Serbia–Montenegro			
Sierra Leone			Yes
Somalia			Yes
South Africa	Yes	1992–1993	No
Soviet Union			
Spain			
Sri Lanka			Yes
Sudan			Yes
Syria			Yes
Tadjikistan			
Tanzania			

Country	Reconciliation	Date	Recurrent Conflict
Thailand			
Turkey			Yes
Uganda			Yes
United States			
Uruguay	Yes	1985	No
Venezuela			Yes
Vietnam, North			
Vietnam, South			Yes
Yemen	Yes	1970	Yes
Yemen, South			Yes
Yugoslavia			Yes
Zaire			Yes
Zambia			Yes
Zimbabwe			Yes

Appendix B
Interstate War and Reconciliation

The analytical approach of the preliminary investigation consisted of the following five steps:

1. Identify the interstate wars that would have created belligerents that might subsequently reconcile.

2. Identify pairs of countries that opposed each other to determine specific dyads that might reconcile.

3. Generate time series plots for each of those dyads.

4. Find any reconciliation events that occurred between members of the dyads.

5. Demarcate the time of the reconciliation events on the appropriate plots.

The result of executing these five steps is a before-and-after picture of bilateral relations between former belligerents that experienced a reconciliation event.

To accomplish those steps, we combined three sets of information. The first was a catalogue of interstate wars from 1888 to 1991. This file contains interstate wars that were fought in the time period potentially relevant to our events databases, whose data span the period 1948 to 1992, and participants of those wars. We obtained our list of wars and major participants—and thus dyads—from the Militarized Interstate Disputes (MIDS) data set (version 2.10) that is available on the Internet at http://www.polsci.binghamton/edu/peace(s)/mid_data. htm and whose nature is described in articles by Gochman and Moaz and Gochman and Leng.[1] From that data set we extracted a list of fifty-three interstate wars. That list and the other lists generated for the preliminary investigation are available from the authors or can be retrieved from the

Internet at `http://www.inta.gatech.edu/peter/reconcile.html`. From that list we identified 114 country dyads for whom reconciliation was feasible at least in principle. Dyad members had to have fought each other in at least one war. In many instances they had fought multiple wars in the time frame of the study.

The time period 1888 to 1991 for the list of wars is not obvious and merits explanation. We used it to address time lags. The end year was chosen because a war had to have concluded before a reconciliation event, and since the events data we had in all but a few cases ended in 1992, 1991 was the last practicable year. The start year was determined by first selecting an upper limit in the time delay for what can be considered a reconciliation. To make that selection, the question was, how far in the past can a war have taken place for a reconciliation to be meaningful? That the participants in the war had still to be alive is one possible criterion. A gap of sixty years is a reasonable upper limit for participants in a war still to be in positions to make a reconciliation for their countries (18 years old as soldiers and 78 years old as statesmen). In that light, sixty years is a plausible upper limit.[2] Because our events data sets that record bilateral relations begin at 1948, a sixty-year delay puts us back to wars beginning as early as 1888.

The second set of information was reconciliation events. We assembled a data set of these between countries in dyads identified from the MIDS data set. These data were collected by the authors from historiographic study of each of the countries and their relationships with their dyadic partners subsequent to the wars between them. We then coded each dyad for reconciliation or its absence.

The third set of information was the status or condition over time of the relationship between dyad countries. This status is measured in terms of the behavior of each country toward its partner. We obtained measures of these relationships from four sources. The first two are the COPDAB and WEIS data sets.[3] Both are well known and have been used for a number of studies. They store in chronological sequence the history of reported cooperative and hostile acts directed from individual countries to other individual countries. COPDAB covers the period 1948–1978, and WEIS 1966–1992. Although the data sets differ in many significant ways, they are broadly similar in how they track the behavior of countries toward each other.[4] With the advent of the Goldstein scale (1992) for the WEIS coding scheme, both data sets now have numeric values for each event that measures the degree of cooperativeness or hostility of the event.[5] Thanks to the numeric scales, it is a straightforward matter to generate comparable time series plots for the relationships.

We accessed two additional, similar data sets to obtain data more recent than 1992. The Levant data set (available at http://www.ukans.edu/ ~keds/) contains a chronology of dyadic, interstate events in the Middle East from April 1979 to February 1997 (at the time of this writing) condensed to their WEIS code values.[6] An ancillary data file has those events summed for each month and converted to Goldstein scale values. We used the ancillary data set. In addition, we received data from the PANDA data set pertaining to a number of dyads for the period 1984 to 1995.[7] These data for all but a small subset of events had been coded to the Goldstein scale. One of the authors converted that subset manually; decisions made regarding the coding of those events are available from the authors.

From these data sets we selected flows pertaining to conflict dyads that we identified from the MIDS data set. In combination with reconciliation events data, the time series of these flows provide the information with which we generated plots and determine whether a reconciliation event corresponded with a change in relations between countries. The task of combining different kinds of data reduced the sample significantly. Table 1.2 identifies which dyads are addressed by any of the four chronological events data sets and the reconciliation events data set.

To address our research question—does a reconcilation event appreciably change the level of conflict between former belligerents—our primary goal in this first study was simple visual analysis. To obtain a picture of the impact of reconciliation, our procedure was as follows: plot the dyadic relationships over time; for those cases that had reconciliations, demarcate the time of reconciliation on the plot; and visually inspect the plots to determine if they indicate a change corresponding to the reconciliation. Our reasoning was that if we (or anyone else) could not see a change, it would be hard to convince anyone that a change had occurred because of a reconciliation, and further investigation into whether and why reconciliation has an impact on bilateral relations would be difficult to justify.

Method for Generating Visual Analysis Plots

One of the authors wrote FORTRAN programs to extract the appropriate data from three of the events data sets to generate time-series plots. (The fourth data set, the data file ancillary to the Levant data set, already had the data in the form required for analysis.) The programs effectively accomplished two tasks. The first program extracted from data sets those events that were directed from one selected country to another (for the WEIS data set converted those events to numerical values using the Goldstein scale),[8] separately summed numerical values for cooperative and conflictual events for each month, and calculated a monthly weighted net conflict (conflict minus cooperation) measure. The result of running this program would be a file containing monthly cooperation, conflict, and net conflict flows from one country to another for those months for which there were any events between countries.

The second program padded data files with zeros for those months for which there were no reported events, so that the plots would be linear from the first month of recorded events within the file to the last month of recorded events.[9] The padded data files were then imported into Excel on a Macintosh, and the time series were plotted. For dyads for which we found a reconciliation event, a line was drawn on the plots demarcating the time of the event.

The resulting plots contain spikes or vertical bars that portray the level or intensity of cooperative, conflictual, and net conflictual interaction for each month for which interaction was reported. The figures we used presented plots of only the net conflictual measure. For the purpose of our study, the scale of the vertical axis of the figures was not as important as was any change in the nature of the spikes around the time of the reconciliation event.

Limitations of Data Constraining Visual Analysis

Unfortunately, only a limited number of cases offered clear visual evidence of the impact of reconciliation. The temporal span or window of relationship data (primarily 1948–1992 with a few instances up to 1995 or 1997) was, in many instances, in the wrong place to allow for accurate comparisons between preconflict and postconflict relations. Of the twenty-one reconciliation events in the period 1948–1995, nine occurred in 1951–1952 (cases 3–11 in table 1.2) and two in 1994–1995 (cases 14 and 15 in table 1.2), periods effectively at the end of the time series plots. In these cases we found it impossible to determine adequately whether a change occurred in behavior between preconflict and postconflict periods because observations were insufficient between 1948 and 1952 or after 1994 to provide a sound reference point for comparison. Furthermore, of the ten remaining cases, two (cases 17 and 18 in table 1.2) had insufficient data to create a meaningful graphic representation of the relationship.

As discussed in the text, despite these limitations, we found, through visual inspection of the eight workable reconciliation cases, five dyads for which a reconciliation event signaled improvement in bilateral relations (cases 1, 2, 12, 16, and 20 in table 1.2). See figures 1.2 to 1.6 (USSR–West Germany, India–China, Egypt–Israel, China–Vietnam, and Poland–West Germany) for illustrations. Figure 1.3, although not a strong case because of sparse data, does display a shift in the ratio of conflictual as opposed to cooperative months when the reconciliation event is used as a divider. Figure 1.4 provides strong evidence that the reconciliation between Egypt and Israel led to improved relations. Peaks of hostile relations between the countries before reconciliation far exceed those for the months of hostile relations after that time. Figure 1.5 shows that the relationship between reconciliation and dyadic relations may be more complicated than a simple before-after step-down in net conflict. Although net conflict is indeed lower after reconciliation, initial observation suggests that the improvement in relations really began considerably (perhaps 30 months) earlier. This outcome may indicate that in some instances a reconciliation event is only one step in a process of improving relations, rather than a turning point or breakthrough. Also of interest is figure 1.6, which portrays the relationship between Poland and West Germany. It indicates that an improvement in relations corresponding with reconciliation was followed by deterioration of relations, such that by seven years later cooperative relations had vanished. This outcome is of interest because it illustrates another possible facet of the relationship between reconciliation and dyadic relations. A reconciliation event may mark a breakthrough or turning point in relations, but the positive effect of that event is not long lasting. Even figure 1.2, whereas it depicts a real improvement in relations after reconciliation, indicates that the impact of reconciliation can erode over time.

Three dyads (cases 13, 18, and 21 in table 1.2) did not provide visual evidence that reconciliation leads to reduced conflict between belligerents. Figures 1.7 to 1.9 (United Kingdom–Argentina, Cambodia–Vietnam, Honduras–El Salvador) give little or no indication that relations improved or deteriorated after the reconciliation event.

Notes

Chapter 1

1. *Hsün Tsu,* trans. Burton Watson (New York: Columbia University Press, 1963).

2. Pierre L. van den Berghe, *The Ethnic Phenomenon* (New York: Elsevier, 1981), p. 6.

3. "Order" refers to the creation of "logical, symbolic, effective hierarchies . . . which enable society and culture to form organized units." Georges Balandier, "An Anthropology of Violence and War," *International Social Science Journal,* vol. 38, no. 4, 1986, pp. 499–511.

4. Johan Galtung, "After Violence: 3 Rs, Reconstruction, Reconciliation, Resolution," available on the World Wide Web at http://www.transcend.org/ TRRECBAS.html, 2001.

5. Louis Kriesberg, *Constructive Conflicts: From Escalation to Resolution* (Boston: Rowman & Littlefield, 1998), pp. 351–352.

6. Frans de Waal, *Peacemaking among Primates* (Cambridge: Harvard University Press, 1989), p. 5.

7. Robert Hendrikson, *Encyclopedia of Word and Phrase Origins* (London: Macmillan Press, 1987), p. 90.

8. "How Can Past Sins Be Absolved," *World Press Review,* vol. 44, no. 2, 1997, pp. 6–9.

9. Hendrick Smith, "Treaty Impact Still Unknown," *New York Times,* March 17, 1979, p. A1.

10. Claudio Cioffi-Revilla, "Origins and Evolution of War and Politics," *International Studies Quarterly,* vol. 40, 1996, p. 8.

11. Lewis F. Richardson, *Statistics of Deadly Quarrels,* Quincy Wright and Carl C. Liernau, eds. (Pittsburgh: Boxwood Press, 1960).

12. The notion of international society (or society of states) we take from Hedley Bull. As discussed in chapter 3, international society "exists when a group of states, conscious of certain common interests and common values, form a society in the sense that they conceive themselves to be bound by a common set of rules

in their relations with one another, and share in the workings of common institutions." Hedley Bull, *The Anarchical Society* (New York: Columbia University Press, 1977), p. 13.

13. Events data typically store in chronological sequence the history of reported cooperative and hostile acts directed from individual countries to other individual countries.

14. For an explanation of limitations in data in producing meaningful plots, see appendix B.

15. The weighted net conflict measure aggregated to monthy values used here corresponds to the description found in Rafael Reuveny and Heejoon Kang, "International Conflict and Cooperation: Splicing COPDAB and WEIS Series," *International Studies Quarterly*, vol. 40, no. 2, 1996, pp. 281–306.

16. The controlled comparative method has certain distinct advantages as well. The problem of reliability and validity may be smaller than in large N studies because the analyst has a small number of cases to thoroughly consider and is less dependent on data one cannot properly evaluate. Arend Lijphart, "The Comparable-Case Strategy in Comparative Research," *Comparative Political Studies*, vol. 8, July 1975, pp. 157–177.

17. Alexander George, "Case Study and Theory Development," paper presented to the second annual symposium on information processing in organizations, Carnegie–Mellon University, October 15–16, 1982.

18. Louis Kriesberg, *Constructive Conflicts*, pp. 198–199.

19. Later in the same study, Kriesberg concluded: "A basic finding of this analysis is that transforming transitions come about when a new way of thinking about the conflict becomes dominant in each of the primary adversaries. They each come to believe that the strategy they had been pursuing cannot triumph or they cannot gain more by continuing it, and an accomodative strategy promises to offer a better alternative." Ibid., p. 217. Emotions are occasionally noted as factors important to conflict resolution. They are generally treated as irrational or unrational factors and made exogenous to any theoretical explanation. Johan Galtung noted, "Something else may be running their minds in addition to cognitions of utilities and probabilities, their products and the sum thereof. That something is usually referred to as emotions." Johan Galtung, "After Violence."

20. Tony Armstrong, *Breaking the Ice: Rapprochment between East and West Germany, the United States, China, Israel, and Egypt* (Washington, DC: U.S. Institute of Peace, 1993), pp. 21–24; Samuel S. Komorita, "Concession-Making and Conflict Resolution," *Journal of Conflict Resolution*, vol. 17, no. 4, 1973, pp. 745–763.

21. James D. Fearon, "Deterrence and the Spiral Model: The Role of Costly Signals in Crisis Bargaining," paper presented at the annual convention of the American Political Science Association, San Francisco, California, August 30–September 2, 1990; James D. Fearon, "Domestic Political Audiences and the Escalation of International Disputes," *American Political Science Review*, vol. 88, no. 3, 1994, pp. 577–592. Fearon's model is designed for democratic societies. We extrapolate on his insight to consider audience effects more generally.

22. J. David Singer, "Threat Perception and National Decision-Makers," in Dean G. Pruitt and Richard C. Snyder, eds., *Theory and Research on the Causes of War* (Englewood Cliffs, NJ: Prentice-Hall, 1969), pp. 39–42.

23. A hurting stalemate is characterized by long periods of pain and suffering that leave no choice but to seek a negotiated accommodation. I. William Zartman and Johannes Aurik, "Power Strategies and De-escalation," in Louis Kriesberg and Stuart J. Thorson, eds., *Timing the De-escalation of International Conflicts* (Syracuse, NY: Syracuse University Press, 1991), pp. 152–581; Louis Kriesberg, *Social Conflict* (2nd ed.) (Englewood Cliffs, NJ: Prentice-Hall, 1982); Louis Kriesberg, "Carrots, Sticks, De-Escalation: U.S.–Soviet and Arab–Israeli Relations," *Armed Forces and Society*, vol. 13, no. 3, 1987, pp. 403–423; Dean G. Pruitt and Paul V. Olczak, "A Multimodal Approach to Seemingly Intractable Conflict," in Barbara Bennedict Bunker and Jeffrey Z. Rubin, eds., *Conflict, Cooperation, and Justice: Essays Inspired by the Work of Morton Deutsch* (San Francisco: Jossey-Bass, 1995), pp. 59–92.

24. Yehuda Amir, "Contact Hypothesis in Ethnic Relations," *Psychological Bulletin*, vol. 71, 1969, pp. 319–342; Miles Hewstone and Rupert Brown, "Contact Is Not Enough: An Intergroup Perspective on the Contact Hypothesis," in Miles Hewstone and Rupert Brown, eds., *Contact and Conflict in Intergroup Encounters* (Oxford: Blackwell, 1986); Walter G. Stephen, "Intergroup Contact: Introduction," *Journal of Social Issues*, vol. 41, no. 3, 1995, pp. 1–8.

25. Ronald J. Fisher, *The Social Psychology of Intergroup and International Conflict Resolution* (New York: Springer-Verlag, 1990), p. 242.

26. See, for example, Christopher R. Mitchell, "A Willingness to Talk: Conciliatory Gestures and De-Escalation," *Negotiation Journal*, vol. 7, no. 4, 1991, pp. 405–429.

27. See Charles E. Osgood, *An Alternative to War or Surrender* (Urbana: University of Illinois Press, 1962).

28. See Svenn Lindshold, "GRIT: Reducing Distrust through Carefully Introduced Conciliation," in Stephen Worchel and William G. Austin, eds., *Psychology of Intergroup Relations* (Chicago: Nelson-Hall, 1986), pp. 305–322; Charles E. Osgood, *An Alternative to War or Surrender*; Dean G. Pruitt and Peter J. Carnevalle, *Negotiation and Social Conflict* (Buckingham, UK: Open University Press and Pacific Grove, CA: Brooks/Cole, 1993); Christopher R. Mitchell, "A Willingness to Talk."

29. Christopher R. Mitchell, "A Willingness to Talk."

30. Ibid.

31. See Charles E. Osgood, *An Alternative to War or Surrender*; Judy P. Gahagan and James T. Tedechi, "Strategy and Credibility of Promises in the Prisoners Dilemma," *Journal of Conflict Resolution*, vol. 12, 1968, pp. 224–234; S. Lindshold, R. Bennett, and M. Wagner, "Retaliation Level as Foundation for Subsequent Conciliation," *Behavioral Science*, vol. 21, 1976, pp. 13–18.

32. See Charles E. Osgood, *An Alternative to War or Surrender*.

33. For a different view of signaling see Amotz Zahavi and Avishag Zahavi, *The Handicap Principle* (New York: Oxford University Press, 1997).

34. Kirsten Renwick Monroe and Kristen Hill Maher, "Psychology and the Rational Actor Theory," *Political Psychology,* vol. 16, no. 1, 1995, pp. 1–21, at p. 2.

35. Bruce Bueno de Mesquita, *The War Trap* (New Haven, CT: Yale University Press, 1981), p. 5. Similarly, Ted Rober Gurr explains "If the parties in separatist wars recognize that the costs of accomodation are probably less than the costs of prolonged conflict, it is only a short step to mutual decisions to settle . . ." "Ethnic Warfare on the Wane," *Foreign Affairs,* May/June 2000, pp. 52–64, at p. 57.

36. William H. Riker, "Implications from the Disequilbrium of Majority Rule for the Study of Institutions," *American Political Science Review,* vol. 74, no. 43, 1980, pp. 432–447.

37. George Tsebelis, *Nested Games* (Berkeley: University of California Press, 1990), pp. 32, 40.

38. Donald P. Green and Ian Shapiro, eds., *Pathologies of Rational Choice* (New Haven, CT: Yale University Press, 1994), pp. 3–4.

39. For an intradisciplinary critique, see Richard Lebow and Janice Stein, "Rational Deterrence Theory: I Think Therefore I Deter," *World Politics,* vol. 41, 1987, pp. 208–224; Donald P. Green and Ian Shapiro, *Pathologies of Rational Choice Theory.*

40. Kirsten Renwick Monroe and Kristen Hill Maher, "Psychology and Rational Actor Theory," p. 6.

41. See Herbert Simon, "Rational Choice and the Structure of the Environment," *Psychology Review,* vol. 63, 1956, pp. 129–138; Amos Tversky and Daniel Kahneman, "Judgment under Uncertainty: Heuristics and Biases," *Science,* vol. 185, September 1974, pp. 1124–1131.

42. See Arthur Lupin, Mathew D. McCubbins, and Samuel L. Popkin, eds., *Elements of Reason: Cognition, Choice and the Bounds of Rationality* (Cambridge, UK: Cambridge University Press, 2000); George E. Marcus, W. Russell Neuman, and Michael McKuen, eds., *Affective Intelligence and Political Judgment* (Chicago: University of Chicago Press, 2000); Jeff Goodwin, James M. Jasper, and Francesca Polletta, eds., *Passionate Politics* (Chicago: University of Chicago Press, 2001).

43. See, for example, George Tsebelis, *Nested Games.*

44. This argument is developed by economist Milton Friedman. "The Methodology of Positive Economics," in Milton Friedman, ed., *Essays in Positive Economics* (Chicago: University of Chicago Press, 1953).

45. Leda Cosmides and John Tooby, "Evolutionary Psychology: A Primer," available on the World Wide Web at http://www.psych.ucsb.edu/research/cep/primer.htm, 1999.

46. Gottfried Leibniz, "Elements of a Calculus," in George Henry Radcliffe Parkinson, ed., *Leibniz, Logical Papers—A Selection* (Oxford: Clarendon Press, 1965); Alfred North Whitehead and Bertrand Russell, *Principles of Mathematics* (2nd ed.) (Cambridge, UK: Cambridge University Press, 1925), vol. 1.

47. Barry Schwartz, *The Battle for Human Nature* (New York: W. W. Norton, 1986), p. 57. Rationality thus has a more limited meaning today than it did in

ancient times. It does not mean "reasonable" in any general sense. Rather it only means that choice is in some sense controlled by the actor's current expectations of the outcomes of his actions, and by his preferences. Those expectations and preferences can be highly unreasonable.

48. For an integration of self-interest and emotion in a behaviorial model, see Robert H. Frank, *Passions within Reason* (New York: W. W. Norton, 1988).

49. The capability to solve the sociality problem through reconciliation is not necessarily limited to humans. Frans de Waal and Filippo Aureli wrote that after conflict, "nonhuman primates engage in nonaggressive reunions . . . now widely known as reconciliations." Reconciliation, they suggest restores valuable relationships disturbed by the conflict. "Conflict Resolution and Distress Alleviation in Monkeys and Apes," in C. Sue Carter, Izja Lederhendler, and Brian Kirkpatrick, eds., *The Integrative Neurobiology of Affiliation* (New York: New York Academy of Sciences, 1997), pp. 317–328, at p. 317.

50. Hannah Arendt, *The Human Condition* (Chicago: University of Chicago Press, 1989), p. 237.

51. Evolutionary psychology seeks to understand the nature of the specific information-processing problems humans faced over evolutionary history, and to develop and test hypotheses of psychological adaptations (mechanisms and behavior) that may have developed as solutions to these recurrent problems. See David M. Buss, *Evolutionary Psychology: The New Science of the Mind,* (Boston: Allyn & Bacon, 1999).

52. Evolution is both a fact, that is, a process widely recognized as true, and a theory, structures of ideas about the mechanisms that bring about evolution, that are much debated in biology. See "Evolution, Science and Society: Evolutionary Biology and the National Research Agenda," (draft), December 23, 1998, Douglas J. Futuyma, ed., sponsored by the A. P. Sloan Foundation and the National Science Foundation, p. 2.

53. Growing evidence from neuroscience shows the mind to be divisible. Both noninvasive studies and studies resulting from injury or brain damage show different neurological substrates serving different cognitive functions. For a summary, see Denise Dellarosa Cummins and Colin Allen, eds., *Evolution of Mind* (New York: Oxford University Press, 1998), pp. 3–29.

54. "Evolved" means our existing "mental circuits" are the product of the process of evolution—descent with modification—due to changes in gene frequency found in a population. A gene is a hereditary unit that can be passed on unaltered for many generations. The collection of genes in a species' population is known as the gene pool. Gene pool frequencies (more precisely, the frequency of alleles, variant forms of genes) typically change because of mutation, migration, random genetic drift, and natural selection.

55. Hirschfeld and Gelman defined a domain as "a body of knowledge that identifies and interprets a class of phenomena assumed to share certain properties and to be of a distinct and general type." A domain functions as a stable response to a set of recurring and complex problems faced by the organism. This response involves difficult-to-access perceptual, encoding, retrieval, and inferential pro-

cesses dedicated to that solution. Lawrence A. Hirschfeld and Susan A. Gelman, "Overview," in Lawrence A. Hirschfeld and Susan A. Gelman, eds., *Mapping the Mind* (Cambridge, UK: Cambridge University Press, 1994), p. 21.

56. "Adaptations are mechanisms or systems of properties crafted by natural selection to solve specific problems posed by regularities of physical, chemical, developmental, ecological, demographic, social, and informational environments encountered by ancestral populations during the course of a species's or population's evolution . . ." John Tooby and Leda Cosmides, "The Psychological Foundations of Culture," in J. Barkow, L. Cosmides, and J. Tooby, eds., *The Adapted Mind* (New York: Oxford University Press, 1992), p. 62. To call a trait an adaptation is not a comment on its current utility but on its history. Elliott Sober, *Philosophy of Biology* (Boulder, CO: Westview Press, 1999), p. 83.

57. By natural selection, Darwin meant that an organism's interaction with its environment set up a feedback mechanism whereby nature selects one organism design over another, the fitter one, depending on how well the design solves an adaptive problem (a problem that affects reproduction). A design is fitter if it allows an organism to solve problems in a way that will facilitate its ability or likelihood of propagation. More precisely, "Trait X is fitter than trait Y if and only if X has a higher probability of survival and/or a greater expectation of reproductive success than Y." Elliot Sober, *Philosophy of Biology*, p. 70. What natural selection predicts is that the fittest of the traits actually represented in a population will become common. Ibid., p. 38. Darwin's insights together with Mendelian genetics give us a neo-Darwinian definition of natural selection as differential reproductive success of preexisting classes of genetic variants in the gene pool.

58. Humans lived in small bands of hunter-gatherer societies for several hundred thousand years, and their ancestors foraged for even longer epochs, whereas modern civilization as we know it—agriculture, governments, cities, et cetera—are the novel products of the last ten to twelve thousand years. See Roger Masters, *The Nature of Politics* (New Haven, CT: Yale University Press, 1989), p. 18. Human civilization has been superimposed on a species with a much longer history of cooperative competition in small groups. Ibid., p. 21.

59. More precisely, adaptive problems occur again and again during the evolution of a species, and their solutions affect, however remotely, the reproduction of individuals. Leda Cosmides and John Tooby, "Better than Rational: Evolutionary Psychology and the Invisible Hand," *American Economic Review*, vol. 84, no. 2, 1994, p. 329. On adaptive specialization in learning, see P. Rozin and J. W. Kalat, "Specific Hunger and Person Avoidance as Adaptive Specializations of Learning," *Psychological Review*, vol. 78, 1971, pp. 459–486.

60. Leda Cosmides and John Tooby, "Origins of Domain Specificity," in *Mapping the Mind*, pp. 86–87.

61. On specially equipped cognitive abilities of infants, see Richard N. Aslin, David B. Risoni, and Peter W. Jusczyk, "Auditory Development and Speech Perception in Infancy," in Marshall M. Haith and Joseph J. Campos, eds., *Handbook of Child Psychology: vol. 2, Infancy and Developmental Psychology (4th ed.)* (New York: Wiley, 1983), pp. 573–687; Peter D. Eimas, Joanne L. Miller, and Peter W. Juscyzk, "On Infant Speech Perception and the Acquisition of Lan-

guage," in Stevan Harnad, ed., *Categorical Perception: The Groundwork of Cognition* (Cambridge, MA: Cambridge University Press, 1987), pp. 161–195; Jean M. Mandler and Patricia J. Bauer, "The Cradle of Categorization: Is the Basic Level Basic," *Cognitive Development*, vol. 3, 1988, pp. 247–264; Elizabeth S. Spelke, "The Origins of Physical Knowledge," in Lawrence Weiskrantz, ed., *Thought without Knowledge* (Oxford: Clarendon Press, 1998), pp. 168–184; Elizabeth S. Spelke, "Principles of Object Perception," *Cognitive Science*, vol. 14, 1990, pp. 28–56.

62. Leda Cosmides and John Tooby, *Evolutionary Psychology*, p. 11.

63. John Tooby and Leda Cosmides, "The Psychological Foundations of Culture," p. 102, p. 166. Noam Chomsky elaborated one of the first, and perhaps best known, accounts of domain-specific reasoning: human language-acquisition faculty. Chomsky asserted that the mental mechanism for language faculty (1) is different from mechanisms governing other domains of thought, (2) reflects humans' biological endowment, and (3) cannot be attributed to the operation of a general learning mechanism. Noam Chomsky, *Language and Problems of Knowledge* (Cambridge: MIT Press, 1988); Lawrence A. Hirschfeld and Susan A. Gelman, *Mapping the Mind*, p. 7.

64. Ibid. A variety of works have studied specific problem-solving capabilities of the human mind. See, for example, John Bowlby, *Attachment and Loss* (New York: Basic Books, 1969, 1973); Paul Ekman, *Emotion in the Human Face* (2nd ed.) (Cambridge, UK: Cambridge University Press, 1984); Isaac M. Marks, *Fears, Phobias, and Rituals* (New York: Oxford University Press, 1987); David M. Buss, "Sex Differences in Human Mate Preferences: Evolutionary Hypotheses Tested in 37 Cultures," *Behavioral and Brain Sciences*, vol. 12, 1989, pp. 1–49; Donald Symons, *The Evolution of Human Sexuality* (New York: Oxford University Press, 1979); Simon Baron-Cohen, *Mindblindness: An Essay on Autism and the Theory of the Mind* (Cambridge: MIT Press, 1995); Renee Baillargeon, "Representing the Existence and the Location of Hidden Objects: Object Permanence in 6- and 8-Month Old Infants," *Cognition*, vol. 23, 1986, pp. 21–41; Leda Cosmides, "Cognitive Adaptations for Social Exchange," in *The Adapted Mind*; J. Garcia, "Learning without Memory," *Journal of Cognitive Neuroscience*, vol. 2, 1990, pp. 287–305; Lawrence A. Hirschfeld and Susan A. Gelman, *Mapping the Mind*; Mark Johnson and John Morton, *Biology and Cognitive Development: The Case of Face Recognition* (Oxford: Blackwell, 1991); Alan Leslie, "Some Implications of Pretense for the Development of Theories of Mind," in Janet W. Astington, Paul L. Harris, and David R. Olson, eds., *Developing Theories of the Mind* (New York: Cambridge University Press, 1988); Ellen M. Markman, *Categorization and Naming in Children* (Cambridge: MIT Press, 1989); Steven Pinker, *The Language Instinct* (New York: Morrow, 1994); Elizabeth S. Spelke, "Principles of Object Perception," pp. 29–56.

65. Neuroscience also suggests the human mind possesses plasticity; the ability to reprogram its mental circuits to establish new processing patterns to meet new challenges or to meet old challenges in new ways after injury to an existing circuit.

66. David M. Buss, "Evolutionary Psychology: A New Paradigm for Psychological Science," *Psychological Inquiry*, vol. 6, no. 1, 1995, p. 7.

67. For the evolutionary psychologist, the domain-specific mind is "better than rational." Leda Cosmides and John Tooby, "Better than Rational: Evolutionary Psychology and the Invisible Hand." Cosmides and Tooby explain that machines limited to general rational procedures are computationally weak relative to those with particular problem-solving mechanisms. "The difference between domain-specific methods and domain-independent ones is akin to the difference between experts and novices: experts can solve problems faster and more efficiently than novices because they already know a lot about the problem domain." Leda Cosmides and John Tooby, *Evolutionary Psychology*.

68. Andrew Wells, "Evolutionary Psychology and Theories of Cognition Architecture," in Charles Crawford and Dennis L. Krebs, eds., *Handbook of Evolutionary Psychology* (Mahwah, NJ: Erlbaum, 1998), pp. 335–364. Specifically, domain-general psychological mechanisms could not have promoted evolutionary fitness because

1. What counts as fit behavior differs from domain to domain so there is no domain-general criterion of success or failure that correlates with fitness.

2. Adaptive courses of action can be neither deduced nor learned by general criteria, because they depend on statistical relationships among features of the environment, behavior, and fitness that emerge over many generations and are, therefore, not observable during a single lifetime.

3. Combinatorial explosion paralyzes any truly domain-general system when encountering real world complexity.

Leda Cosmides and John Tooby, *Mapping the Mind*, p. 91.

69. Ibid., p. 243; "Who Knows How the Mind Works," *Nature*, vol. 335, October 6, 1988, pp. 489–491.

70. Tooby and Cosmides, *The Adapted Mind*, p. 113.

71. See, for example, Magda B. Arnold, *Emotion and Personality* (New York: Columbia University Press, 1960); Magda B. Arnold, *The Nature of Emotion* (London: Penguin Books, 1968); Iranäus Eibl-Eibesfeldt, *Ethology: The Biology of Behavior* (2nd ed.) (New York: Holt, Rinehart & Winston, 1975).

72. Daniel Tranel, Antoine Bechara, and Antonio Damasio, "Decision-Making and the Somatic Marker Hypothesis," in Michael S. Garraniga, ed., *The New Cognitive Neurosciences* (Cambridge: MIT Press, 1999), pp. 1047–1061, at p. 1049.

73. John Tooby and Leda Cosmides, *The Adapted Mind*, p. 99.

74. Stanley Schachter, "The Interaction of Cognitive and Physiological Determinants of Emotional State," in Leonard Berkowitz, ed., *Advances in Social Psychology*, vol. 1 (New York: Academic Press, 1964).

75. Donald T. Kenrick, Edward K. Sadalle, and Richard C. Keefe, "Evolutionary Cognitive Psychology: The Missing Heart of Modern Cognitive Science," in *Handbook of Evolutionary Psychology*, pp. 485–514, at p. 488.

76. Carroll E. Izard, *The Face of Emotion* (New York: Appleton-Century-Crofts, 1971); Robert Plutchik, "A General Psychoevolutionary Theory of Emotion," in Robert Plutchik and Henry Kellerman, eds., *Emotion: Theory, Research and Experience*, vol. 1 (New York: Academic Press, 1980), pp. 3–32.

77. Joseph LeDoux, *The Emotional Brain* (New York: Simon & Schuster, 1996).

78. According to the frustration-aggression hypothesis, frustration supposedly leads to a heightened state of physiological arousal or drive, which, under certain environmental conditions, may lead to aggression. Leonard Berkowitz, *Aggression: A Social Psychological Analysis* (New York: McGraw-Hill, 1962). On the distinction between anger and aggression, see Charles D. Spielberger, Gerald Jacobs, Sheryl Russell, and R. Crane, "Assessment of Anger: The State-Trait Anger Scale," in James N. Butcher and Charles D. Spielberger, eds., *Advances in Personality Assessment* (vol. 2) (Hillsdale, NJ: Erlbaum, 1983), pp. 159–187. This definition of aggression differs from its political use, which mean an unprovoked attack. See Ralph K. White, *Fearful Warriors* (New York: Free Press, 1984), p. 130. For an account of the role of shame and anger leading to cycles of recurrent conflict, see Thomas J. Scheff, *Bloody Revenge: Emotions, Nationalism and War* (Boulder, CO: Westview Press, 1994).

79. Paul A. Cardis, *The Psychology and Measurement of Revenge,* master's thesis, University of Northern Iowa, July 1993, pp. 13–14. Revenge is thought to have both internal and external goals. Externally, it is the search for justice or rectification of injury. Internally, revenge is a defense against sorrow, repressed grief, anxiety, or loss of self-esteem. See Michael Franz Basch, "The Significance of a Theory of Affect in Psychoanalytic Technique," in Theodore Shapiro and Robert N. Emde, eds., *Affect: A Psychoanalytic Perspective* (Madison, CT: International Universities Press, 1992), pp. 291–303; Silvan Solomon Tomkins, *Affect, Imagery, and Consciousness* (2 vols.) (New York: Springer, 1962–1963).

80. Empathy implies taking the role of the other without losing one's identity. Components of empathy are accurately perceiving another's feelings and thoughts; experiencing those feelings and thoughts as if they were one's own; distinguishing one's own thoughts and feelings from those of the other person; and communicating the experience of empathy to the other. Louis Kriesberg, *Constructive Conflicts,* p. 184.

81. John Bowlby *Attachment and Loss* (vol. 2); Roy F. Baumeister and Mark R. Leary, "The Need to Belong: Desire for Interpersonal Attachments as a Fundamental Human Motivation," *Psychological Bulletin,* vol. 117, no. 3, 1995, pp. 497–529. At a minimum, it is maintained that affiliation permits development of a social environment and differentiation of tasks that aid the survival of all group-affiliated members. See, for example, Frans de Waal, *Peacemaking among Primates.* Affiliation is not always the preferred choice, however; for example, when another threatens injury or worse. See H. C. J. Godfray, "The Evolution of Forgiveness," *Nature,* vol. 355, no. 16, 1992, pp. 206–207. Studies in political science and sociology have also probed the desire for affinity. See, for example, James Q. Wilson, *Political Organizations* (New York: Basic Books, 1973); Amitai Etzioni, *Comparative Analysis of Complex Organizations,* 2nd ed. (New York: Free Press, 1975).

82. Joseph W. Elder, "Expanding Our Options: The Challenge of Forgiveness," in Robert Enright and Joanna North, eds., *Exploring Forgiveness,* (Madison: University of Wisconsin Press, 1998), p. 161.

83. Louis Kriesberg, "Coexistence and the Reconciliation of Communal Conflicts," in Eugene Weiner, ed., *The Handbook of Interethnic Coexistence* (New York: Continuum, 1998), p. 184.

84. Ibid., p. 185.

85. Richard Fitzgibbons, "Anger and the Healing Power of Forgiveness: A Psychiatrist's View," in *Exploring Forgiveness*, p. 64. Hannah Arendt proposed that vengeance is the "natural, automatic reaction to transgression and which . . . can be expected and even calculated." Forgiveness, she maintains, is unpredictable, it "is the only reaction which does not merely re-act but acts anew and unexpectedly, unconditioned by the act which provoked it . . ." *The Human Condition*, p. 241.

86. Joanna North, "The 'Ideal' of Forgiveness: A Philosopher's Exploration," in *Exploring Forgiveness*, p. 17 (emphasis in the original).

87. Richard Fitzgibbons, "Anger and the Healing Power of Forgiveness," p. 64.

88. Forgiveness allegedly reduces negative feelings and promotes well-being and mental health in the forgiver. See Robert D. Enright, D. L. Eastin, S. Golden, Isidoros Sarinopoulos, and Suzanne Freedman, "Interpersonal Forgiveness within the Helping Professions: An Attempt to Resolve Differences of Opinion," *Counseling and Values*, vol. 36, 1992, pp. 84–103; Robert D. Enright and R. L. Zell, "Problems Encountered when We Forgive One Another," *Journal of Psychology and Christianity*, vol. 8, no. 1, 1989, pp. 52–60; R. P. Fitzgibbons, "The Cognitive and Emotive Uses of Forgiveness in the Treatment of Anger," *Psychotherapy*, vol. 23, 1986, pp. 629–633; D. Hope, "The Healing Paradox of Forgiveness," *Psychotherapy*, vol. 24, 1987, pp. 240–244; Robin Casarjian, *Forgiveness: A Bold Choice for a Peaceful Heart* (New York: Bantam, 1992); Mica B. Estrada-Hollenbeck, *Forgiving in a World of Rights and Wrongs: Victims' and Perpetrators' Roles in Resolving Interpersonal Conflicts through Forgiveness*, Ph.D. dissertation, Harvard University, 1996; Nicolas Tavuchis, *Mea Culpa* (Stanford, CA: Stanford University Press, 1991), p. 17.

89. Joanna North, "The 'Ideal' of Forgiveness," p. 26.

90. Louis Kriesberg, "Coexistence and the Reconciliation of Communal Conflicts," p. 185.

91. Hannah Arendt, *The Human Condition*, p. 241.

92. Donald W. Shriver, Jr., *An Ethic for Enemies*, (New York: Oxford University Press, 1995), p. 8.

93. Ibid., p. 20. See also Felicidad Oberholzer, *The Transformation of Evil into Sin and Sin into Sorrow and Forgiveness: Lessons from Analytic Psychology and Theology*, Ph.D. dissertation, Graduate Theological Union, Berkeley, CA, 1984, pp. 219, 232.

94. Hannah Arendt, *The Human Condition*, p. 241. Lily Gardner Feldman also notes, "The English term 'reconciliation' has two German equivalents: *Versöhnung* and *Aussöhnung,* conveying respectively a philosophical/emotional aspect and a practical/material element." Lily Gardner Feldman, "The Principle and Practice of 'Reconciliation' in German Foreign Policy: Relations with France,

Israel, Poland and the Greek Republic," *International Affairs*, vol. 75, no. 2, 1999, pp. 333–355, at p. 334.

95. Donald W. Shriver, Jr., *An Ethic for Enemies*, pp. 7–8.

96. Nigel Biggar, "Can We Reconcile Peace with Justice?," *World of Forgiveness*, vol. 2, no. 4, 1999, p. 1.

97. Donald W. Shriver, Jr., *An Ethic for Enemies*, p. 8.

98. Hannah Arendt, *The Human Condition*, p. 243.

99. Cited in Donald W. Shriver, Jr., *An Ethic for Enemies*, p. 8.

100. Lyman T. Lundeen, "Forgiveness and the Human Relationship," in Leroy Aden and David G. Benner, eds., *Counseling and the Human Predicament* (Grand Rapids, MI: Baker Book House, 1989), pp. 188–189.

101. Louis Kriesberg, "Coexistence and the Reconciliation of Communal Conflicts," p. 185.

102. Robert D. Enright and Joanna North, eds. *Exploring Forgiveness*, p. 7; James O'Connell, "The Essence of Forgiveness," *Peace Review*, vol. 7, no. 3/4, 1995, pp. 457–462. Where forgiveness can be unilateral, reconciliation is always mutual and thus serves a social relationship. See Walter Wink, *When the Powers Fall: Reconciliation in the Healing of Nations* (Minneapolis: Fortress, 1998).

103. Many studies of civil conflict also cite the importance of restructuring identity as part of a process of national reconciliation. See Herbert C. Kelman, "Transforming the Relationship Between Former Enemies," in Robert Rothstein, ed., *After the Peace: Resistence and Reconciliation* (Boulder, CO: Lynne Reinner, 1999), pp. 193–205; Franke Wilmer, "The Social Construction of Conflict and Reconciliation in the Former Yugoslavia," *Social Justice*, vol. 25, no. 4, 1998, pp. 90–113.

104. Louis Kriesberg, "Coexistence and the Reconciliation of Communal Conflicts," pp. 186–187.

Chapter 2

1. "The Star-Splitter," in Edward Connery Lathem, ed., *The Poetry of Robert Frost* (New York: Holt, Reinhart & Winston, 1975), p. 177.

2. Todd Eisenstadt and Daniel Garcia, "Colombia: Negotiations in a Shifting Pattern of Insurgency," in I. William Zartman, ed., *Elusive Peace* (Washington, DC: Brookings, 1995).

3. Gabriel Marcela and Donald Schultz, "War and Peace in Colombia," *Washington Quarterly*, vol. 22, no. 3, 1999, pp. 213–228; Mark Chernick, *Insurgency and Negotiations: Defining the Boundaries of the Political Regime in Colombia*, Ph.D. dissertation, Columbia University, 1991, p. 57.

4. Michael Shifter, "Colombia at War," *Current History*, vol. 98, no. 626, 1999, pp. 116–121.

5. Ibid.

6. Charles Dunbar, "The Unification of Yemen: Process, Politics, and Prospects," *Middle East Journal,* vol. 46, Summer 1992, pp. 456–476 at p. 466.

7. J. E. Peterson, *Yemen: The Search for a Modern State* (Baltimore: Johns Hopkins University Press, 1982), p. 105.

8. Robert D. Burrowes, "The Yemen Arab Republic's Legacy and Yemeni Unification," *Arab Studies Quarterly,* vol. 14, Fall 1992, pp. 41–68.

9. J. E. Peterson, *Yemen: The Search for a Modern State,* p. 107–109.

10. Rene Lemarchand, "Chad: The Roots of Chaos," *Current History,* vol. 80, no. 470, 1981, pp. 414–418, 436–438.

11. Samuel Decalo, "Regionalism, Political Decay, and Civil Strife in Chad," *Journal of Modern African Studies,* vol. 18, no. 1, 1980, pp. 23–56, at p. 45.

12. Sam C. Nolutshungu, *Limits of Anarchy: Intervention and State Formation in Chad* (Charlottesville: University of Virginia Press, 1996), p. 74.

13. Peter Rosenblum, "Pipeline Politics in Chad," *Current History,* vol. 99, no. 637, 2000, pp. 195–199.

14. Ibid.

15. Sam C. Nolutshungu, *Limits of Anarchy.*

16. "Chad Government Declares Unilateral Ceasefire in War with Rebels," *Deutsche Presse-Agentur,* July 13, 1995; "Two Chad Opposition Groups Join Forces Against Government," *Agence France Presse,* August 1, 1995.

17. Howard W. French, "Chad: Every Silver Lining Has a Cloud; Colonial Legacies/Oil Find and Elections Could Mean Trouble," *International Herald Tribune,* June 12, 1996.

18. "Chadian Rebel Activity Government Forces Kill 28 Rebels," *Agence France Presse,* March 23, 1999.

19. Sam C. Nolutshungu, *Limits to Anarchy,* p. 2.

20. Edward Schumacher, "Argentina and Democracy," *Foreign Affairs,* vol. 63, no. 3, 1984, pp. 1070–1095.

21. Luis Moreno Ocampo, "Beyond Punishment: Justice in the Wake of Massive Crimes in Argentina," *Journal of International Affairs,* vol. 52, no. 2, 1999, pp. 669–690.

22. Elizabeth Jelin, "The Politics of Memory: The Human Rights Movement and the Construction of Democracy in Argentina," *Latin American Perspectives,* vol. 21, no. 2, 1994, pp. 38–58.

23. Edward Schumacher, "Argentina and Democracy," pp. 1070–1095.

24. Wendy Hunter, *State and Soldier in Latin America: Redefining the Military's Role in Argentina, Brazil and Chile* (Washington, DC: U.S. Institute of Peace, 1996).

25. Georgie Anne Geyer, "Uruguay's Travail," *Courier-Journal,* April 25, 1989, p. 10A.

26. Alexandra Barahona de Brito, *Human Rights and Democratization in Latin America* (Oxford: Oxford University Press, 1997).

27. Jonathan Steele, "A Kind of Liberation," *Guardian*, December 4, 1998, p. 21.

28. Thomas P. Rowan, "Chile: Country Background Report," *Congressional Reference Report* (Washington, DC: Congressional Research Service, 1991).

29. Margaret Popkin and Naomi Roht-Arriaza, "Truth as Justice: Investigatory Commission on Latin America," *Law and Social Inquiry*, vol. 20, no. 1, 1995, pp. 79–117.

30. Aryeh Neier, "Watching Rights: Argentina and Chile," *Nation*, vol. 251, no. 17, 1990, p. 588.

31. "Pinochet's Legacy to Chile: The Reckoning," *Economist*, September 18, 1999, pp. 36–37.

32. Margaret Popkin and Naomi Roht-Arriaza, "Truth as Justice," pp. 79–117.

33. Peter Hakim and Jeffrey Puryear, "Human Rights Lessons in Chile," *Christian Science Monitor*, May 31, 1991, p. 19.

34. Chapultepec Agreements between the Government of El Salvador and the FMLN, chapter 1, "Armed Forces," section 5, "End to Impunity," in *United Nations El Salvador Agreements: The Path to Peace* (San Salvador: United Nation Department of Public Information, no. 1208-92614, July 12, 1992).

35. Mike Kaye, "The Role of Truth Commissions in the Search for Justice, Reconciliation and Democratization: The Salvadoran and Honduran Cases," *Journal of Latin American Studies*, vol. 29, no. 3, 1997, pp. 693–716.

36. Laura Nuzzi O'Shaughnessy and Michael Dodson, "Political Bargaining and Democratic Transition: A Comparison of Nicaragua and El Salvador," *Journal of Latin American Studies*, vol. 31, no. 1, 1999, pp. 99–127.

37. Tim Golden, "Can the Truth Help Salvador Outlive Hate?," *New York Times*, March 21, 1993, section 4, p. 1.

38. Georgie Anne Geyer, "The Amazing New 'Center' in Central America," *Washington Quarterly*, vol. 22, no. 3, 1999, pp. 197–211.

39. Martin Rupiya, "War and Peace in Mozambique," *Accord*, available on the World Wide Web at http://www.c-r.org/accord/acc_moz/rupiya.html, December 1, 1999.

40. "Mozambique: Church Group to Play a Role in Peace Process," *Inter Press Service*, September 18, 1991.

41. Jim Wurst, "Beating Swords into . . . Furniture," *Bulletin of the Atomic Scientists*, vol. 53, no. 3, 1997, pp. 17–18.

42. Dinis S. Sengulane and Jaime Pedro Goncalves, "A Calling for Peace," *Accord*, available on the World Wide Web at http://www.c-r.org/accord/acc_moz/sengulane.html, December 1, 1999.

43. Ibid.

44. Heike Schneider, "Mozambique: One of the Secret Success Stories of Africa," *Deutsche Presse-Agentur*, October 22, 1996.

45. "Burying the Past in Mozambique, *New York Times*, December 11, 1999, section A, p. 18.

46. I. William Zartman, "Negotiating the South African Conflict," in I. William Zartman, ed., *Elusive Peace,* p. 150.

47. David Ottaway, *Chained Together* (New York: Times Books, 1993), p. 62.

48. David J. Whitaker, *Conflict and Reconciliation in the Contemporary World* (London: Routledge, 1999), p. 32.

49. Quoted in Lyn S. Graybill, "South Africa's Truth and Reconciliation Commission: Ethical and Theological Perspectives," *Ethics and International Affairs,* vol. 12, 1999, pp. 43–62, at p. 47.

50. "Burying South Africa's Past," *Economist,* vol. 345, no. 1, 1997, pp. 21–23, at p. 22.

51. Paul van Zyl, "Dilemmas of Transitional Justice: The Case of South Africa's Truth and Reconciliation Commission," *Journal of International Affairs,* vol. 52, no. 2, 1999, pp. 647–666, at p. 651.

52. Kate Dunn, "The Heavy Weight of Truth," *Macleans,* vol. 111, no. 45, 1998, p. 32.

53. National Commission for Protection of Human Rights, *Honduras: The Facts Speak for Themselves* (New York: Human Rights Watch/Americas and Center for Justice and International Law, 1994).

54. Mark J. Ruhl, "Doubting Democracy in Honduras," *Current History,* vol. 96, no. 607, 1997, p. 82.

55. Aryeh Neier, "What Should Be Done about the Guilty?," *New York Review of Books,* 1990, pp. 32–34.

56. Priscilla Hayner, "The Past as Predator," (draft), October 9, 1998.

57. Margaret Popkin and Naomi Roht-Arriaza, "Truth as Justice," pp. 79–117.

58. John Sobrino, "Theological Reflections on the Report of the Truth Commission," in Charles Harper, ed., *Impunity: An Ethical Perspective* (Geneva: World Council of Churches Publication, 1996).

59. Priscilla Hayner, "Commissioning the Truth: Further Research Questions," *Third World Quarterly,* vol. 17, no. 1, 1996, pp. 19–30.

60. Guillermo O'Donnell and Philippe Schmitter, "Transitions from Authoritarian Rule: Tentative Conclusions about Uncertain Democracies," in Neil J. Kritz, ed., *Transitional Justice:* (vol. I) *General Considerations* (Washington, DC: U.S. Institute of Peace, 1995), p. 59.

61. Luiz Perez Aguirre, "Reconciliation, Justice, and Forgiveness," in Charles Harper, ed., *Impunity: An Ethical Perspective.* (Geneva: World Council of Churches, 1996), pp. 40–48.

62. Priscilla Hayner, "The Past as Predator."

63. Luiz Perez Aguirre, "Reconciliation, Justice, and Forgiveness."

64. Guillermo O'Donnell and Philippe C. Schmitter, "Transitions from Authoritative Rule: Tentative Conclusions about Uncertain Democracies," p. 59.

65. Ibid., p. 64.

66. Samuel P. Huntington, "The Third Wave: Democratization in the Late 20th Century," in Neil J. Kritz, ed., *Transitional Justice.* (Washington, DC: U.S. Institute of Peace, 1995), pp. 69–70.

67. Frederick Luskin, "Practicing Forgiveness as a Person and as a Society," "Talk of the Nation" (radio broadcast), April 20, 1999.

68. Gregory L. Jones, "Truth and Consequences in South Africa: Documenting the Horrors of Apartheid," *Christianity Today,* vol. 43, no. 4, 1999, p. 59.

69. Richard Lewis Siegel, "Transitional Justice: A Decade of Debate and Experience," *Human Rights Quarterly,* vol. 20, 1998, pp. 431–454.

70. David J. Whitaker, *Conflict and Reconciliation in the Contemporary World,* p. 33.

71. David Pion-Berlin, "To Persecute or Pardon? Human Rights Decisions in the Latin American Cone," in *Transitional Justice,* p. 83.

72. Edward O. Wilson, *Consilience: The Unity of Knowledge* (New York: Knopf, 1998).

Chapter 3

1. Quoted in Robert Wright, *Nonzero* (New York: Pantheon Books, 2000).

2. Many of those working at the "third image" or structural level do not, by definition, recognize reconciliation events—symbolic and purposeful acts by agents representing states—as important to understanding interstate conflict. Even those who look for the origins of international conflict in individuals, and from this point of departure draw inferences to the behavior of groups (such as states), have rarely directly considered the role of reconciliation in international relations. There are some recent exceptions. See, for example, Alice Ackermann, "Reconciliation as a Peacebuilding Process in Postwar Europe," *Peace and Change,* vol. 19, no. 3, 1994, pp. 229–251; Lily Gardner Feldman, "The Principle and Practice of 'Reconciliation' in German Foreign Policy," pp. 333–356.

3. See Georges Balandier, "An Anthropology of Violence and War," *International Social Science Journal,* vol. 38, no. 4, 1986, pp. 499–511.

4. According to Hedley Bull, in contrast to international *society,* an "international system is formed when two or more states have sufficient contact between them, and have sufficient impact on one another's decisions, to cause them to behave, at least in some measure, as parts of a whole." *The Anarchical Society,* pp. 9–10.

5. This middle road is often termed the "English school" of international relations because its modern proponents were predominantly British writers who reacted to predominantly American realists. See K. J. Holsti, "America Meets the 'English School': State Interests in International Society," *Mershon International Studies Review,* vol. 41, 1997, pp. 275–280.

6. Hedley Bull, *The Anarchical Society,* p. 13.

7. Martin Wight, "Western Values in International Relations," in Martin Wight and Herbert Butterfield, eds., *Diplomatic Investigation* (London: Allen & Unwin, 1966), pp. 96–97.

8. Evan Luard, *Types of International Society* (New York: Free Press, 1976).

9. Hedley Bull, *The Anarchical Society*.

10. Evan Luard, *Types of International Society*, p. 49.

11. Walter Laqueur, *Russia and Germany: A Century of Conflict* (Boston: Little, Brown, 1985), pp. 21–23.

12. Ibid., p. 285.

13. Angela E. Stent, *Russia and Germany Reborn: Unification, the Soviet Collapse, and the New Europe* (Princeton, NJ: Princeton University Press, 1999), p. 21.

14. Ibid.

15. Angela E. Stendt, *Russia and Germany Reborn*, p. 99.

16. Serge Schmemann, "Evolution in Europe: Two Germanys Unite After 45 Years with Jubilation and a Vow of Peace," *New York Times*, October 3, 1990, p. 1.

17. Angela E. Stendt, *Russia and Germany Reborn*, pp. 119–124.

18. Ibid., pp. 127–146.

19. David Remnick, "West Germans, Soviets Initial 20-Year Treaty of Friendship," *Washington Post*, September 14, 1990, p. A18.

20. Neville Maxwell, *India's China War* (London: Jonathan Cape, 1970), pp. 20–21.

21. Sujit Dutta, "Sino–Indian Diplomatic Negotiations: A Preliminary Assessment," available on the World Wide Web at http://www.idsa-india.org/an-mar9-2.html, 1999.

22. Ibid.

23. Dawa Norbu, "Tibet in Sino–Indian Relations," *Asian Survey*, vol. 37, no. 11, 1997, pp. 1088–1099.

24. Ibid.

25. Ibid.

26. "Hands Across the Himalayas," *Economist*, July 12, 1980, p. 15.

27. Sujit Dutta, "Sino–Indian Diplomatic Negotiations."

28. Ibid.

29. David Housego, "Reconciliation in the Air as Li Peng Visits India," *Financial Times*, December 11, 1991, p. 6.

30. Howard M. Sachar, *Egypt and Israel* (New York: Richard Marek, 1981), pp. 48–60.

31. Ibid., pp. 160–161.

32. Ibid., p. 166.

33. Ibid.

34. Ibid., p. 183.

35. Ibid.

36. Ibid., p. 215.

37. Raymond Carroll, *Anwar Sadat* (New York: Franklin Watts, 1982), p. 80.

38. Ibid., p. 82.

39. Speech to the Israeli Knesset on November 20, 1977, printed in Anwar el-Sadat, *In Search of Identity* (New York: Harper & Row, 1977), pp. 330–343.

40. Melvin A. Friedlander, *Sadat and Begin: The Domestic Politics of Peacemaking* (Boulder, CO: Westview Press, 1983), pp. 252–253.

41. Mark Tessler, "The Camp David Accords and the Palestinian Problem," in *Israel, Egypt, and the Palestinians: From Camp David to Intifada,* Ann Mosely Lesch and Mark Tessler eds., (Bloomington: Indiana University Press, 1989), pp. 3–5.

42. Melvin A.Friedlander, *Sadat and Begin,* p. 228–231.

43. Raymond Carroll, *Anwar Sadat,* p. 88.

44. Yitzhak Oron, "Ten Years after the Signing of the Treaty: Egypt, the Anchor of Peace," *Jerusalem Post,* March 24, 1989.

45. Melvin A. Friedlander, *Sadat and Begin,* p. 81.

46. Anwar Sadat, *In Search of Identity,* p. 311

47. Yitzhak Oron, "Ten Years After the Signing of the Treaty."

48. Amer Ramses, "Sino–Vietnamese Normalization in the Light of the Crisis of the Late 1970s," *Pacific Affairs,* vol. 67, no. 3, 1994, p. 357.

49. Ibid., pp. 29–42.

50. Ibid., pp. 39–40.

51. Ibid., p. 45.

52. Ibid., pp. 140–144.

53. Stephen J. Hood, *Dragons Entangled: Indochina and the China–Vietnam War* (Armonk, NY: M. E. Sharpe, 1992), pp. 150–155.

54. Yvonne Preston, "Vietnam and China Forced into Friendship," *Financial Times,* November 6, 1991, p. 4.

55. Amer Ramses, "Sino–Vietnamese Normalization in the Light of the Crisis of the Late 1970s," pp. 365–367.

56. "China and Vietnam: Read Their Lips," *Economist,* September 29, 1990, pp. 36–37.

57. "In China's Shadow," *Economist,* March 16, 1991, p. 31.

58. W. W. Kulski, *Germany and Poland: From War to Peaceful Relations* (Syracuse, NY: Syracuse University Press, 1976), p. 28.

59. "The History of Poland—The Second World War," available on the World Wide Web at http://www.kasprzyk.demon.co.uk/www/WW2.html, 1999.

60. W. W. Kulski, *Germany and Poland,* pp. 45–57.

61. "Willy Brandt," available on the World Wide Web at http://www.bham.ac.uk/IGS/course/brandt.htm, 2000.

62. Monica Scislowska, "Poles, Germany Mend War Wounds: Border Ceremony Commemorates 60th Anniversary of First Attack," *Ottawa Citizen,* September 2, 1999, p. A8.

63. Patricia Clough, "Far Right Stops Bonn Extending Olive Branch," *Independent,* June 5, 1989, p. 8.

64. Robert J. McCartney, Germany Bitter Memories Still Sow Bonn-Warsaw Relations," *Washington Post* September 1, 1989, p. A23.

65. Francine S. Kiefer, "Germans Move to Reassure Eastern Europe," *Christian Science Monitor,* June 19, 1991, p. 4.

66. Wladyslaw Czaplinski, "The New Polish–German Treaties," *American Journal of International Law,* vol. 86, January 1992, pp. 163–173.

67. Great Britain's claim rested on its claim of settlement on the western island and on the Falklands/Malvinas continuously since 1833.

68. David A. Welch, "Remember the Falklands?," *International Journal,* Summer 1997, pp. 485–486.

69. Ibid., pp. 491–492; Max Hastings and Simon Jenkins, *The Battle for the Falklands* (New York: W. W. Norton, 1983), pp. 6–7.

70. "Chronicle of the Falklands/Malvinas History and War," available on the World Wide Web at http://www.yendor.com/vanished/falklands-war.html.

71. David A. Welch, "Remember the Falklands?," pp. 494–498. A Peruvian plan for third-party administration of the island tentatively approved by Argentine President Galteri in May 1982, failed when a British submarine sank the Argentine warship *General Belgrano,* resulting in 400 casualties. The attack occurred outside the war zone as the ship was returning to the Argentine mainland. This fact, and the loss of life, scuttled the peace initiative and remained a rallying cry for Argentine claims against the British after the war.

72. "Chronicle of the Falklands/Malvinas History and War."

73. James Nelson Goodsell, "Falklands Prompts Argentine Reshuffle," *Christian Science Monitor,* June 18, 1982, p. 1; Hugh O'Shaughnessy and Jimmy Burns, "Galtieri Ousted in Bloodless Coup by Armed Forces," *Financial Times,* June 18, 1982, p. 2.

74. Christian Tyler, "Doubts over Lifting of Argentina Sanctions," *Financial Times,* August 15, 1983, p. 2.

75. Klaus Dodds, "Towards Rapprochement? Anglo–Argentine Relations and the Falklands/Malvinas in the Late 1990s," *International Affairs,* vol. 74, no. 3, 1998, p. 620.

76. Ibid., p. 619.

77. Alexander MacLeod, "Britain Lifts Three-Year-Old Trade Ban on Argentine Goods," *Christian Science Monitor,* July 23, 1985, p. 11.

78. Argentina seized victory in the match, and one player announced that they had "avenged the Malvinas." Bill Center, "Maradona, Argentina Top England," *San Diego Union Tribune,* June 23, 1986, p. C1; Norman Chad, "England Ousted by Argentina; Maradona's 2 Goals Lead 2–1 Cup Win," *Washington Post,* June 23, 1986, p. C1.

79. "Security Council Heard Argentinian Complaint against United Kingdom, Takes No Action," *UN Chronicle,* vol. 25, no. 2, 1998, p. 62.

80. "Argentina and United Kingdom Asked to Resolve Future of Falklands Malvinas," *UN Chronicle,* vol. 25, no. 1, 1988, p. 71. Resolution 42/19 was approved 114 to 5, with Argentina voting yes and the United Kingdom voting no.

81. Klaus Dodds, "Towards Rapprochement?," p. 630.

82. Peter Truell, "U.S. Is Attempting to Nudge Argentina and Britain Toward a Reconciliation," *Wall Street Journal,* August 28, 1989, p. 1.

83. "Argentina: Government Satisfied with Negotiations with Britain," *Inter Press Service,* October 23, 1989; Anton La Guardia and Patrick Watts, "Anglo–Argentine Travel Ban Lifted as Diplomatic Ice Thaws," *Daily Telegraph,* April 10, 1990, p. 9.

84. Tim McGirk, "Britain and Argentina Agree on Diplomatic Ties," *Independent,* February 16, 1990, p. 11.

85. Ibid.

86. Charles Miller, "Falkland Islanders Promise Cold Reception for Argentines," *Press Association Newsfile,* March 2, 1990.

87. Clifford Krauss, "Falkland Pact Is Protested on Both Sides of the Dispute," *New York Times,* July 31, 1999, p. A5.

88. "Best of Friends Again, Almost," *Economist,* vol. 319, no. 7711, 1991, p. 54.

89. "The Americas: Bubbling Up," *Economist,* vol. 347, no. 8066, 1998, p. 35.

90. Alistair McQueen, "16 Years on, Falklands Enemies Bury the Hatchet," *Evening Standard,* October 28, 1998, p. 4; "Menem's Visit to Britain; Views from Argentina and the Falkland Islands About the War," *Guardian,* October 31, 1998, p. 6.

91. "Argentina: Government Satisfied with Negotiations with Britain," *Inter Press Service,* October 23, 1989.

92. "The Falklands; Ending the Affair," *Economist,* October 28, 1989, p. 48; Peter Ford. "Argentina and UK Face Last Obstacle to Restoring Links," *Independent,* February 14, 1990, p. 11.

93. The Argentine Investigatory Commission, set up under the Argentine Ministry of Defense in 1982, did consider some investigations into British war crimes during the conflict, especially in response to a British investigation that many Argentines found lacking. However, the commission "got off to a troubled start," and after initial investigation it opted not to open a full investigation under the Geneva Convention. See James Nelson Goodsell, "Argentina Investigates Falklands War, but how Thoroughly?" *Christian Science Monitor,* December 7, 1982, p. 3.

94. "Argentina, United Kingdom Decide to Re-establish Diplomatic Relations," *UN Chronicle,* June 1990, p. 28.

95. Argentina's Foreign Minister Guido Di Tella sent Christmas cards to all the islanders and President Menem offered to clear the mines left behind by the war. The islanders blocked all such advances. "No Mr. President, that's Our Business," *Economist,* vol. 330, no. 7849, 1994, p. 48.

96. Klaus Dodds, "Toward Rapprochement?," p. 628.

97. Wilford P. Deac, *Road to the Killing Fields: The Cambodian War of 1970–1975* (College Station: Texas A&M University Press, 1997) pp. 22–23.

98. Steven J. Hood, *Dragons Entangled: Indochina and the China-Vietnam War,* p. 40.

99. Wilford P. Deac, *Road to the Killing Fields,* pp.74–75.

100. Keith B. Richburg, "Cambodian Peace Talks under Way; Warring Guerrilla Factions Meet with Vietnam for First Time," *Washington Post,* July 26, 1988, p. A1.

101. Chris Pomery, "Anxiety as Hanoi's Troops Start Their Cambodia Pull-out," *Times* (London), September 22, 1989.

102. "The High Price of Peace in Cambodia," *New York Times,* October 24, 1991, p. A24.

103. Lee Kim Chew, "Vietnam Watching Khmer Rouge's Return Closely," *Straits Times* (Singapore), September 20, 1996, p. 50.

104. Amanda Hickman, "Moment of Truth: Will Cambodia Confront the Past?," *In These Times,* April 11, 1999, p. 20.

105. "Vietnam Leader in Cambodia to Improve Ties," *Seattle Times,* June 9, 1999, p. A12.

106. Andrew F. Moore, "Ad Hoc Chambers of the International Court and the Question of Intervention," *Case Western Reserve Journal of International Law,* vol. 24, no. 3, 1992, pp. 667–699.

107. Tom Buckley, *Violent Neighbors: El Salvador, Central America, and the United States* (New York: Times Books, 1984), p. 8.

108. James A. Morris, *Honduras: Caudillo Politics and Military Rulers* (Boulder, CO: Westview Press, 1984), pp. 110–111.

109. David Kirby, "Centuries Old Border War Continues," *B. C. Cycle,* May 17, 1989.

110. Juan De Onis, "El Salvador and Honduras Reach a Border Agreement," *New York Times,* October 18, 1980, p. A10.

111. David Kirby, "Centuries Old Border War Continues."

112. "Security Council Heard Argentinian Complaint against United Kingdom, Takes No Action," *UN Chronicle,* vol. 25, no. 62, December 1988, p. 77.

113. Barbara F. Walter, "The Critical Barrier to Civil War Settlement," *International Organization,* vol. 51, no. 3, 1997, pp. 335–364, at p. 335.

114. Ibid., p. 338.

115. As Clausewitz reminds us, "even the most civilized nations can be passionately inflamed against each other. We should therefore miss the truth if we ascribed war among civilized men to a purely rational act of governments and conceived it as continuously reducing the element of passion . . ." Karl Von Clausewitz, *War, Politics and Power* (Chicago: Gateway, 1962), p. 65.

Chapter 4

1. David Hume, *Moral and Political Philosophy* (New York: Hafner Press, 1948), pp. 24–25.

2. More precisely, we now know that different mental faculties or functions are localized in different regions of the brain. But mental functions are not strictly speaking functions of brain areas; they are more accurately the product of a particular brain system, parts or all of which are found in certain areas of the brain.

3. Long ago, Freud recognized that there was more to the mind than conscious thought, that the mind included an emotional unconscious, an insight supported by modern neuroscience. A growing body of neuroscience evidence supports the proposition that a great deal of human mental processing occurs outside conscious awareness, including emotional appraisal of external stimuli. See Joseph LeDoux, *The Emotional Brain* (New York: Simon & Schuster, 1996); Antonio R. Damasio, *The Feeling of What Happens* (New York: Harcourt Brace, 1999).

4. Neta C. Crawford, "The Passion of World Politics," *International Security,* vol. 24, no. 4, 2000, pp. 116–156, at p. 122.

5. Richard D. Lane, Lynne Nadel, John B. Allen, and Alfred W. Kasniak, "The Study of Emotion from the Perspective of Cognitive Neuoroscience," in Richard D. Lane and Lynn Nadel, eds. *Cognitive Neuroscience of Emotion* (New York: Oxford University Press, 2000), p. 5. Real-time images of brain activity are possible with new technologies such as positron emission (PET) scans and functional magnetic resonance imaging (fMRI). These tools allow investigators to estimate subcortical locations and degree of neural dynamics as a function of psychological and behavioral states.

6. Richard J. Davidson, "Cognitive Neuroscience Needs Affective Neuroscience (and Vice Versa)," *Brain and Cognition,* vol. 42, 2000, pp. 89–92, at p. 91.

7. Antonio Damasio, "A Second Chance for Emotion," in Richard Lane and Lynn Nadel, eds., *Cognitive Neuroscience of Emotion,* pp. 12–23.

8. "Strategic reasoning" means voluntary choice of controlled processing routines to meet a particular goal.

9. Peter J. Lang, Margaret M. Bradley, and Bruce N. Cuthburt, "Emotion, Motivation, and Anxiety: Brain Mechanisms and Psychophysiology," *Biological Psychiatry,* vol. 44, 1998, pp. 1248–1263.

10. Antonio Damasio, *The Feeling of What Happens,* p. 53.

11. Ibid., pp. 37, 70.

12. David Goleman, *Emotional Intelligence* (New York: Bantam Books, 1995), p. 5. Jon Elster raises a qualification, arguing that certain emotions—sadness and grief and aesthetic emotions—do not seem to have action tendencies. Jon Elster, "Rationality and the Emotions," *Economic Journal,* vol. 106, September 1996, pp. 1386–1397, at p. 1388.

13. Jaak Panksepp, *Affective Neuroscience: The Foundations of Human and Animal Emotions* (New York: Oxford University Press, 1998), p. 47.

14. Antonio Damasio, *The Feeling of What Happens,* p. 285.

15. Joseph LeDoux, *The Emotional Brain,* pp. 40, 71.

16. Ibid., p. 127

17. Ibid. For example, freezing, the suspension of movement, is an innate fear response that can be triggered by either natural or learned triggers.

18. Gerald L. Clore and Andrew Ortony, "Cognition in Emotion: Always, Sometimes, or Never?," in Richard D. Lane and Lynn Nadel, eds., *Cognitive Neuroscience of Emotion,* pp. 24–61.

19. Paul Ekman lists characteristics that distinguish basic emotions from one another and from other affective phenomena: distinctive universal signals, presence in other primates, distinctive physiology, distinctive universals in antecedent events, coherence among emotional response, quick onset, brief duration, automatic appraisal, and unbidden occurrence. "An Argument for Basic Emotions," *Cognition and Emotion,* vol. 6, 1992, pp. 172–175. Earlier, Robert Plutchik, proposed a set of "primary emotions" that are physiologically elemental; found consistently across cultures; emerge at birth or in the first year of life; and express the actor's most important adaptational tasks. *Emotion: A Psychoevolutionary Synthesis* (New York: Harper & Row, 1980).

20. See Sylvan Tomkins, *Affect, Imagery, Consciousness* (New York: Springer, 1962); Carroll Izard, "Basic Emotions, Relations among Emotions, and Emotion-Cognition Relations," *Psychology Review,* vol. 99, 1992, pp. 561–565; Paul Ekman, "Expression and the Nature of Emotion," in K. Scherer and P. Ekman, eds., *Approaches to Emotion* (Hillsdale, NJ: Erlbaum, 1992), pp. 319–343.

21. Joseph LeDoux, *The Emotional Brain,* p. 16

22. Jaak Panksepp, *Affective Neuroscience,* p. 123. Elster's study of emotion and rationality makes a similar distinction between what he called protoemotions, which are universal, and proper emotions, which are akin to what neuroscientists call feelings, and have a basis in protoemotion. Elster concluded, "it follows that there are no emotions in any society that are 'nothing but' social constructions, that is, entirely disassociated from universal features of the human condition." Jon Elster, *Alchemies of the Mind: Rationality and the Emotions* (Cambridge: Cambridge University Press, 1999), p. 260.

23. Joseph LeDoux, *The Emotional Brain,* p. 127.

24. See Elster, *Alchemies of the Mind,* p. 241.

25. W. B. Cannon, "The James-Lange Theory of Emotion: A Critical Examination and an Alternative Theory," *American Journal of Psychology,* vol. 39, 1927,

pp. 106–124; R. S. Lazarus, *Emotion and Adaptation* (Oxford University Press, 1991); P. N. Johnson-Laird and K. Oatley, "Basic Emotions, Rationality, and Folk Theory," *Cognition and Emotion,* vol. 6, 1992, pp. 201–223.

26. Antonio Damasio, *The Feeling of What Happens,* pp. 53–54.

27. Joseph LeDoux, *The Emotional Brain,* p. 69.

28. Joseph LeDoux, "Emotional Memory Systems in the Brain," *Behavioral Brain Research,* vol. 58, nos. 1–2, 1998, pp. 69–79.

29. Paul Ekman, "An Argument for Basic Emotions," pp. 169–200.

30. Joseph LeDoux, *The Emotional Brain,* p. 36.

31. David Goleman, *Emotional Intelligence,* p. 5.

32. Joseph LeDoux, *The Emotional Brain,* p. 165.

33. Paul MacLean, *The Triune Brain in Evolution: Role in Paleocerebral Functions* (New York: Plenum, 1990).

34. Neurons (brain cells) are composed of three parts: a cell body, an axon, and some dendrites. Typically, information from other neurons comes into a brain cell by way of the dendrites (but the cell body or axon can also receive inputs). Each cell receives inputs from many other cells. When the neuron receives enough inputs at the same time, it will fire an action potential (an electrical charge) down the axon. Although a neuron usually has only one axon, it branches extensively, allowing many other neurons to be influenced. When the action potential reaches the axon terminals, a chemical called a neurotransmitter is released. The neurotransmitter diffuses from the terminal to the dendrites of adjacent neurons and contributes to the firing of action potentials in these. The space between the axon terminal of one cell and its neighbors is called the synapse. For this reason, communication between neurons is referred to as synaptic transmission. Joseph LeDoux, *The Emotional Brain,* p. 139.

35. A whole host of neurochemicals transfer information throughout the brain. Much of this neurochemical language remains to be explained. One author estimated, however, that up to 98 percent of our bodies internal communication is the result of these chemicals, not synapses. C. Pert, *Molecules of Emotions* (New York: Charles Scribner, 1997). Another writer compared this chemical communication to huge bullhorns that broadcast to wide areas of the brain and body in comparison with the synaptic communication that he calls the "cell phones" of brain communication. Eric Jensen, *Teaching with the Brain in Mind* (Alexandria, VA: ASCD, 1998), p. 15.

36. Antonio Damasio, "A Second Chance for Emotion," p. 16.

37. Joseph LeDoux, *The Emotional Brain,* p. 140.

38. Ibid.

39. See C. Pert, *Molecules of Emotion.*

40. Joseph LeDoux, "Emotional Memory and the Brain," *Scientific American,* June 1994, pp. 50–57.

41. See Richard D. Lane, Lynn Nadel, John B. Allen, and Alfred W. Kasniak, "The Study of Emotion from the Perspective of Cognitive Neuroscience." pp. 3–11.

42. Karin Mogg and Brendan P. Bradley, "Selective Attention and Anxiety: A Cognitive–Motivational Perspective," in Tim Dalgleish and M. Power, eds., *Handbook of Cognition and Emotion* (New York: Wiley, 1999).

43. P. M. Niedenthal and M.B. Setterlund, "Emotional Congruence in Perception," *Personality and Social Psychological Bulletin,* vol. 20, no. 4, 1994, pp. 401–411.

44. C. S. Kitayama, "Impairment of Perception by Positive and Negative Affect," *Cognition and Emotion,* vol. 5, 1991, pp. 255–274.

45. Richard S. Lazarus, *Emotion and Adaptation,* p. 16.

46. Joseph LeDoux, *The Emotional Brain,* p. 19.

47. J. Hooper and D. Teresi, *The Three Pound Universe: The Brain from Chemistry of the Mind to New Frontiers of the Soul* (New York: Dell, 1986).

48. Robert Zajonc, "Feeling and Thinking: Preferences Need No Inferences," *American Psychologist,* vol. 35, 1980, pp. 151–175.

49. Ibid., p. 151.

50. Daniel Tranel, Antoine Bechara, and Antonio Damasio, "Decision Making and the Somatic Marker Hypothesis," in Michael S. Garraniga, ed., *The New Cognitive Neurosciences,* pp. 1047–1061, at p. 1049.

51. Ibid.

52. Joseph LeDoux, *The Emotional Brain,* p. 69.

53. See generally, William James, *The Principles of Psychology* (New York: Henry Holt, 1890); Sven Christianson, ed., *The Handbook of Emotional Memory: Research and Theory* (Hillsdale, NJ: Erlbaum, 1992). See also, J. L. McGaugh, L. Cahill, and B. Roozendaal, "Involvement of the Amygdala in Memory Storage: Interaction with Other Brain Systems," *Proceedings of the National Academy of Sciences USA,* vol. 93, 1996, pp. 13508–13514 (stories with emotional content are remembered better than similar stories lacking emotional implications); U. Neisser, E. Winograd, E. Bergman, A. Schrieber, S. Palmer, and M. S. Wilson, "Remembering the Earthquake: Direct Experience versus Hearing the News," *Memory,* vol. 4, 1996, pp. 337–357 (earthquake eyewitnesses have stronger recollection of collateral facts than newspaper readers); G. Stratton, "Retroactive Hyperamnesia and other Emotional Effects on Memory," *Psychological Review,* vol. 26, 1919, pp. 474–486 (accident eyewitnesses have stronger recall than those recalling learned facts); J. N. Bohannon, "Flashbulb Memories of the Space Shuttle Disaster: A Tale of Two Theories," *Cognition,* vol. 29, 1988, pp. 179–196 (recollection of disaster strongly imprinted in memory).

54. S. Christianson, "Emotional Stress and Eyewitness Memory: A Critical Review," *Psychological Bulletin,* vol. 112, no. 2, 1992, pp. 284–309.

55. L. B. Cahill, B. Prins, M. Weber, and J. McGaugh, "Adrenergic Activation and Memory for Emotional Events," *Nature,* vol. 371, no. 6499, 1994, pp. 702–704. An individual subjected to extreme or repeated emotional trauma, however, can develop psychogenic amnesia that inhibits explicit recall of events.

56. Sven Christianson and Elizabeth Engelberg, "Organization of Emotional Memories," in Tim Dalgleish and M. Power, eds., *Handbook of Emotion and Cognition* (New York: Wiley, 1999), pp. 145–170.

57. Richard J. Davidson, "Cognitive Neuroscience Needs Affective Neuroscience (and Vice Versa)," pp. 89–92.

58. See Antonio Damasio, *Descartes' Error* (New York: Putnam & Sons, 1994); J.C. Pearce, *Evolution's End* (San Francisco: Harper Collins, 1992).

59. Antonio Damasio, *The Feeling of What Happens*, pp. 40–41.

60. Ibid., pp. 41–42.

61. Robert Zajonc, "Feeling and Thinking," p. 169.

62. Ibid.

63. Jaak Panksepp, *Affective Neuroscience*, p. 301.

64. Robert Zajonc, "Feeling and Thinking," p. 172.

65. Patricia Churchland and Terrence Sejnowski, "Neural Representation and Neural Computation," in L. Nadel, L. Cooper, M. Harnish, and P. Culicover, eds., *Neural Connections, Mental Computation* (Cambridge: MIT Press, 1989), pp. 15–48.

66. Donald P. Green and Ian Shapiro, eds., *Pathologies of Rational Choice*, p. 24.

67. Ibid., p. 25. Jon Elster notes that discerning multiple equilibria is useful in that it eliminates some alternative explanation, even if it does not discern only one option. Jon Elster, *Rational Choice* (New York: New York University Press, 1986), p. 19.

68. Sidney Verba stated that psychological variables should be added to the rationality assumption only when it yields greater explanatory power. Sidney Verba, "Assumptions of Rationality and Non-Rationality in Models of the International System," in *The International System: Theoretical Essays*, Klaus Knorr and Sidney Verba, eds. (Princeton, NJ: Princeton University Press, 1961), pp. 93–117.

69. "The words selfish and altruistic have connotations in everyday use that biologists do not intend. Selfish simply means behaving in such a way that one's own inclusive fitness is maximized; altruistic means behaving in such a way that another's fitness is increased at the expense of one's own." Chris Colby, *Introduction to Evolutionary Biology*, version 2, available on the World Wide Web at http://www.talkorigins.org/origins/faqs-evolution.html, 1999.

70. Within evolutionary biology, there has been a debate over whether the basic unit of survival is the individual, the group, or the species. Most evolutionary psychologists, however, reject the notion of group-maximizing behavior as a realistic starting point, relying instead on individual self-interest. Thus, altruism within one's group or species is problematic.

71. Pierre L. van den Berghe, *The Ethnic Phenomenon*, pp. 6–7.

72. Elliott Sober, *Philosophy of Biology*, p. 90.

73. William D. Hamilton, "The Genetical Evolution of Social Behavior," *Journal of Theoretical Biology*, vol. 7, 1964, pp. 1–52.

74. R. Axelrod and W. Hamilton, "The Evolution of Cooperation," *Science,* vol. 211, 1981, pp. 1390–1396.

75. Robert L. Trivers, "The Evolution of Reciprocal Altruism," *Quarterly Review of Biology,* vol. 46, March 1971, pp. 35–57.

76. Gary R. Johnson, "Kin Selection, Socialization, and Patriotism: An Integrating Theory," *Politics and the Life Sciences,* vol. 4, no. 2, 1986, pp. 127–140.

77. Roger D. Masters, *The Nature of Politics* (New Haven, CT: Yale University Press, 1989), pp. 178–179.

78. See, for example, Kenneth Waltz, who contends that if states did not approximate rationality, they would not survive. Kenneth Waltz, *Theory of International Politics* (Reading, MA: Addison-Wesley, 1979).

79. Robert Jervis, for example, maintained that units composed of many individuals appear more irrational than individual decision makers because they may pursue contradictory goals, suffer from various forms of organizational or institutional incapacity, or be led by different groups with different preferences. Miles Kahler, "Rationality in International Relations," *International Organization,* vol. 52, no. 4, 1998, pp. 919–941, at p. 930, citing Robert Jervis, "Rational Deterrence: Theory and Evidence," *World Politics,* vol. 41, 1989, pp. 183–207.

80. Miles Kahler, "Rationality in International Relations," pp. 931–936. From a more sociological perspective, Louis Kriesberg and others made a similar point: collectivities are not unitary, they are socially and culturally constructed, a product of humans' symbol-making capacities, and social outcomes can be seen as a result of interaction among such groups. Personal correspondence, May 17, 2000.

81. James M. Buchanan and Gordon Tullock, *The Calculus of Consent* (Ann Arbor: University of Michigan Press, 1962), p. 13.

82. See Jon Elster, *Rational Choices,* pp. 1–33.

83. Michael T. Hannan and John H. Freeman, "The Population Ecology of Organizations," *American Journal of Sociology,* vol. 83, 1977, pp. 929–964.

84. Oliver Williamson, "The Economics of Organizations: The Transaction Cost Approach," *American Journal of Sociology,* vol. 87, 1981, pp. 548–577.

85. Graham Allison, *Essence of Decision* (Boston: Little, Brown, 1971); J. Bender and T. H. Hammond, "Rethinking Allison's Models," *American Political Science Review,* vol. 86, 1992, pp. 301–322.

86. See Mica B. Estrada-Hollenbeck, *Forgiving in a World of Rights and Wrongs,* pp. 98–117; Donald W. Shriver, Jr., *An Ethic for Enemies,* p. 221; Felicidad Oberholzer, *The Transformation of Evil,* pp. 266, 275–276; Nicolas Tavuchis, *Mea Culpa,* pp. 100–101.

87. Jack S. Levy, "Prospect Theory and the Cognitive-Rational Debate," in Nehemia Geva and Alex Mintz, eds., *Decision-Making on War and Peace: The Cognitive-Rational Debate* (Boulder, CO: Lynn Rienner, 1997), pp. 33–50, at p. 44.

88. As noted, modern techniques are making the operation of the contemporary mind more transparent. As this research progresses, we will have greater evidence,

if not greater certainty, as to whether and to what extent, human problem solving (rationality) is more aptly characterized as universal reasoning or as emotionally assisted, domain-specific reasoning.

89. Alexander Rosenberg, *Philosophy of Social Science,* 2nd ed. (New York: Westview Press, 1995), pp. 170–171.

90. Imre Lakatos's, "Falsification and the Methodology of Scientific Research Programmes," in *Criticism and the Growth of Knowledge,* Imre Lakatos and Alan Musgrave, eds. (Cambridge, UK: Cambridge University Press, 1970), pp. 91–195.

91. Albert Bandura, *Aggression: A Social Learning Analysis* (Englewood Cliffs, NJ: Prentice-Hall, 1973); Claire Armon-Jones, "The Thesis of Constructivism," in Rom Harré, ed. *Construction of Emotions* (Oxford: Blackwell, 1986), pp. 32–55.

92. Neta C. Crawford, "The Passion of World Politics," *International Security,* vol. 24, no. 4, 2000, pp. 116–156.

93. Glen Chafetz, Benjamin Frankel, and Michael Spirtas, "Tracing the Influence of Identity," in *The Origins of National Interest,* Glen Chafetz and Michael Spirtas, eds. (London: Frank Cass, 1999), p. viii. See also, Erik Erikson, "The Problem of Ego Identity," in Maurice R. Stein, Arthur J. Vidich, and David M. White, eds., *Identity and Anxiety* (Glencoe, IL: Free Press, 1960), p. 30.

94. Work with animals illustrates, for example, that in some cases, one's biological identity can be socially reconstituted. In one study, eliminating a higher-ranking vervet monkey in a dominance hierarchy caused an increase in seretonin (a brain chemical that contributes to well-being and esteem) in the second-ranked monkey. Michael McGuire, M. Raleigh, and G. Brammer, "Sociopharmacology," *Annual Review of Pharmacological Toxicology,* vol. 22, 1982, pp. 643–661.

95. Antonio Damasio, "A Second Chance for Emotion," p. 17.

96. Joshua S. Goldstein, "The Emperor's New Genes: Sociobiology and War," *International Studies Quarterly,* vol. 31, 1987, pp. 33–43, at p.34.

97. See, for example, Clifford Geertz, *The Interpretation of Cultures* (New York: Basic Books, 1973).

98. Robin Fox, *The Search for Society* (New Brunswick, NJ: Rutgers University Press, 1989). See also Carl N. Degler, *In Search of Human Nature* (New York: Oxford University Press, 1991); Donald E. Brown, *Human Universals* (Philadelphia: Temple University Press, 1991).

99. Clair Armon-Jones, "The Thesis of Constructivism," pp. 32–55.

100. For an example of intriguing work that blends universal human psychological factors with cultural variables in understanding problem solving, see Incheol Choi, Richard Nisbett, and Ara Norenzayan, "Causal Attribution Across Cultures: Variation and Universality," *Psychological Bulletin,* vol. 125, no. 1, 1999, pp. 47–63.

101. "Culture," Clifford Geertz defines as "an historically transmitted pattern of meanings embodied in symbols," used to "communicate, perpetuate, and develop

their knowledge about and attitudes toward life." Clifford Geertz, *The Interpretation of Cultures,* 1973, cited in Richard S. Lazarus, *Emotion and Adaptation,* p. 355. Richard Lazarus goes on to define social structures as "detailed patterns of social relationships and transactions among people who occupy different roles and statuses within a social system."

102. See Edward O. Wilson, *On Human Nature* (New York: Bantam Books, 1978); Joshua S. Goldstein, "The Emperor's New Genes."

103. See, for example, T. J. Bouchard, "Genes, Environment, and Personality," *Science,* vol. 264, 1994, p. 1700–1701.

104. Joshua S. Goldstein, "The Emperor's New Genes," p. 42.

105. Roger D. Masters, *The Nature of Politics,* p. 112.

106. Leda Cosmides and John Tooby, *Evolutionary Psychology: A Primer,* p. 19.

107. Natalie Angier, "Do Races Differ? Not Really, Genes Show," *New York Times,* August 22, 2000, pp. D1, 6.

108. David Buss, "Evolutionary Psychology: A New Paradigm in Psychological Science," *Psychological Inquiry,* vol. 6, no, 1, 1995, pp. 1–30, at p. 9.

109. Ibid.

110. Ibid., p. 10.

Chapter 5

1. Alexander George, *Bridging the Gap: Theory and Practice in Foreign Policy* (Washington, DC: U.S. Institute of Peace, 1993), pp. 117–141.

2. Social science research is not of the scientific quality that would permit one to predict the success or failure of a strategy in every situation. Systematic examination of a strategy in past cases can, however, identify for policy makers conditions that favor (or impede) its successful operation, leading to conditional generalizations, or what George calls "generic knowledge."

3. Ibid.

4. Barbara F. Walter, "The Critical Barrier to Civil War Settlement," *International Organization,* vol. 51, no. 3, 1997, pp. 335–364, at p. 335. Generally, see earlier works, such as George Modelski, "International Settlement of Internal War," in James Rosenau, ed., *International Aspects of Civil Strife* (Princeton, NJ: Princeton University Press, 1964); Paul Pillar, *Negotiating Peace: War Termination as a Bargaining Process* (Princeton, NJ: Princeton University Press, 1983).

5. Barbara F. Walter, "The Critical Barrier to Civil War Settlement," p. 335.

6. Ted Robert Gurr, "Ethnic Warfare on the Wane," *Foreign Affairs,* May/June, 2000, pp. 52–64.

7. Arnold Wolfers, *Discord and Collaboration* (Baltimore: Johns Hopkins University Press, 1962), pp. 47–65.

8. Cited in Joseph Lopreato, *Human Nature and Biocultural Evolution* (Boston: Allen & Unwin, 1984), p. 142.

9. Robert Frank, *Passions within Reason* (New York: W. W. Norton, 1988).

10. Neta Crawford, "The Passion of World Politics."

Appendix B

1. Charles S. Gochman and Zeev Moaz, "Militarized Interstate Disputes 1816–1976," *Journal of Conflict Resolution*, vol. 28, no. 4, 1984, pp. 585–615; Charles S. Gochman and Russell J. Leng, "Militarized Disputes, Incidents and Crises: Identification and Classification," *International Interactions*, vol. 14, no. 2, 1988, pp. 157–163.

2. We chose such a long lag because choosing anything less than 60 years between a war and a reconciliation was problematic. When one looks at reports such as that in the October 1, 1997, *New York Times* describing how the Roman Catholic Church in France has only now (and the French government only two years earlier) apologized to the Jewish community in France for what it did or did not do to the Jews during World War II, events as long ago as 57 years, 60 years is not an unreasonable number. Roger Cohen, "French Church Issues Apology to Jews on War," *New York Times*, October 1, 1997, p. 5. Or similarly, events such as Helmut Kohl apologizing to the Czech people in January 1997 for actions begun in 1938, or German President Roman Herzog apologizing in April 1997 to the Spanish people for the role Germany played in the Spanish Civil War (1936–1939) do not lead us to believe that 60 years is an unreasonable upper limit. It is true that none of our cases of reconciliation emerged from those earlier wars, but when we began this study, we did not know that. Our goal was to capture as many cases as we could.

3. Edward E. Azar, "The Conflict and Peace Data Bank (COPDAB) Project," *Journal of Conflict Resolution*, vol. 24, 1980, pp. 143–152; Edward E. Azar, *The Codebank of the Conflict and Peace Data Bank (COPDAB)* (Chapel Hill: University of North Carolina Department of Political Science, 1980); John L. Davies and Chad K. McDaniel, "A New Generation of International Event-Data," *International Interactions*, vol. 20, nos. 1–2, 1994, pp. 55–78; Rodney G. Tomlinson, "Monitoring WEIS Event Data in Three Dimensions," in Richard L. Merritt, Robert G. Mewcaster, and Dina A. Zinnes, eds., *International Event Data Developments: DDIR Phase II* (Ann Arbor: University of Michigan Press, 1993), pp. 55–85; Rodney G. Tomlinson, *World Event/Interaction Survey (WEIS) User's Guide*, 8th revision (draft), 1996.

4. Rafael Reuveny and Heejoon Kang, "Internatioanl Conflict and Cooperation: Splicing COPDAB and WEIS Series," pp. 281–306.

5. Joshua S. Goldstein, "A Conflict-Cooperation Scale for WEIS Events Data," *Journal of Conflict Resolution*, vol. 36, no. 2, 1992, pp. 369–385.

6. Philip A. Schrodt and Deborah J. Gerner, "Empirical Indicators of Crisis Phase in the Middle East," *Journal of Conflict Resolution*, vol. 41, no. 4, 1997, pp. 529–552.

7. Joe Bond and Doug Bond, *Panda Codebook* (Cambridge: Harvard University Center for International Affairs, 1995).

8. The Goldstein scale contains numerical values for 61 WEIS events. The version of WEIS we received in the fall of 1996 contains 63 events. The two additional events are 022 (COM2) pessimistic comment on situation and 024 (COM4) optimistic comment on situation. We gave event 022 a value of -0.5 and event 024 a value of 0.5.

9. The source code for the FORTRAN programs can be found on the Web site for Brecke (http://www.inta.gatech.edu/peter/reconcile.html).

References

Ackermann, Alice (1994), "Reconciliation as a Peacebuilding Process in Postwar Europe," *Peace and Change,* 19: 229–251.

Agence France Presse (1995), "Two Chad Opposition Groups Join Forces against Government," August 1.

Agence France Presse (1999), "Chadian Rebel Activity: Government Forces Kill 28 Rebels," March 23.

Aguirre, Luiz Perez (1996), "Reconciliation, Justice and Forgiveness," in Charles Harper, ed., *Impunity: An Ethical Perspective,* Geneva: World Council of Churches, pp. 40–48.

Allison, Graham (1971), *Essence of Decision,* Boston: Little, Brown.

Amir, Yehuda (1969), "Contact Hypothesis in Ethnic Relations," *Psychological Bulletin,* 71: 319–342.

Angier, Natalie (2000), "Do Races Differ? Not Really, Genes Show," *New York Times,* August 22, pp. D1, 6.

Arendt, Hannah (1989), *The Human Condition,* Chicago: University of Chicago Press.

Armon-Jones, Claire (1986), "The Thesis of Constructivism," in Rom Harré, ed., *Construction of Emotions,* Oxford: Blackwell, pp. 32–55.

Armstrong, Tony (1993), *Breaking the Ice,* Washington, DC: U.S. Institute of Peace.

Arnold, Magda B. (1960), *Emotion and Personality,* New York: Columbia University Press.

Arnold, Magda B. (1968), *The Nature of Emotion,* London: Penguin Books.

Aslin, Richard N., David B. Risoni, and Peter W. Jusczyk (1983), "Auditory Development and Speech Perception in Infancy," in Marshall M. Haith and Joseph J. Campos, eds., *Handbook of Child Psychology:* Vol. 2, *Infancy and Developmental Psychology,* 4th ed., New York: Wiley, pp. 573–687.

Axelrod, R. and W. Hamilton (1981), "The Evolution of Cooperation," *Science,* 211: 1390–1396.

Azar, Edward E. (1980), "The Conflict and Peace Data Bank (COPDAB) Project," *Journal of Conflict Resolution,* 24: 143–152.

Azar, Edward E. (1980), *The Codebook of the Conflict and Peace Data Bank (COPDAB).* Chapel Hill: University of North Carolina at Chapel Hill.

Baillargeon, Renee (1986), "Representing the Existence and the Location of Hidden Objects: Object Permanence in 6- and 8-Month Old Infants," *Cognition,* 23: 21–41.

Balandier, Georges (1986), "An Anthropology of Violence and War," *International Social Science Journal,* 38: 499–511.

Bandura, Albert (1973), *Aggression: A Social Learning Analysis,* Englewood Cliffs, NJ: Prentice-Hall.

Barkow, J., L. Cosmides, and J. Tooby, eds. (1992), *The Adapted Mind: Evolutionary Psychology and the Generation of Culture,* New York: Oxford University Press.

Baron-Cohen, Simon (1995), *Mindblindness: An Essay on Autism and the Theory of the Mind,* Cambridge: MIT Press.

Basch, Michael Franz (1992), "The Significance of a Theory of Affect in Psychoanalytic Technique," in Theodore Shapiro and Robert N. Emde, eds., *Affect: A Psychoanalytic Perspective,* Madison, CT: International Universities Press, pp. 291–303.

Baumeister, Roy F. and Mark R. Leary (1995), "The Need to Belong: Desire for Interpersonal Attachments as a Fundamental Human Motivation," *Psychological Bulletin,* 117: 497–529.

Bender, J. and T. H. Hammond (1992), "Rethinking Allison's Models," *American Political Science Review,* 86: 301–322.

Berkowitz, Leonard (1962), *Aggression: A Social Psychological Analysis,* New York: McGraw-Hill.

Biggar, Nigel (1999), "Can We Reconcile Peace with Justice?" *World of Forgiveness,* 2: 27–30.

Bohannon, J. N. (1988), "Flashbulb Memories of the Space Shuttle Disaster: A Tale of Two Theories," *Cognition,* 29: 179–196.

Bond, Joe and Doug Bond (1995), *Panda Codebook.* Cambridge: Harvard University Center for International Affairs.

Bouchard, T. J. (1994), "Genes, Environment, and Personality," *Science,* 264: 1700–1701.

Bowlby, John (1969, 1973), *Attachment and Loss,* 2 vols., New York: Basic Books.

"Willy Brandt," available on the World Wide Web at http://www.bham.ac.uk/IGS/course/brandt.htm.

Brecke, Peter (1999), "Violent Conflicts 1400 A.D. to the Present in Different Regions of the World," paper prepared for the 1999 Meeting of the Peace Science Society (International), Ann Arbor, MI, October 8–10.

Brown, Donald E. (1991), *Human Universals*, Philadelphia: Temple University Press.

Buchanan, James M. and Gordon Tullock (1962), *The Calculus of Consent*, Ann Arbor: University of Michigan Press.

Buckley, Tom (1984), *Violent Neighbors: El Salvador, Central America, and the United States*, New York: Times Books.

Bueno de Mesquita, Bruce (1981), *The War Trap*, New Haven, CT: Yale University Press.

Bull, Hedley (1977), *The Anarchical Society*, New York: Columbia University Press.

Burrowes, Robert D. (1992), "The Yemen Arab Republic's Legacy and Yemeni Unification," *Arab Studies Quarterly*, 14: 41–68.

Buss, David M. (1989), "Sex Differences in Human Mate Preferences: Evolutionary Hypotheses Tested in 37 Cultures," *Behavioral and Brain Sciences*, 12: 1–49.

Buss, David M. (1995), "Evolutionary Psychology: A New Paradigm for Psychological Science," *Psychological Inquiry*, 6: 1–30.

Buss, David M. (1999), *Evolutionary Psychology: The New Science of the Mind*, Boston: Allyn & Bacon.

Cahill, L. B., B. Prins, M. Weber, and J. McGaugh (1994), "Adrenergic Activation and Memory for Emotional Events," *Nature*, 371: 702–704.

Cannon, W. B. (1927), "The James-Lange Theory of Emotion: A Critical Examination and an Alternative Theory," *American Journal of Psychology*, 39: 106–124.

Cardis, Paul A. (1993), *The Psychology and Measurement of Revenge*, master's thesis, University of Northern Iowa.

Carroll, Raymond (1982), *Anwar Sadat*, New York: Franklin Watts.

Casarjian, Robin (1992), *Forgiveness: A Bold Choice for a Peaceful Heart*, New York: Bantam.

Center, Bill (1986), "Maradona, Argentina Top England," *San Diego Union Tribune*, June 23, p. C1.

Chad, Norman (1986), "England Ousted by Argentina; Maradona's 2 Goals Lead 2–1 Cup Win," *Washington Post*, June 23, p. C1.

Chafetz, Glen, Benjamin Frankel, and Michael Spirtas (1999), "Tracing the Influence of Identity," in Glen Chafetz and Michael Spirtas, eds., *The Origins of National Interest*, London: Frank Cass.

Chapultepec Agreements between the Government of El Salvador and the FMLN (1992), chapter 1, "Armed Forces," section 5, "End to Impunity," in United Nations, *El Salvador Agreements: The Path to Peace*, San Salvador: United Nations Department of Public Information, no. 1208-92614, July 12.

Chernick, Mark (1991), *Insurgency and Negotiations: Defining the Boundaries of the Political Regime in Colombia*, Ph.D. dissertation, Columbia University.

Chew, Lee Kim (1996), "Vietnam Watching Khmer Rouge's Return Closely," *Straits Times* (Singapore), September 20, p. 50.

Choi, Incheol, Richard Nisbett, and Ara Norenzayan (1999), "Causal Attribution Across Cultures: Variation and Universality," *Psychological Bulletin,* 125: 47–63.

Chomsky, Noam (1988), *Language and Problems of Knowledge,* Cambridge: MIT Press.

"Chronicle of the Falklands/Malvinas History and War" (2002), February 20, available on the World Wide Web at http://www.yendor.com/vanished/falklands-war.html.

Christianson, Sven, ed. (1992), *The Handbook of Emotional Memory: Research and Theory,* Hillsdale, NJ: Erlbaum.

Christianson, Sven (1992), "Emotional Stress and Eyewitness Memory: A Critical Review," *Psychological Bulletin,* 112: 284–309.

Christianson, Sven and Elizabeth Engelberg (1999), "Organization of Emotional Memories," in Tim Dalgleish and M. Power, eds., *Handbook of Emotion and Cognition,* New York: Wiley, pp. 145–170.

Churchland, Patricia and Terrence Sejnowski (1989), "Neural Representation and Neural Computation," in L. Nadel, L. Cooper, M. Harnish, and P. Culicover eds., *Neural Connections, Mental Computation,* Cambridge: MIT Press, pp. 15–48.

Cioffi-Revilla, Claudio (1996), "Origins and Evolution of War and Politics," *International Studies Quarterly,* 40: 1–22.

Clausewitz, Karl Von (1965), *War Politics and Power,* Chicago: Gateway.

Clore, Gerald L. and Andrew Ortony (1999), "Cognition in Emotion: Always, Sometimes, or Never?" in Richard D. Lane and Lynn Nadel, eds., *Cognitive Neuroscience of Emotion,* New York: Oxford University Press, pp. 24–61.

Clough, Patricia (1989), "Far Right Stops Bonn Extending Olive Branch," *Independent,* June 5, p. 8.

Cohen, Roger (1997), "French Church Issues Apology to Jews on War," *New York Times,* October 1, p. 5.

Colby, Chris (1999), "Introduction to Evolutionary Biology," version 2, available on the World Wide Web at http://www.talkorigins.org/origins/faqs-evolution.html.

Cosmides, Leda (1992), "Cognitive Adaptations for Social Exchange," in J. Barkow, L. Cosmides, and J. Tooby, eds., *The Adapted Mind: Evolutionary Psychology and the Generation of Culture,* New York: Oxford University Press, pp. 163–228.

Cosmides, Leda and John Tooby (1994), "Origins of Domain Specificity," in Lawrence A. Hirschfeld and Susan A. Gelman, eds., *Mapping the Mind,* Cambridge, UK: Cambridge University Press, pp. 85–116.

Cosmides, Leda and John Tooby (1994), "Better than Rational: Evolutionary Psychology and the Invisible Hand," *American Economic Review,* 84: 27–32.

Cosmides, Leda and John Tooby (1998), "Evolutionary Psychology: A Primer," available on the World Wide Web at http://www.psych.ussb.edu/research/cep/primer.htm.

Crawford, Neta C. (2000), "The Passion of World Politics," *International Security,* 24: 116–156.

Cummins, Denise Dellarosa and Colin Allen, eds., (1998). *Evolution of Mind,* New York: Oxford University Press.

Czaplinski, Wladyslaw (1992), "The New Polish–German Treaties," *International Journal of International Law,* 86: 163–173.

Damasio, Antonio (1994), *Descarte's Error,* New York: Putnam.

Damasio, Antonio R. (1999), *The Feeling of What Happens,* New York: Harcourt Brace.

Damasio, Antonio, "A Second Chance for Emotion," in Richard Lane and Lynn Nadel, eds., *Cognitive Neuroscience of Emotion,* New York: Oxford University Press, pp. 12–23.

Davidson, Richard J. (2000), "Cognitive Neuroscience Needs Affective Neuroscience (and Vice Versa)," *Brain and Cognition,* 42: 89–92.

Davies, John L. and Chad K. McDaniel (1994), "A New Generation of International Event-Data," *International Interactions,* 20: 55–78.

Deac, Wilford P. (1997), *Road to the Killing Fields: The Cambodian War of 1970–1975,* College Station: Texas A&M University Press.

De Brito, Alexandra Barahona (1997), *Human Rights and Democratization in Latin America,* Oxford: Oxford University Press.

Decalo, Samuel (1980), "Regionalism, Political Decay, and Civil Strife in Chad," *Journal of Modern African Studies,* 18: 23–56.

Degler, Carl N. (1991), *In Search of Human Nature,* New York: Oxford University Press.

Deutsche Presse-Agentur (1995), "Chad Government Declares Unilateral Ceasefire in War with Rebels," July 13.

De Waal, Frans (1989), *Peacemaking among Primates,* Cambridge: Harvard University Press.

De Waal, Frans and Filippo Aureli (1997), "Conflict Resolution and Distress Alleviation in Monkeys and Apes," in C. Sue Carter, Izga Lederhendler, and Brian Kirkpatrick, eds., *The Integrative Neurobiology of Affiliation,* New York: New York Academy of Sciences, pp. 119–130.

Dodds, Klaus (1998), "Towards Rapprochement? Anglo–Argentine Relations and the Falklands/Malvinas in the Late 1990s," *International Affairs,* 74: 619–630.

Dunbar, Charles (1992), "The Unification of Yemen: Process, Politics, and Prospects," *Middle East Journal,* 46: 456–476.

Dunn, Kate (1998), "The Heavy Weight of Truth," *Macleans,* vol. 111, no. 45, pp. 32.

Dutta, Sujit, "Sino–Indian Diplomatic Negotiations: A Preliminary Assessment," available on the World Wide Web at http://www.idsa-india.org/an-mar9-2.html.

Economist (1980), "Hands Across the Himalayas," July 12, p. 15.

Economist (1989), "The Falklands; Ending the Affair," October 28, p. 48

Economist (1990), "China and Vietnam: Read Their Lips," September 29, pp. 36–37.

Economist (1991), "Best of Friends Again, Almost," June 15, p. 54.

Economist (1991), "In China's Shadow," March 16, p. 31.

Economist (1994), "No Mr. President, That's Our Business," February 5, p. 48.

Economist (1997), "Burying South Africa's Past," November 1, pp. 21–23.

Economist (1998), "The Americas: Bubbling Up," May 2, p. 35.

Economist (1999), "Pinochet's Legacy to Chile: The Reckoning," September 18, pp. 36–37.

Eibl-Eibesfeldt, I. (1975), *Ethology: The Biology of Behavior*, 2nd ed., New York: Holt, Rinehart & Winston.

Eimas, Peter D., Joanne L. Miller, and Peter W. Juscyzk (1987), "On Infant Speech Perception and the Acquisition of Language," in Stevan Harnad, ed., *Categorical Perception: The Groundwork of Cognition*, Cambridge: Cambridge University Press, pp. 161–195.

Eisenstadt, Todd and Daniel Garcia (1995), "Colombia: Negotiations in a Shifting Pattern of Insurgency," in I. William Zartman, ed., *Elusive Peace*, Washington, DC: Brookings, pp. 265–298.

Ekman, Paul (1984), *Emotion in the Human Face*, 2nd ed., Cambridge, UK: Cambridge University Press.

Ekman, Paul (1992), "An Argument for Basic Emotions," *Cognition and Emotion*, 6: 169–200.

Ekman, Paul (1992), "Expression and the Nature of Emotion," in K. Scherer and P. Ekman, eds., *Approaches to Emotion*, Hillsdale, NJ: Erlbaum, pp. 319–343.

Elder, Joseph W. (1998), "Expanding Our Options: The Challenge of Forgiveness," in Robert D. Enright and Joanna North, eds., *Exploring Forgiveness*, Madison: University of Wisconsin Press, pp. 150–164.

Elster, Jon (1986), *Rational Choice*, New York: New York University Press.

Elster, Jon (1996), "Rationality and the Emotions," *Economic Journal*, 106: 1386–1397.

Elster, Jon (1999), *Alchemies of the Mind: Rationality and the Emotions*, Cambridge, UK: Cambridge University Press.

Enright, Robert D. and R. L. Zell (1989), "Problems Encountered when We Forgive One Another," *Journal of Psychology and Christianity*, 8: 52–60.

Enright, Robert D., D. L. Eastin, S. Golden, Isidoros Sarinopoulos, and Suzanne Freedman (1992), "Interpersonal Forgiveness within the Helping Professions: An Attempt to Resolve Differences of Opinion," *Counseling and Values*, 36: 84–103.

Enright, Robert D. and Joanna North, eds. (1998), *Exploring Forgiveness,* Madison: University of Wisconsin Press.

Erikson, Erik (1960), "The Problem of Ego Identity," in Maurice R. Stein, Arthur J. Vidich, and David M. White, eds., *Identity and Anxiety,* Glencoe, IL: Free Press, pp. 37–87.

Estrada-Hollenbeck, Mica B. (1996), *Forgiving in a World of Rights and Wrongs: Victims' and Perpetrators' Roles in Resolving Interpersonal Conflicts through Forgiveness,* Ph.D. dissertation, Harvard University.

Etzioni, Amitai (1975), *Comparative Analysis of Complex Organizations,* 2nd ed., New York: Free Press.

Fearon, James D. (1990), "Deterrence and the Spiral Model: The Role of Costly Signals in Crisis Bargaining," paper presented at the annual convention of the American Political Science Association, San Francisco, CA, August 30–September 2.

Fearon, James D. (1994), "Domestic Political Audiences and the Escalation of International Disputes," *American Political Science Review,* 88: 577–592.

Feldman, Lily Gardner (1999), "The Principle and Practice of 'Reconciliation' in German Foreign Policy: Relations with France, Israel, Poland and the Greek Republic," *International Affairs,* 75: 333–355.

Fisher, Ronald J. (1990), *The Social Psychology of Intergroup and International Conflict Resolution,* New York: Springer-Verlag.

Fitzgibbons, R. P. (1986), "The Cognitive and Emotive Uses of Forgiveness in the Treatment of Anger," *Psychotherapy,* 23: 629–633.

Fitzgibbons, Richard (1998), "Anger and the Healing Power of Forgiveness: A Psychiatrist's View," in Robert D. Enright and Joanna North, eds., *Exploring Forgiveness,* Madison: University of Wisconsin Press, pp. 63–74.

Ford, Peter (1990), "Argentina and UK Face Last Obstacle to Restoring Links," *Independent,* February 14, p. 11.

Fox, Robin (1989), *The Search for Society,* New Brunswick, NJ: Rutgers University Press.

Frank, Robert H. (1988), *Passions within Reason,* New York: W. W. Norton.

French, Howard W. (1996), "Chad: Every Silver Lining Has a Cloud; Colonial Legacies/Oil Find and Elections Could Mean Trouble," *International Herald Tribune,* June 12, electronic version.

Friedlander, Melvin A. (1983), *Sadat and Begin,* Boulder, CO: Westview Press.

Friedman, Milton (1953), "The Methodology of Positive Economics," in Milton Friedman, ed., *Essays in Positive Economics,* Chicago: University of Chicago Press, pp. 3–43.

Frost, Robert (1975), "The Star-Splitter," in Edward Connery Lathem, ed., *The Poetry of Robert Frost,* New York: Holt, Reinhart & Winston, p. 177.

Futuyama, Douglas J., ed. (1998), "Evolution, Science and Society: Evolutionary Biology and the National Research Agenda," draft, December 23.

Gahagan, Judy P. and James T. Tedechi (1968), "Strategy and Credibility of Promises in the Prisoners Dilemma," *Journal of Conflict Resolution*, 12: 224–234.

Galtung, Johan (2000), "After Violence: 3 Rs, Reconstruction, Reconciliation, Resolution," available on the World Wide Web at http://www.transcend.org/TRRECBAS.HTML

Garcia, J. (1990), "Learning without Memory," *Journal of Cognitive Neuroscience*, 2: 287–305.

Geertz, Clifford (1973), *The Interpretation of Cultures*, New York: Basic Books.

George, Alexander (1982), "Case Study and Theory Development," presented at the second annual symposium on Information Processing in Organizations, Carnegie Mellon University, October 15–16.

George, Alexander (1993), *Bridging the Gap: Theory and Practice in Foreign Policy*, Washington, DC: U.S. Institute of Peace.

Geyer, Georgie Anne (1989), "Uruguay's Travail," *Courier-Journal*, April 25, p. 10A.

Geyer, Georgie Anne (1999), "The Amazing New 'Center' in Central America," *Washington Quarterly*, 22: 197–211.

Gochman, Charles S. and Zeev Moaz (1984), "Militarized Interstate Disputes, 1816–1976," *Journal of Conflict Resolution*, 28: 585–615.

Gochman, Charles S. and Russell J. Leng (1988), "Militarized Disputes, Incidents, and Crises: Identification and Classification," *International Interactions*, 14: 157–163.

Godfray, H. C. J. (1992), "The Evolution of Forgiveness," *Nature*, 355: 206–207.

Golden, Tim (1993), "Can the Truth Help Salvador Outlive Hate?" *New York Times*, March 21, section 4, p. 1.

Goldstein, Joshua S. (1987), "The Emperor's New Genes: Sociobiology and War," *International Studies Quarterly*, 31: 33–43.

Goldstein, Joshua S. (1992), "A Conflict-Cooperation Scale for WEIS Events Data," *Journal of Conflict Resolution*, 36: 369–385.

Goleman, David (1995), *Emotional Intelligence*, New York: Bantam Books.

Goodsell, James Nelson (1982), "Falklands Prompts Argentine Reshuffle," *Christian Science Monitor*, June 18, p. 1.

Goodsell, James Nelson (1982), "Argentina Investigates Falklands War, but How Thoroughly?" *Christian Science Monitor*, December 7, p. 3.

Goodwin, Jeff, James M. Jasper, and Francesca Polletta, eds. (2001), *Passionate Politics*, Chicago: University of Chicago Press.

Graybill, Lyn S. (1999), "South Africa's Truth and Reconciliation Commission: Ethical and Theological Perspectives," *Ethics and International Affairs*, 12: 43–62.

Green, Donald P. and Ian Shapiro, eds., (1994), *Pathologies of Rational Choice*, New Haven, CT: Yale University Press.

Guardian (1998), "Menem's Visit to Britain; Views from Argentina and the Falkland Islands About the War," October 31, p. 6.

Gurr, Ted Robert (2000), "Ethnic Warfare on the Wane," *Foreign Affairs*, May/June, pp. 52–64.

Hakim, Peter and Jeffrey Puryear (1991), "Human Rights Lessons in Chile," *Christian Science Monitor*, May 31, p. 19.

Hamilton, William D. (1964), "The Genetical Evolution of Social Behavior," *Journal of Theoretical Biology*, 7: 1–52.

Hannan, Michael T. and John H. Freeman (1977), "The Population Ecology of Organizations," *American Journal of Sociology*, 83: 929–964.

Hastings, Max and Simon Jenkins (1983), *The Battle for the Falklands*, New York: W. W. Norton.

Hayner, Priscilla (1996), "Commissioning the Truth: Further Research Questions," *Third World Quarterly*, 17: 19–30.

Hayner, Priscilla (1998), "The Past as Predator," draft, October 9.

Hendrikson, Robert (1987), *Encyclopedia of Word and Phrase Origins*, London: Macmillan Press, p. 90.

Hewstone, Miles and Rupert Brown (1986), "Contact Is Not Enough: An Intergroup Perspective on the Contact Hypothesis," in Miles Hewstone and Rupert Brown, eds., *Contact and Conflict in Intergroup Encounters*, Oxford: Blackwell, pp. 1–44.

Hickman, Amanda (1999), "Moment of Truth: Will Cambodia Confront the Past?" *In These Times*, April 11, p. 20.

Hirschfeld, Lawrence and Susan A. Gelman, eds. (1994), *Mapping the Mind*, Cambridge, UK: Cambridge University Press.

"The History of Poland—The Second World War," available on the World Wide Web at http://www.kasprzyk.demon.co.uk/www/WW2.html.

Holsti, K. J. (1997), "America Meets the 'English School': State Interests in International Society," *Mershon International Studies Review*, 41: 275–280.

Hood, Stephen J. (1992), *Dragons Entangled: Indochina and the China–Vietnam War*, Armonk, NY: M. E. Sharpe.

Hooper, J. and D. Teresi (1991), *The Three Pound Universe: The Brain from Chemistry of the Mind to New Frontiers of the Soul*, New York: Dell.

Hope, D. (1987), "The Healing Paradox of Forgiveness," *Psychotherapy*, 24: 240–244.

Housego, David (1991), "Reconciliation in the Air as Li Peng Visits India," *Financial Times*, December 11, p. 6.

Hsün Tsu, *Hsün Tsu* (1963), trans. Burton Watson, New York: Columbia University Press.

Hume, David (1948), *Moral and Political Philosophy,* New York: Hafner Press.

Hunter, Wendy (1996), *State and Soldier in Latin America: Redefining the Military's Role in Argentina, Brazil and Chile,* Washington, DC: U.S. Institute of Peace.

Huntington, Samuel P. (1995), "The Third Wave: Democratization in the Late 20th Century," in Neil J. Kritz, ed., *Transitional Justice,* Washington, DC: U.S. Institute of Peace, pp. 69–89.

Inter Press Service (1989), "Argentina: Government Satisfied with Negotiations with Britain," October 23.

Inter Press Service (1991), "Mozambique: Church Group to Play a Role in Peace Process," September 18.

Izard, Carroll (1971), *The Face of Emotion,* New York: Appleton-Century-Crofts.

Izard, Carroll (1992), "Basic Emotions, Relations among Emotions, and Emotion-Cognition Relations," *Psychology Review,* 99: 561–565.

James, William (1890), *The Principles of Psychology,* New York: Henry Holt.

Jelin, Elizabeth (1994), "The Politics of Memory: The Human Rights Movement and the Construction of Democracy in Argentina," *Latin American Perspectives,* 21: 38–58.

Jensen, Eric (1998), *Teaching with the Brain in Mind,* Alexandria, VA: ASCD.

Jervis, Robert (1989), "Rational Deterrence: Theory and Evidence," *World Politics,* 41: 183–207.

Johnson, Gary R. (1986), "Kin Selection, Socialization, and Patriotism: An Integrating Theory," *Politics and the Life Sciences,* 4: 127–140.

Johnson, Mark and John Morton (1991), *Biology and Cognitive Development: The Case of Face Recognition,* Oxford: Blackwell.

Johnson-Laird, P. N. and K. Oatley (1992), "Basic Emotions, Rationality, and Folk Theory," *Cognition and Emotion,* 6: 201–223.

Jones, Gregory L. (1999), "Truth and Consequences in South Africa: Documenting the Horrors of Apartheid," *Christianity Today,* 43: 59.

Kahler, Miles (1998), "Rationality in International Relations," *International Organization,* 52: 919–941.

Kaye, Mike (1997), "The Role of Truth Commissions in the Search for Justice, Reconciliation and Democratization: The Salvadoran and Honduran Cases," *Journal of Latin American Studies,* 29: 693–716.

Kelman, Herbert C. (1999), "Transforming the Relationship Between Former Enemies," in Robert Rothstein, ed., *After the Peace: Resistence and Reconciliation,* Boulder, CO: Lynne Rienner, pp. 193–205.

Kenrick, Donald T., Edward K. Sadalle, and Richard C. Keefe (1998), "Evolutionary Cognitive Psychology: The Missing Heart of Modern Cognitive Science," in Charles Crawford and Dennis L. Krebs, eds., *Handbook of Evolutionary Psychology*, Mahwah, NJ: Erlbaum, pp. 485–514.

Kiefer, Francine S. (1991), "Germans Move to Reassure Eastern Europe," *Christian Science Monitor*, June 19, p. 4.

Kirby, David (1989), "Centuries Old Border War Continues," *B. C. Cycle*, May 17.

Kitayama, C. S. (1991), "Impairment of Perception by Positive and Negative Affect," *Cognition and Emotion*, 5: 255–274.

Komorita, S. S. (1973), "Concession-Making and Conflict Resolution," *Journal of Conflict Resolution*, 17: 745–763.

Krauss, Clifford (1999), "Falkland Pact Is Protested on Both Sides of the Dispute," *New York Times*, July 31, p. A5.

Kriesberg, Louis (1982), *Social Conflict*, 2nd ed., Englewood Cliffs, NJ: Prentice-Hall.

Kriesberg, Louis (1987), "Carrots, Sticks, De-Escalation: U.S.–Soviet and Arab–Israeli Relations," *Armed Forces and Society*, 13: 403–423.

Kriesberg, Louis (1998), "Coexistence and the Reconciliation of Communal Conflicts," in Eugene Weiner, ed., *The Handbook of Interethnic Coexistence*, New York: Continuum, pp. 182–198.

Kriesberg, Louis (1998), *Constructive Conflicts: From Escalation to Resolution*, Boston: Rowman & Littlefield.

Kulski, W. W. (1976), *Germany and Poland: From War to Peaceful Relations*, Syracuse, NY: Syracuse University Press.

La Guardia, Anton and Patrick Watts (1990), "Anglo–Argentine Travel Ban Lifted as Diplomatic Ice Thaws," *Daily Telegraph*, April 10, p. 9.

Lakatos, Imre (1970), "Falsification and the Methodology of Scientific Research Programmes," in Imre Lakatos and Alan Musgrave, eds., *Criticism and the Growth of Knowledge*, Cambridge, UK: Cambridge University Press, pp. 91–195.

Lane, Richard D., Lynne Nadel, John B. Allen, and Alfred W. Kasniak (2000), "The Study of Emotion from the Perspective of Cognitive Neuroscience," in Richard D. Lane and Lynn Nadel, eds., *Cognitive Neuroscience of Emotion*, New York: Oxford University Press, pp. 3–11.

Lang, Peter J., Margaret M. Bradley, and Bruce N. Cuthburt (1998), "Emotion, Motivation, and Anxiety: Brain Mechanisms and Psychophysiology," *Biological Psychiatry*, 44: 1248–1263.

Lazarus, R. S. (1991), *Emotion and Adaptation*, New York: Oxford University Press.

Lebow, Richard and Janice Stein (1987), "Rational Deterrence Theory: I Think Therefore I Deter," *World Politics*, 41: 208–224.

LeDoux, Joseph (1993), "Emotional Memory Systems in the Brain," *Behavioral Brain Research*, 58: 69–79.

LeDoux, Joseph (1994), "Emotional Memory and the Brain," *Scientific American,* June, pp. 50–57.

LeDoux, Joseph (1996), *The Emotional Brain,* New York: Simon & Schuster.

Leibniz, Gottfried (1965), "Elements of a Calculus," in George Henry Radcliffe Parkinson, ed., *Leibniz, Logical Papers—A Selection,* Oxford: Clarendon Press, pp. 17–24.

Lemarchand, Rene (1981), "Chad: The Roots of Chaos," *Current History,* 80: 414–418, 436–438.

Leslie, Alan (1988), "Some Implications of Pretense for the Development of Theories of Mind," in Janet W. Astington, Paul L. Harris, and David R. Olson, eds., *Developing Theories of the Mind,* New York: Cambridge University Press, pp. 19–46.

Levy, Jack S. (1997), "Prospect Theory and the Cognitive-Rational Debate," in Nehemia Geva and Alex Mintz, eds., *Decision-Making on War and Peace: The Cognitive-Rational Debate,* Boulder, CO: Lynne Rienner, pp. 33–50.

Lijphart, Arend (1975), "The Comparable-Case Strategy in Comparative Research," *Comparative Political Studies,* 8: 157–177.

Lindshold, S., R. Bennett, and M. Wagner (1976), "Retaliation Level as Foundation for Subsequent Conciliation," *Behavioral Science,* 21: 13–18.

Lindshold, Svenn (1986), "GRIT: Reducing Distrust through Carefully Introduced Conciliation," in Stephen Worchel and William G. Austin, eds., *Psychology of Intergroup Relations,* Chicago: Nelson-Hall, pp. 305–322.

Lopreato, Joseph (1984), *Human Nature and Biocultural Evolution,* Boston: Allen & Unwin.

Luard, Evan (1976), *Types of International Society,* New York: Free Press.

Lundeen, Lyman T. (1989), "Forgiveness and the Human Relationship," in Leroy Aden and David G. Benner, eds., *Counseling and the Human Predicament,* Grand Rapids, MI: Baker Book House, pp. 188–189.

Lupin, Arthur, Mathew D. McCubbins, and Samuel L. Popkin, eds. (2000), *Elements of Reason: Cognition, Choice and the Bounds of Rationality,* Cambridge, UK: Cambridge University Press.

Luskin, Frederick (1999), "Practicing Forgiveness as a Person and as a Society," "Talk of the Nation," radio broadcast, April 20.

MacLean, Paul (1990), *The Triune Brian in Evolution: Role in Paleocerebral Functions,* New York: Plenum.

MacLeod, Alexander (1985), "Britain Lifts Three-Year-Old Trade Ban on Argentine Goods," *Christian Science Monitor,* July 23.

Mandler, Jean M. and Patricia J. Bauer (1988), "The Cradle of Categorization: Is the Basic Level Basic," *Cognitive Development,* 3: 247–264.

Marcela, Gabriel and Donald Schultz (1999), "War and Peace in Colombia," *Washington Quarterly,* 22: 213–228.

Marcus, George E., W. Russell Neuman, and Michael McKuen, eds. (2000), *Affective Intelligence and Political Judgment,* Chicago: University of Chicago Press.

Markman, Ellen M. (1989), *Categorization and Naming in Children,* Cambridge: MIT Press.

Marks, Isaac M. (1987), *Fears, Phobias, and Rituals,* New York: Oxford University Press.

Masters, Roger D. (1989), *The Nature of Politics,* New Haven, CT: Yale University Press.

Maxwell, Neville (1970), *India's China War,* London: Jonathan Cape.

McCartney, Robert J. (1989), "Germany Bitter Memories Still Sour Bonn–Warsaw Relations," *Washington Post,* September 1, p. A23.

McGaugh, J. L., L. Cahill, and B. Roozendaal (1993), "Involvement of the Amygdala in Memory Storage: Interaction with Other Brain Systems," *Proceedings of the National Academy of Sciences USA,* 93: 13508–13514.

McGirk, Tim (1990), "Britain and Argentina Agree on Diplomatic Ties," *Independent,* February 16, p. 11.

McGuire, Michael, M. Raleigh, and G. Brammer (1982), "Sociopharmacology," *Annual Review of Pharmacological Toxicology,* 22: 643–661.

McQueen, Alistair (1998), "16 Years on, Falklands Enemies Bury the Hatchet," *Evening Standard,* October 28, p. 4.

Miller, Charles (1990), "Falkland Islanders Promise Cold Reception for Argentines," *Press Association Newsfile,* March 2.

Mitchell, Christopher R. (1991), "A Willingness to Talk: Conciliatory Gestures and De-Escalation," *Negotiation Journal,* 7: 405–429.

Modelski, George (1964), "International Settlement of Internal War," in James Rosenau, ed., *International Aspects of Civil Strife,* Princeton, NJ: Princeton University Press, pp. 122–153.

Mogg, Karin and Brendan P. Bradley (1999), "Selective Attention and Anxiety: A Cognitive–Motivational Perspective," in Tim Dalgleish and M. Power, eds., *Handbook of Cognition and Emotion,* New York: Wiley, pp. 145–170.

Monroe, Kristen Renwick and Kristen Hill Maher (1995), "Psychology and the Rational Actor Theory," *Political Psychology,* 16: 1–21.

Moore, Andrew F. (1992), "Ad Hoc Chambers of the International Court and the Questions of Intervention," *Case Western Reserve Journal of International Law,* 24: 667–699.

Morris, James A. (1984), *Honduras: Caudillo Politics and Military Rulers,* Boulder, CO: Westview Press.

National Commission for Protection of Human Rights (1994), *Honduras: The Facts Speak for Themselves,* New York: Human Rights Watch/Americas and Center for Justice and International Law.

Nature (1988), "Who Knows How the Mind Works," 335: 489–491.

Neier, Aryeh (1990), "What Should Be Done about the Guilty," *New York Review of Books,* pp. 32–34.

Neier, Aryeh (1990), "Watching Rights: Argentina and Chile," *Nation,* 251: 588.

Neisser, U., E. Winograd, E. Bergman, A. Schrieber, S. Palmer, and M.S. Wilson (1996), "Remembering the Earthquake: Direct Experience versus Hearing the News," *Memory,* 4: 337–357.

New York Times (1991), "The High Price of Peace in Cambodia," October 24, p. A24.

New York Times (1999), "Burying the Past in Mozambique," December 11, section A 18.

Niedenthal, P. M. and M. B. Setterlund (1994), "Emotional Congruence in Perception," *Personality and Social Psychological Bulletin,* 20: 401–411.

Nolutshungu, Sam C. (1996), *Limits of Anarchy: Intervention and State Formation in Chad,* Charlottesville: University of Virginia Press.

Norbu, Dawa (1997), "Tibet in Sino–Indian Relations," *Asian Survey,* 37: 1088–1099.

North, Joanna (1998), "The 'Ideal' of Forgiveness: A Philosopher's Exploration," in Robert D. Enright and Joanna North, eds., *Exploring Forgiveness,* Madison: University of Wisconsin Press.

Oberholzer, Felicidad (1984), *The Transformation of Evil into Sin and Sin into Sorrow and Forgiveness: Lessons from Analytic Psychology and Theology,* Ph.D. dissertation, Graduate Theological Union, Berkeley, CA.

Ocampo, Luis Moreno (1999), "Beyond Punishment: Justice in the Wake of Massive Crimes in Argentina," *Journal of International Affairs,* 52: 669–690.

O'Connell, James (1995), "The Essence of Forgiveness," *Peace Review,* 7: 457–462.

O'Donnell, Guillermo and Philippe Schmitter (1995), "Transitions from Authoritarian Rule: Tentative Conclusions About Uncertain Democracies," in Neil J. Kritz, ed., *Transitional Justice,* Washington, DC: U.S. Institute of Peace, pp. 57–132.

Onis, Juan De (1980), "El Salvador and Honduras Reach a Border Agreement," *New York Times,* October 18, p. A10.

Oron, Yitzhak (1989), "Ten Years after the Signing of the Treaty: Egypt, the Anchor of Peace," *Jerusalem Post,* March 24.

O'Shaughnessy, Hugh and Jimmy Burns (1982), "Galtieri Ousted in Bloodless Coup by Armed Forces," *Financial Times,* June 18, p. 2.

O'Shaughnessy, Laura Nuzzi and Michael Dodson (1999), "Political Bargaining and Democratic Transition: A Comparison of Nicaragua and El Salvador," *Journal of Latin American Studies,* 31: 99–127.

Osgood, Charles E. (1962), *An Alternative to War or Surrender,* Urbana: University of Illinois Press.

Ottaway, David (1993), *Chained Together,* New York: Times Books.

Panksepp, Jaak (1998), *Affective Neuroscience: The Foundations of Human and Animal Emotions,* New York: Oxford University Press.

Pearce, J. C. (1993), *Evolution's End,* San Francisco: Harper Collins.

Pert, C. (1997), *Molecules of Emotion,* New York: Scribner.

Peterson, J. E. (1982), *Yemen: The Search for a Modern State,* Baltimore: Johns Hopkins University Press.

Pillar, Paul (1983), *Negotiating Peace: War Termination as a Bargaining Process,* Princeton, NJ: Princeton University Press.

Pinker, Steven (1994), *The Language Instinct,* New York: Morrow.

Pion-Berlin, David (1995), "To Persecute or Pardon? Human Rights Decisions in the Latin American Cone," in Neil J. Kritz, ed., *Transitional Justice,* Washington, DC: U.S. Institute of Peace, pp. 1–56.

Plutchik, Robert (1980), *Emotion: A Psychoevolutionary Synthesis,* New York: Harper & Row.

Plutchik, Robert (1980), "A General Psychoevolutionary Theory of Emotion," in Robert Plutchik and Henry Kellerman, eds., *Emotion: Theory, Research and Experience,* vol. 1, New York: Academic Press, pp. 3–32.

Pomery, Chris (1989), "Anxiety as Hanoi's Troops Start Their Cambodia Pull-out," *Times* (London), September 22.

Popkin, Margaret and Naomi Roht-Arriaza (1995), "Truth as Justice: Investigatory Commission on Latin America," *Law and Social Inquiry,* 20: 79–117.

Preston, Yvonne (1991), "Vietnam and China Forced into Friendship," *Financial Times,* November 6, p. 4.

Pruitt, Dean G. and Peter J. Carnevalle (1993), *Negotiation and Social Conflict,* Buckingham, UK: Open University Press, and Pacific Grove, CA: Brooks/Cole.

Pruitt, Dean G. and Paul V. Olczak (1995), "A Multimodal Approach to Seemingly Intractable Conflict," in Barbara Bennedict Bunker and Jeffrey Z. Rubin, eds., *Conflict, Cooperation, and Justice: Essays Inspired by the Work of Morton Deutsch,* San Francisco: Jossey-Bass, pp. 59–92.

Ramses, Amer (1994), "Sino–Vietnamese Normalization in the Light of the Crisis of the Late 1970s," *Pacific Affairs,* 67: 357–367.

Remnick, David (1990), "West Germans, Soviets Initial 20-Year Treaty of Friendship," *Washington Post,* September 14, p. A18.

Reuveny, Rafael and Heejoon Kang (1996), "International Conflict and Cooperation: Splicing COPDAB and WEIS Series," *International Studies Quarterly,* 40: 281–306.

Richardson, Lewis F. (1960), *Statistics of Deadly Quarrels,* Quincy Wright and Carl C. Lienau, eds., Pittsburgh: Boxwood Press.

Richburg, Keith B. (1988), "Cambodian Peace Talks under Way; Warring Guerrilla Factions Meet with Vietnam for First Time," *Washington Post,* July 26, p. A1.

Riker, William H. (1980), "Implications from the Disequilbrium of Majority Rule for the Study of Institutions," *American Political Science Review*, 74: 432–447.

Rosenberg, Alexander (1995), *Philosophy of Social Science*, 2nd ed., New York: Westview Press.

Rosenblum, Peter (2000), "Pipeline Politics in Chad," *Current History*, 99: 195–199.

Rowan, Thomas P. (1991), "Chile: Country Background Report," *Congressional Reference Report*, Washington, DC: Congressional Research Service.

Rozin, P. and J. W. Kalat (1971), "Specific Hunger and Person Avoidance as Adaptive Specializations of Learning," *Psychological Review*, 78: 459–486.

Ruhl, Mark J. (1997), "Doubting Democracy in Honduras," *Current History*, 96: 81–86.

Rupiya, Martin (1999), "War and Peace in Mozambique," *Accord*, September 19, available on the World Wide Web at http://www.c-r.org/accord/accmoz/rupiya.html.

Sachar, Howard M. (1981), *Egypt and Israel*, New York: Richard Marek.

Sadat, Anwar el (1977), *In Search of Identity*, New York: Harper & Row.

Schachter, Stanley (1964), "The Interaction of Cognitive and Physiological Determinants of Emotional State," in Leonard Berkowitz, ed., *Advances in Social Psychology*, vol. 1, New York: Academic Press, pp. 49–80.

Scheff, Thomas J. (1994), *Bloody Revenge: Emotions, Nationalism and War*, Boulder, CO: Westview Press.

Schneider, Heike (1996), "Mozambique: One of the Secret Success Stories in Africa," *Deutsche Presse-Agentur*, October 22, financial pages.

Schrodt, Philip A. and Deborah J. Gerner (1997), "Empirical Indicators of Crisis Phase in the Middle East," *Journal of Conflict Resolution*, 41: 529–552.

Schumacher, Edward (1984), "Argentina and Democracy," *Foreign Affairs*, 63: 1070–1095.

Schwartz, Barry (1986), *The Battle for Human Nature*, New York: W. W. Norton.

Scislowska, Monica (1999), "Poles, Germany Mend War Wounds: Border Ceremony Commemorates 60th Anniversary of First Attack," *Ottawa Citizen*, September 2, p. A8.

Seattle Times (1999), "Vietnam Leader in Cambodia to Improve Ties," June 9, p. A12.

Sengulane, Dinis S. and Jaime Pedro Goncalves (1999), "A Calling for Peace," *Accord*, December 1, available on the World Wide Web at http://www.c-r.org/accord/acc_moz/sengulane.html.

Shifter, Michael (1999), "Colombia at War," *Current History*, 98: 116–121.

Shriver, Donald W. Jr. (1995), *An Ethic for Enemies*, New York: Oxford University Press.

Siegel, Richard Lewis (1998), "Transitional Justice: A Decade of Debate and Experience," *Human Rights Quarterly,* 20: 431–454.

Simon, Herbert (1956), "Rational Choice and the Structure of the Environment," *Psychology Review,* 63: 129–138.

Singer, J. David (1969), "Threat Perception and National Decision-Makers," in Dean G. Pruitt and Richard C. Snyder, eds., *Theory and Research on the Causes of War,* Englewood Cliffs, NJ: Prentice-Hall, pp. 39–42.

Smith, Hendrick (1979), "Treaty Impact Still Unknown," *New York Times,* March 17, p. A1.

Sober, Elliott (1999), *Philosophy of Biology,* Boulder, CO: Westview Press.

Sobrino, John (1996), "Theological Reflections on the Report of the Truth Commission," in Charles Harper, ed., *Impunity: An Ethical Perspective,* Geneva: World Council of Churches Publications, pp. 118–135.

Spelke, Elizabeth S. (1990), "Principles of Object Perception," *Cognitive Science,* 14: 28–56.

Spelke, Elizabeth S. (1998), "The Origins of Physical Knowledge," in Lawrence Weiskrantz, ed., *Thought without Knowledge,* Oxford: Clarendon Press, pp. 168–184.

Spielberger, Charles D., Gerald Jacobs, Sheryl Russell, and R. Crane (1983), "Assessment of Anger: The State-Trait Anger Scale," in James N. Butcher and Charles D. Spielberger, eds., *Advances in Personality Assessment,* vol. 2, Hillsdale, NJ: Erlbaum, pp. 159–187.

Steele, Jonathan (1998), "A Kind of Liberation," *Guardian,* December 4, p. 21.

Stent, Angela E. (1999), *Russia and Germany Reborn: Unification, the Soviet Collapse, and the New Europe,* Princeton, NJ: Princeton University Press.

Stephen, Walter G. (1995), "Intergroup Contact: Introduction," *Journal of Social Issues,* 41: 1–8.

Stratton, G. (1919), "Retroactive Hyperamnesia and other Emotional Effects on Memory," *Psychological Review,* 26: 474–486.

Symons, Donald (1979), *The Evolution of Human Sexuality,* New York: Oxford University Press.

Tavuchis, Nicolas (1991), *Mea Culpa,* Stanford, CA: Stanford University Press.

Tessler, Mark (1989), "The Camp David Accords and the Palestinian Problem," in Ann Mosely Lesch and Mark Tessler eds., *Israel, Egypt, and the Palestinians: From Camp David to Intifada,* Bloomington: Indiana University Press, pp. 3–22.

Tomkins, Silvan Solomon (1962–1963), *Affect, Imagery, and Consciousness,* 2 vols., New York: Springer.

Tomlinson, Rodney G. (1993), "Monitoring WEIS Event Data in Three Dimensions," in Merritt, Richard L., Robert G. Muncaster, and Dina A. Zinnes, eds., *International Event Data Developments: DDIR Phase II,* Ann Arbor: University of Michigan Press, pp. 55–85.

Tomlinson, Rodney G. (1996), *World Event/Interaction Survey (WEIS) User's Guide*, 8th revision, draft.

Tooby, John and Leda Cosmides (1992), "The Psychological Foundations of Culture," in J. Barkow, L. Cosmides, and J. Tooby, eds., *The Adapted Mind: Evolutionary Psychology and the Generation of Culture*, New York: Oxford University Press, pp. 19–136.

Tranel, Daniel, Antoine Bechara, and Antonio Damasio (1999), "Decision-Making and the Somatic Marker Hypothesis," in Michael S. Garraniga, ed., *The New Cognitive Neurosciences*, Cambridge: MIT Press, pp. 1047–1061.

Trivers, Robert L. (1971), "The Evolution of Reciprocal Altruism," *Quarterly Review of Biology*, 46: 35–57.

Truell, Peter (1989), "U.S. Is Attempting to Nudge Argentina and Britain Toward a Reconciliation," *Wall Street Journal*, August 28, p. 1.

Tsebelis, George (1990), *Nested Games*, Berkeley: University of California Press.

Tversky, Amos and Daniel Kahneman (1974), "Judgment under Uncertainty: Heuristics and Biases," *Science*, 185: 1124–1131.

Tyler, Christian (1983), "Doubts over Lifting of Argentina Sanctions," *Financial Times*, August 15, p. 2.

UN Chronicle (1990), "Argentina, United Kingdom Decide to Re-establish Diplomatic Relations," 27: 28.

UN Chronicle (1992), "El Salvador Agreements: The Path to Peace," 29: 77.

UN Chronicle (1998), "Security Council Heard Argentinian Complaint against United Kingdom, Takes No Action," 25: 62.

van den Berghe, Pierre L. (1981), *The Ethnic Phenomenon*, New York: Elsevier.

van Zyl, Paul (1999), "Dilemmas of Transitional Justice: The Case of South Africa's Truth and Reconciliation Commission," *Journal of International Affairs*, 52: 647–666.

Verba, Sidney (1961), "Assumptions of Rationality and Non-Rationality in Models of the International System," in Klaus Knorr and Sidney Verba, eds., *The International System: Theoretical Essays*, Princeton, NJ: Princeton University Press, pp. 93–117.

Walter, Barbara F. (1997), "The Critical Barrier to Civil War Settlement," *International Organization*, 51: 335–364.

Waltz, Kenneth (1979), *Theory of International Politics*, Reading, MA: Addison-Wesley.

Welch, David A. (1997), "Remember the Falklands?," *International Journal*, 52: 485–498.

Wells, Andrew (1998), "Evolutionary Psychology and Theories of Cognition Architecture," in Charles Crawford and Dennis L. Krebs, eds., *Handbook of Evolutionary Psychology*, Mahwah, NJ: Erlbaum, pp. 335–364.

Whitaker, David J. (1999), *Conflict and Reconciliation in the Contemporary World*, London: Routledge.

White, Ralph K. (1984), *Fearful Warriors*, New York: Free Press.

Whitehead, Alfred North and Bertrand Russell (1925), *Principles of Mathematics*, vol. 1, 2nd ed., Cambridge, UK: Cambridge University Press.

Wight, Martin (1966), "Western Values in International Relations," in Martin Wight and Herbert Butterfield, eds., *Diplomatic Investigation*, London: Allen & Unwin, pp. 89–131.

Williamson, Oliver (1981), "The Economics of Organizations: The Transaction Cost Approach," *American Journal of Sociology*, 87: 548–577.

Wilmer, Franke (1998), "The Social Construction of Conflict and Reconciliation in the Former Yugoslavia," *Social Justice*, 25: 90–113.

Wilson, Edward O. (1978), *On Human Nature*, New York: Bantam Books.

Wilson, Edward O. (1998), *Consilience: The Unity of Knowledge*, New York: Knopf.

Wilson, James Q. (1973), *Political Organizations*, New York: Basic Books.

Wink, Walter (1998), *When the Powers Fall: Reconciliation in the Healing of Nations*, Minneapolis: Fortress.

Wolfers, Arnold (1962), *Discord and Collaboration*, Baltimore: Johns Hopkins University Press.

Worchel, Stephen and William G. Austin, eds. (1986), *Psychology of Intergroup Relations*, Chicago: Nelson-Hall.

World Press Review (1997), "How Can Past Sins Be Absolved," 44: 6–9.

Wright, Robert (2000), *Nonzero*, New York: Pantheon Books.

Wurst, Jim (1997), "Beating Swords into . . . Furniture," *Bulletin of the Atomic Scientists*, 53: 17–18.

Zahavi, Amotz and Avishag Zahavi (1997), *The Handicap Principle*, New York: Oxford University Press.

Zajonc, Robert (1980), "Feeling and Thinking: Preferences Need No Inferences," *American Psychologist*, 35: 151–175.

Zartman, I. William and Johannes Aurik (1991), "Power Strategies and De-escalation," in Louis Kriesberg and Stuart J. Thorson, eds., *Timing the De-escalation of International Conflicts*, Syracuse, NY: Syracuse University Press, pp. 152–181.

Zartman, I. William (1995), "Negotiating the South African Conflict," in I. William Zartman, ed., *Elusive Peace*, Washington, DC: Brookings, pp. 147–174.

Index